The Climbers' Club
Centenary
Journal

Edited by
Terry Gifford

The Climbers' Club

Published by The Climbers' Club 1997
© Individual authors or The Climbers' Club

ISBN 0-901-601-67-5

A CIP catalogue record for this book is available from the British Library.

Front Cover: Mike Kosterlitz on Scorpio (E2) Clogwyn Du'r Arddu, c.1963.
Photo: Ken Wilson.
Rear Cover: Pete Bailey on Skylon (Hard Severe) Carreg Wastad, June 1961.
Photo: Ken Wilson.

Typeset and prepared for printing by the C.C. Hon. Editor for Wales, Ian Smith.
Printed by BPC, Exeter.

CONTENTS

COMPLETELY TO MY SURPRISE

HIRAETH

THE SPIRIT OF THE AGE

TOASTING THE CLUB

POSTSCRIPT

APPENDIX

EDITORIAL

So, it is finished, this monumental, impossible task that has been so much a team effort. Now the critics crouch amongst the grey, wet boulders out there. But in here, alone in front of the Helyg fire, I have been sustained by the querulous ghosts of this place. Their voices have made this final, silent vigil of selection a surprisingly exciting one. Their words, arguing eloquently, wittily with each other, have made this a book which I hope will leave members greatly amused, rather proud and not a little in awe.

It is slowly getting dark again.

Be cautious, critics. A. B. has the Helyg poker in his hand.

Not that the task has turned me mad, you understand. (Laptops like this, for reasons we barely begin to understand, are incapable of lying.) I *have* come through the thickening mist that even now descends the flanks of Gallt yr Ogof.

I keep going to the door. It clears my mind of guilt for those I've not included. I am strangely comforted by the Helyg boulder. It will be here, like those other articles, to comfort the next Editor of a *Centenary Journal.*

For there is much more where this came from. Ask those members who kindly recommended pieces they search for here in vain. (An Hon. Custodian has just walked in and asked if I've included that piece by A. B. about Craig yr Ysfa, with added plums and pegs. I have.) Eighty one members requested a total of 61 articles. Then Pip Hopkinson read everything up to the Great War, Harold Drasdo read into the 1920s and '30s, Roger Briggs chose the 1940s, Derek Walker made recommendations from the '50s, as did Dave Gregory for the '60s, whilst Roger Salisbury took over Huts and the 1970s, and Tim Noble read the '80s and '90s. For the last year the journals have been my pillow books and constant travel companions. I well remember reading a decade on the plane out to the Banff Mountain Book Festival (Odell on climbs in the Rockies with Smythe, as it happened) and another decade on the flight back. Then suddenly yesterday evening, as I lay my long short-list out on the floor in front of the fire, the 10 groupings started to reveal themselves. One piece began to nudge up against another — Ken Wilson with Marjorie Allen, Dave Hope with Geoff Milburn — that sort of thing. It was, as I say, rather exciting.

There is something here from the first *Journal* to the present day. Sheer quality of writing has been my first, frankly subjective, criterion for selection. Humorous insight has been my second. (I hope admirers of Kevin Fitzgerald are satisfied at last and that they will now recommend to each other C. E. Benson, Raymond Lister and Mrs O'Malley.) By following these criteria, historical balance and the climbing record have, as suspected, been quite capable of looking after themselves. I have taken the liberty of making extracts from longer pieces and occasionally giving a more appropriate title to the extract. Authors and dates will enable the originals to be traced. There will be gaps, inevitably, but the least I hoped for was a good read for members. I crave indulgence from those outwith the spirit of this place, its caricatures by French, oxygen equipment trials by Hunt and life-saving karabiner donated by Band. And I have not forgotten the poker. (The Hon. Custodian on the other side of the fire complains gruffly that it has disappeared. He does not realise why.)

Of the Club's long record of heated debates I have chosen to give most extended coverage to the issue of access to Scottish game-farming estates since the concern of 1901 remains unresolved. On other debates members might have hoped to relive here, Mrs O'Malley, Marjorie and Jancis can speak for themselves in these pages.

Finally, before I retire to Cobden's Hotel to buy your Hon. Custodian a pint for the pains suffered on our behalf (which have obviously been so great as to reduce his size and even bow his legs a little) let me acknowledge the bullies. Their voices have the foremost place here. And rightly so, I hear you echo. For without the year-long cajoling of the Editor we would be a poorer club. So let us agree that this is not, in fact, an ending, but rather a beginning — a beginning of the work for the next *Centenary Journal* via the next *Journal*. The pen lifted by the members represented here now passes to you. Put an evening aside to make a small effort. "Be active!" as A. B. used to say.

The Hon. Custodian is grunting in the doorway for his pint. He's staring at those boulders out there in the dark. And where did that poker in his hand appear from?

December 1996, Helyg
Terry Gifford

ALREADY FAMOUS

Many outstanding articles from the *Climbers' Club Journal* have already been anthologised in *The Games Climbers Play* and in *Mirrors in the Cliffs*. I have tried to avoid reproducing here all but the essential pieces, but, for the record, here is a complete list of articles from our *Journals* which have contributed to the success of these anthologies:

The Games Climbers Play contains:
'Surely We're Off The Route?' (1968) by Kevin Fitzgerald
'Lazy Men's Ways' (1963) and 'A Visit to Saussois' (1966) by Allan Austin
'A Longing for Wales' (1963) by S. Gonzales
'Denn Bleiben Ist Nirgends' (1976) and 'A Valediction' (1973-74) by Jim Perrin
'A Face: A Friend' (1975) by Mike Baker
Quotes from the guidebooks to Tryfan (1937) and Idwal (1940)
Obituary notes for J. M. Archer Thompson by G. W. Young and Professor Orton (1913)
'Punch-up at the Padarn Lake' (titled 'Cae Coch Quarry') (1968) by Harold Drasdo
'A Short Siesta on the Upper Slopes' (1967) by Anon
'Scenery for a Murder' (1939) by J. M. Edwards
'Skills and Safety' (1962) by Robin Hodgkin

Mirrors in the Cliffs contains:
'Taxation no Tyranny' (1979/80) by Jim Perrin
'Beltane Fire' (1979/80) by Geoff Milburn
'Trapdoor Fandango' (1978) by Ron Fawcett.
'On Tree Climbing' (1915) by H. E. L. Porter
'End of a Climb' (1939) by J. M. Edwards

A CHALLENGE FROM THE EDITOR

When I announced in the September 1995 *Newsletter* that John Andrews, great nephew of A.W. Andrews, had given the club copyright to *Selected Poems on West Penwith and Reflections*, privately published by A. W. A. in 1957, and that some of these poems would be appearing in the *Centenary Journal*, I mentioned that a line from one of them had been used in Biven and McDermott's 1968 guidebook *Cornwall Vol 1* - 'Nothing but sea, America and night'. I promptly received a note from Al Alvarez indicating that this line is 'not originally from A.W.A. It is a quote from D.H. Lawrence. Where precisely I'm not too sure. Maybe the 'Nightmare' chapter of *Kangaroo*, maybe a letter. But I'm quite certain it's D. H. L. and I remember quoting it to Peter [Biven] umpteen years ago.'
I have failed to find it in either source. Can anyone locate it?

ACKNOWLEDGEMENTS

President Mark Vallance and Chair of the Publications Sub-Committee Bob Moulton have been very supportive and patient by turns, leaving me just the right amount of slack rope. The three star grading system adopted by the readers of the decades of the *Journal* has helped me surmount a crux of huge proportions. Thanks for fascinating notes from Messrs P. Hopkinson, H. Drasdo, R. Briggs, D. Walker, D. Gregory, R. Salisbury and T. Noble.

The following members kindly offered suggestions of articles for inclusion: J. Neill, C. E. Davies, M. H. Bebbington, G. D. Hughes, M. G. Mortimer, S. Westmacott, D. J. Weaver, N. C. Peacock, H. B. Sales, R. D. Sykes, K. J. Wilson, J. D. Foster, D. Wiggett, J. S. Milledge, K. H. Salter, J. Disley, B. W. Wright, T. R. Briggs, A. G. L Williams, P. M. Clarke, N. Elliott, R. P. Crellin, A. K. Tickle, A. D. Newton, R. Turner, K. V. Latham, G. A. M. Robertson, G. L. Scott-Cowell, P. L. Harrison, L. White, M. R. Sinker, R. Enwright, G. W. White, A. L. Atkinson, D. T. Roscoe, F. Fitzgerald, A. R. Sharp, M. J. Ball, R. Goodier, G. C. Norman, P. R. J. Harding, D. Thomas, E. W. O. Douglas, F. M. Hill, R. J. Isherwood, S. A. Keir, H. Drasdo, P. J. Hardman, J. Perrin, D. G. N. Hunter, M. Vallance, D. E. Hope, M. R. Learoyd, C. R. Davies, P. M. Gerrard, D. Atchison, V. N. Stevenson, J. S. Cleare, G. Bintley, J. H. Thomas, R. Tibawi, J. Burrows, D. W. Matthews, J. D. Heydon, F. E. R. Cannings, M. F. Browell (who suggested his own excellent article), N. Coe, G. H. G. Hughes, A. Boorman, R. A. Hodgkin, H. D. Griffiths, P. H. Bartrum, J. H. Emlyn-Jones, P. D. Hunt, C. Gilbert, P. H. Hopkinson, J. F. Jones, E. M. Viney, K. A. Goodey, P. E. Burt, C. Fishwick, E. Alsford.

Proof-reading was undertaken by M. Vetterlein (lots), D. Gregory (even more), R. D. Moulton, T. Noble and P. Harrison.

Pictures have generously been offered by M. Mortimer, M. Browell, C. J. S. Bonington, G. Band, C. Craggs, D. Atchison, D. Walker, H. Pretty, R. Allen, M. Banks, I. Smith, C. Jackson, J. Curran, B. Molyneux, L. Dickinson, S. Dean, J. Cleare, N. Biven, M. Westmacott, G. Taylor, J. Allison.

K. Wilson was as unstinting with advice as ever and some of it has been taken. However, realising that we **were** going for pictures on the dust jacket, he was again generous in providing not just access at his home, but verbal directions to his photographic archives, despite a damaged jaw and crutches (for his leg) from a post-climbing accident. His two atmospheric cover pictures deserve our warm acknowledgements.

Pip Hopkinson has provided a personal view of the Club's history that has evolved after wide consultation. I appreciate his willingness to collaborate in the editorial process on a text which remains his own.

In the final stages, Ian Smith (with assistance from his wife, Vivienne) has put in a lot of hard work without which the book would never have been ready for production. I have come to witness something of the hours of unacknowledged work that members of the Publications Sub-Committee give to the Club. My warmest personal thanks go to Ian for his invaluable guidance, advice and hours of effort in crafting this book.

Terry Gifford

'Completely to my surprise'

'In March I discovered completely to my surprise that I had become the Editor of this *Journal*'.
John Longland (1973/74)

THE FOUNDING OF THE JOURNAL

GEORGE B. BRYANT
(Vol. 1 No.1 August 1898)

The issue of the first number of the *Journal* offers the earliest opportunity of giving the whole of the members an account of how the Club came to be formed, and of what has taken place up to the present time, and I have been asked by the Editor to put such an account into shape.

The idea had, no doubt, its natural birth at Pen-y-Gwryd, amid surroundings familiar to many of us. In August or September of most years, men who rarely met anywhere else, spent days together on the hills, and found themselves at seven o'clock (more or less) round the well-provided dinner table, dried, clothed, and in their right minds. There, as the inner man got what was overdue to him, and later, when warmth and tobacco had completed his contentment, the work of the day passed into pleasant talk; the older men dropped an encouraging word to the beginners, difficult points were discussed and located, and suggestions made for the next day's climbing. In that congenial atmosphere, where conventionalities were not obtrusive, and the bishop or the man of law shared the sofa with the old shepherd and deferred to his opinions, men of various sorts, but united in their deep love of the mountains, grew to know each other; and there the sense of association, the germ of the Club, struck its first root

Being of British origin, what else could be its first expression but a dinner? The suggestion thrown out that those who had enjoyed these haphazard meetings at Pen-y-Gwryd might bridge the long intervals by a dinner in London met with a warm response, and on the 19th May, 1897, about forty frequenters of the Welsh farm-house foregathered at the "Monico" to recall old times, with the familiar form of Mr. T. S. Halliday in the chair. At this time, doubts were felt whether anything in the nature of a Club would be a success, but a strong desire was shown that the Pen-y-Gwryd dinner should not be dropped, and arrangements were made to repeat it in the following December.

As the time for the second dinner approached, it became abundantly clear that from many quarters an opinion in favour of the formation of a Club was setting in, and it was decided that a proposal in that direction should be brought forward. The dinner was fixed for the 6th December — a date which was not a fortunate one, about twenty-five gentlemen who desired to attend being compelled to absent themselves. The meeting was, nevertheless, a good one and it fell to its lot to lay the foundations of the club.

The resolution, "That a Climbing Club should be formed," was proposed by Mr. Roderick Williams, and seconded by Mr. H. C. Gotch — both, as it happened, Alpine Club men, as well as keen British climbers. Before the chairman put the resolution, the meeting was placed in possession of replies from twenty of the absentees, who had availed themselves of the opportunity given them to state their opinions on the proposal. Of these, fifteen were distinctly in favour of the formation of the Club; four were neutral, or gave a qualified approval; and one expressed inability to join it, if formed. The resolution was then passed, without a dissentient voice. The first general meeting was held on 28th April 1898 at which the President, Mr. C. E. Mathews, proposed the toast of 'Our Club':

"I trust that this dinner may be memorable in mountaineering annals. Forty years ago — a period equal to that during which the children of Israel are said to have wandered in the wilderness — a Club was founded in a modest and unassuming manner, having for its objects the friendship and the worship of the great Alps. It numbered about thirty original members. Its first dinner was attended by twelve men. It published a series of ascents and adventures, and the Club, its members, and its publications received from an undiscerning public, ridicule, disapprobation and contempt.

The critics did not know much about it. There is a story told of a certain undergraduate, not very well up in his Greek, who told his tutor 'that he had a contempt for Plato.' 'I should presume, sir,' said the tutor, 'that yours is a contempt which does not proceed from familiarity.'

Criticism is good for all of us, but it is really valuable in proportion to the honesty and ability and insight of the critic. That Club, with a steadily rising standard of qualification, now numbers over six hundred men; the great hall at the 'Métropole' is not large enough to accommodate the numbers that flock to its winter dinners; and it comprises within its ranks some of the best of the intellectual aristocracy of this country.

It was found, too, that it supplied a great want, and it was shortly imitated all over the world. The time for ridicule soon passed away;
'The seed,
The little seed they laughed at in the dark,
Had risen and cleft the soil',
and the children of the Alpine Club became as the sand which is upon the sea shore in multitude. The Austrians were the first to follow our example, then the Swiss, then the Italians, then the Germans, and finally the French, whose Club has over four thousand members, with a separate organisation in every department of France. Then came independent groups, such as the Société des Touristes de Dauphiné, and the Society of Excursionists of Catalonia. Then we annexed far-distant countries, and started a New Zealand Club, a Caucasian Club, a Norwegian Club, and Heaven knows how many more.

Well, it is said that a man 'who sees only what is just before his eyes loses always the best part of every view', but we have neglected too long the binding together of the lovers of the beautiful scenery at our own doors. The Scottish Mountaineering Club first realised the situation; then the Yorkshire Ramblers; and last year a Pen-y-Gwryd Club was suggested as specially representing Wales; but it seemed to some of us that union was strength, and so the Climbers' Club has been founded, which embraces England, Ireland, and Wales, and yet is open to all lovers of mountaineering in every quarter of the globe.

Well, gentlemen, some of us know what hard work is in the various occupations of our lives. We must have some alterative, and we are all agreed that there is no alterative comparable to mountaineering. It is a sport which combines admirable physical exercise with pleasures of a purely intellectual kind. It is a sport which makes us young again; and, believe me, that writer had real insight who said, 'That country is the happiest whose people longest retain their youth.' It is a sport which brings us face to face with Nature, and puts us in quest of the unknown. Who is there amongst us who does not share in the craving of the old Ulysses to discover something of the unknown'

'To sail beyond the sunset, and the baths
Of all the western stars'?

It is a sport which enables us to throw off the cares and troubles of life, as Christian threw off the burden of sin in Bunyan's famous allegory. It is a sport that from some mysterious cause appeals mainly to the cultivated intellect."

Notes

The Committee, for a time, was somewhat divided as to the advisability of issuing the *Journal* so often as four times a year, there being a feeling in certain quarters that, sooner or later, difficulty will be experienced in obtaining a sufficiency of suitable material; but the Editor has already received such liberal promises of support, that there is every reason to believe that the course adopted will be justified by success. However, in order to make our publication thoroughly interesting, it will be necessary to provide a constant flow of entirely fresh climbing information, and this can only be done by the assistance of all the active members of the Club.

We are arranging for a series of articles upon rock-climbing in the British Isles. The first of the series — on rock-climbing in England — has kindly been undertaken by Mr. Owen Glynne Jones, and will appear in our November number, which will also contain an article on "First Aid in Climbing Accidents", and an account of some practice scrambles in the Derbyshire Peak District, &c., &c.

Con Carey on the much missed Yankee Doodle (E2), Land's End. First climbed by Tom Proctor and Geoff Birtles in 1976, it became one of the classic crack climbing pitches of Britain, but was destroyed by storms in 1989/90. Photo: Ian Smith.

Above: Mark Vallance, current President, in Zion Canyon in 1996. Photo: Mike Browell.
Below: Bob Moulton, long serving member of the Publications Sub-Committeee having acted as Guidebook Editor, Business Manager and Chairman, climbing Central Crack (5c), Under Rockes, Southern Sandstone. Photo: Ian Smith.

Above: Nigel Rogers (left) and John Neill (right). Nigel was *Journal* Editor 1965-69 and John was *Journal* Editor 1959-65, photographed in 1966.
Below: Left to right, John Longland, John Disley and Roger Chorley photographed at Helyg on Saturday 8th June 1985 during the 60th anniversary celebrations of the establishment of the hut. John Longland was *Journal* Editor 1974-76. Photo: Ian Smith.

Rear Admiral Keith Lawder, renowned as a developer of crags in the South West. Seen here aged 76 on Lundy in 1969. Photo: Mike Banks.

ENGLISH CLIMBING
CONSIDERED MAINLY FROM AN ALPINE STANDPOINT
(extract)

OWEN GLYNNE JONES
(Vol. 1 No. 2 November 1898)

A good series of Cumberland climbing photographs were lately at the Schwarzsee, and under the shadow of the noble old Matterhorn, a party of German cragsmen were ridiculing the idea that anything good in their line of sport could be found in England. Whereupon a patriot rose and brought them the photographs. "Ach Gott! these men are terrible, they attempt the impossible!" and they, with strenuous verbal effort, decided that Englishmen at home must be madder than when abroad. Nevertheless, the method of our madness interested them not a little, and they were at any rate convinced that we were not without our training-ground for heavier work in the Alps — our *polytechnik* — where correct principles could be learnt and inwardly digested by the aid of suitable practice.

We cannot ignore the fact that our polytechnic is small and incomplete. Ten years ago, our athletes were few, and the Cumberland fells were large enough for all. But with this terribly rapid growth of the "tooth-and-nail" industry, there has arisen the corresponding demand for technical training in that special subject, and we find that additional space is required for the use of fresh students of mountaineering, and new work of an advanced character for those who have graduated in the ordinary courses. So far as the English school is concerned, we must be prepared to admit without much qualification that there is no more room, and that there are not many problems remaining unsolved.

On the threshold of a new departure, we first members of the English Climbers' Club have good reason to pause and contemplate our responsibilities. The formation of a club, if it does not mean a pledge to justify our pursuit to the outer world, at any rate implies a conviction in us that adverse critics could be silenced with fuller knowledge of what we risk and what we gain. The outer world have every right to enquire into the cause of misadventure that happens to us, every right to blame severely those whose folly or negligence has taken bad luck by the hand and courted disaster. We may be too proud or too indifferent to answer their adverse judgments, but it is well-nigh impossible for even an inveterate climber to remain entirely unaffected by the opinions of his friends and relatives. The experience of the Alpine Club is at our disposal; its champions in dialectic are fortunately ours of necessity, and it remains to act up to our convictions and theirs. Accidents to novices will always set the world barking at our heels; accidents to our tried mountaineers, rare though they must assuredly be, turn our best arguments against us.

All this moralising is very well, but it is not exactly what the Editor required of me. He has let me take the lead in a new climb, and under the pretence of prospecting, I have run out on an unconscionable length of rope before beginning the actual business of the day. And yet here again is a sign of the times; our climbing literature as well as our districts are becoming exhausted. The usual narration of a modern mountaineering achievement suggests an aimless circling round and round in aerial flight, with an apparent forgetfulness of time and object, and then a sudden pounce on the unfortunate little, half-hidden *motif*. It is kept out of sight in the preliminary pages, and then bolted in a paragraph. The veterans with axe and pen are a little hard on all this. They actually expect us to please them, as much as they please us! They have used up all the little climbing jokes; they bar our reference to the pleasures and penalties of nights out, to damp or otherwise unrestful beds, to the matchless excellences of our leaders, to the glories of Alpine sunrises and sunsets, to every type of incident that used to supply them with so much copy. They were frequently inaccurate in matters of climbing detail, probably deeming accuracy incompatible with artistic treatment of their subject. Yet they laugh at our "times," and profess to despise the details that are now-a-days so fully and generously offered them. No wonder the sensitive scribe is tempted to compact his matter into the smallest possible space, and write on other subjects for the rest of his article. We may well envy the pioneers their opportunities, but at the same time we may console ourselves with the reflection that they did much for us. It would be unbecoming to appear thankless. Any more information on English climbing they perhaps think it is impossible to supply, now that nearly every gully and ridge and pinnacle has been written up *in extenso*.

It was a fine sarcasm in a recent paper before the Alpine Club that permeated the allusion to our luckless literary efforts. The author could not, or would not, remember the details of his own climbing expedition, and amusingly contrasted it with the accounts of ascents in England or Wales, or the Coolins of Skye, where it was deemed necessary to know, on starting out from the hotel, which foot to put foremost, and where detail was so elaborate that a stonefall in a gully might call for a new edition. But this same author, in the *role* of scientific exponent of the principles of mountaineering, also studies the subject with microscopic minuteness. His directions to the would-be climber are innumerable. There may be thirty-seven things for an oarsman to think about in each stroke, but a cragsman has a thousand and one. Nor are these directions supplied with examples. We read in his instructive pages of the various aids to stability: how to place our hands, our feet, and the other portions of our anatomy that can be temporarily used as limbs; but we do not know where we are. We have to imagine the situations, or draw on our past experiences. Only those with a past can appreciate the ingenious analysis; those without must wait.

To write realistically about rock climbing is one of the hardest things in the world; and to understand what the writer is striving to explain, when he is narrating the overcoming or circumvention of difficulties, is often almost impossible even with the work of the most gifted authors. Perhaps one of the most explicit, and at the same time, most enjoyable narratives of the kind ever written, is Mummery's chapter on the Grépon, but until the reader has traversed this peak, he will never realize the description sufficiently well to understand the nature of its general design, and of its chief difficulties. This *Journal* must be persuaded to tolerate it, but incomprehensible to all but Cumberland climbers will be the following account of a famous foreign rock climb, illustrated by references to similar passages in our own district.

It was my great pleasure to be taken across the Dent du Requin last August. Its preliminaries were of the ordinary character — easy glacier for two hours, intermittent steep moraine and ice for an hour, much-crevassed glacier for an hour. Then the rock-work began with an hour of the easy parts of the Ennerdale face of Great Gable, minus all vestiges of grass or other vegetation. All members of the party could move together, even when the scrambling was varied by the passage of the Slab-and-Notch Route. This brought us to a shoulder on the main east ridge of the mountain, and in a situation such as the top of the first part of the West Climb on the Pillar Rock, we sat and lunched, and examined the remaining work before us. The highest point was about a hundred and fifty feet above our heads, separated off by a wide and very Savage Gully that descended steeply 1,500 feet to the glacier below. The ridge on which we were seated curved up on our left, like the upper portion of the Needle Ridge, and fifty feet above us it wound across directly towards the final tower, like the horizontal ridge finish of the Shamrock Chimney.

The first party to reach the summit of the Requin descended 400 feet of the Savage Gully, and, bearing across to more broken ground on the other side of the peak, they forced a route up the north face. Our own party adopted a course that involved no long descent. Looking across at the final tower, we could see that it was seamed by a vertical chimney starting from the level of the Shamrock ridge on our left, and extending upwards for 100 feet to an elevated notch on the left side of the tower, close to the highest point. This chimney, an erected "Oblique" Chimney, was divided into two equal portions, of which perhaps only the upper half could be climbed without a fixed rope. At any rate, the lower part had been occasionally attempted, but never achieved. Our route followed the ridge up to the great tower, and skirted the foot of the Oblique Chimney by an easy hand traverse. It then descended the Savage Gully by a crack thirty feet long, to a small resting-place for three, such as that below the pinnacle on the Keswick Brothers' Climb. Thence a Pendlebury Traverse led across nearly to the other side of the Savage Gully, and a steep but easy first pitch of the A Pike's Crag Gully brought us to a secondary buttress that marked the limit of our traversing. Then a succession of chimneys and ledges gradually turning the tower, brought us to the elevated notch at the head of the Oblique Chimney. It must suffice to say that the series started with the outside route up the Needle, a rather wide

Doctor's Chimney, and the direct finish of the great Ennerdale Gully on Gable Crag. Nothing harder was encountered. From the notch there remained a few feet of easy cleft, and a finish up the Y-boulder of Mosedale. The ascent from our breakfasting-place, and the return by means of a doubled rope twice used in the Oblique Chimney, occupied only two hours exclusive of halts — quite a Cumberland time. We had left the hotel at 2 a.m. (unusual for Wastdale!) and were back again at 3.30 p.m. Another party on the mountain, unaccustomed to these importations of English ascents into French territory, decided somewhat early in the day to give up the Requin, and left it to us.

Though the few guides who have climbed the Requin are asking for it a tariff of 300 francs, it does not demand greater skill or strength in its individual pitches, separately considered, than are needed in the English climbs enumerated in the above description. Some may ask why was it that the first party, all men of the highest attainments in mountaineering, took 20 hours from bivouac to summit and back? The answer is simple: they were tired after the long journey out from England, they had to design a route up, and they had the experiences of but a few previous explorers on the mountain. Their second ascent would have been accomplished in half the time; its narration would not have been half so thrilling. Dr. Clinton Dent, in reviewing Mummery's book for the *Alpine Journal,* remarked that such climbs as the Dent du Requin and the "crack" on the Grépon are impossible for men who have not been schooled in the ways of guides of the stamp of Alexander Burgener. We can sympathise with his strong partisanship for the guide that led him ultimately to victory in that long-protracted struggle with the almost unconquerable Grand Dru, but we do not altogether agree with his remark. He should be persuaded to join our club, and take part in some of our guideless meets; for the particular *tours de force* that he quotes, he might learn that a training-school nearer home can be found where no Burgeners are wanted.

While thus running counter to the well-known opinion of an expert, let me venture even a step further. Everybody knows of the Aiguille du Géant, and of the fixed ropes all the way up the interesting finish. Also most climbers will remember that Mr. Leslie Stephen, examining it from Mont Mallet in 1871, remarked that nobody would ever climb it by fair means. So far, indeed, he is right, in that various engineering methods were employed by the first party to mount it, and all succeeding visitors have benefited by the ropes and stanchions they left behind. Yet I am convinced that a party of two men could climb the Aiguille without these aids. The lower crack on the Burgener platten, usually reckoned the stiffest piece on the rock, is less difficult than the direct ascent to the Slingsby Chimney on Scawfell Pinnacle, from the first pitch in Deep Ghyll. The slightly overhanging chimney on the main ridge above the platten, taken by two men, is equalled in severity by many a short English pitch. The higher pinnacle of Robin Hood's Stride in Derbyshire is a match for it.

EDITORIAL
FAITH-HOPE-CHARITY

J. D. MILLS
(1929)

It was half-past eleven. The Honorary Secretary of the Climbers' Club laid aside his cue and passed sadly from the billiard room to the smoking room of the famous mountain inn. There he found an innocent member of the Club busily reading the last issue of the *Journal* and, occasionally, gazing at the dim "Faith — Hope — Charity" on the wall above the mantelpiece. The Honorary Secretary sat down and sighed.

"What is the matter?" said the Innocent Member.

"The *Journal* is the matter," said the Honorary Secretary. "The late Editor is in Africa. I have asked twenty seven different members to take on his job and all have refused."

"Oh!" said the Innocent Member.

And then, being both enthusiasts of the same profession, they discussed, as might have been expected, the nicer points of the Latin language.

It was two o'clock. The Honorary Secretary had just propounded his theory that the motto *Dum spiro spero* was originally uttered from the depths of the Monolith Crack. A tear stood in his right eye.

"What is the matter?" said the Innocent Member.

"The *Journal* is the matter," said the Honorary Secretary. "The late Editor is in Ashanti. I have asked one hundred and eighty seven different members to take on his job and all have refused."

"Oh !" said the Innocent Member.

And then, being both enthusiasts of the same sport, they discussed, as might have been expected, the nicer points of rock-climbing.

It was half-past three. The Innocent Member was just relating how he always vaulted on to the first pitch of the Holly Tree Wall. He noticed two tears rolling down each of the two cheeks of the Honorary Secretary.

"What is the matter?" said the Innocent Member.

"The *Journal* is the matter," said the Honorary Secretary. "The late Editor is cruising on Lake Chad. I have asked three hundred and fifty seven different members to take on his job and all have refused."

"Oh!" said the Innocent Member.

And then, being both human beings, they yawned, as might have been expected, and closed their eyes.

It was five o'clock. The Honorary Secretary turned in his chair and sobbed.

"What is the ... " began the Innocent Member and then stopped. Could he with decency allow the Honorary Secretary to perjure himself further? He coughed discreetly. There was no sign of life. The Honorary Secretary slept.

"Well," whispered the Innocent Member, hoping thereby to salve his conscience and, perhaps, to save the Honorary Secretary's soul, "of course, if you're really in a bad way...(the Honorary Secretary still slept on)... I could... (lowering his voice)... temporarily... take on the job."

The Honorary Secretary sat up at once, eyes wide open. "Done!" he said, quickly, and dashed upstairs, light-heartedly to bed.

A hopeless dawn smiled wanly over the shoulder of Moel Siabod.

LATEST NEWS

E. RAYMOND TURNER
(Vol. II No. 6 December 1899)

Just as we are going to press we hear that an unfortunate party of two were benighted on the Pillar Rock on the last night of the year. We hope to be in a position to give details of their experiences in our next number.

EDITORIAL

T.I.M. LEWIS
(1970/1)

The club has reached an interesting point in its career. Symptomised, unfortunately, by the sad state of the *Journal*, momentum seems to be lacking. Always a decentralised organisation there have been distinct signs of schism in the 'arguings' over admitting women to the club and also the dealings over the publication of guide books. In the former case many of the younger and active members felt that the club was dragging its heels and that its continued practice of holding major meetings in London was a sign of the undue influence of non-climbing members. This latter has been ostensibly changed. It is hoped that the club will pander to the age of 'Women's Lib' with at least the intelligence to realise that they are a different sex but not a different species i.e. let them in now and stop being anachronistic. Over the matter of guide books it is the club's amateur tradition that has been at fault. Several of the members of the newly formed publications sub-committee are successful businessmen in their private lives. It is to be hoped that they run their businesses better than they run the club's. The age of small time publication is past and the club, as a senior and august body, has a high duty to the climbing community to publish guide books of an authoritative nature as it always has done.

In the modern economic climate of inflation this is an expensive business. A grant from the Sports Council to the Climbers' Club to publish guides would be a start. It would have to be through the British Mountaineering Council, and here we can see the path that we have to tread. The B.M.C. has been a paper tiger for years — in fact as long as it remained a bastion of the amateur. The age of the amateur is now dead in British climbing.

There are too many people involved now for the 'Old School Tie' league to work any longer. The B.M.C. have seen this; they have appointed a full time National Officer. The Climbers' Club too had better look to its methods before it becomes a museum piece. If the members of this club do not want this, as some committee members allege, they are kicking against the pricks.

Now is the time to introduce the other strand of my argument. This malaise which affects the club is to be found in a more general form in Britain, with the salient exception of Scotland. There is a general feeling that what we have in this country is nothing but training for the Alps and the Himalaya. We grew out of that theory in the late nineteenth century but it has returned. It has come back because of the spurious 'cool' that climbers affect: no self respecting 'hard man' can be impressed by what goes on in this country any more. Partly this is true because there are so many people climbing at a high standard, but the achievements are still there. What we have in this country is more climbing and climbers to the square inch than anywhere else in the world. Couple this with our purer ethic and high standards and what is there to be ashamed of?

The sense that only the Alps matter and that we cannot take anything on the island too seriously is at the root of the club's difficulties in organising itself. The club ought to make a point of leading the Renaissance of pride in British mountaineering that is long overdue.

If this club, which is the sum of its members, does not look to its own house and get back to the forefront by such twentieth century moves as recognising female members and such 'Seventies' moves as becoming the guide book collator for the country, it will become an even bigger laughing stock than it is now.

Your club is dying. Help save it. It goes hard with the English to be enthusiastic, but get that way soon or you will lose your planet to pollution and your country to the Common Market as well as your club to the dogs.

ON CLIMBING BOOKS

(extract)

C. MYLES MATHEWS
(1912)

> " *'How camest thou by thy burden at first?'*
> *'By reading this book in my hand'.*"

An eminent conductor, exasperated to candour, possibly by some more than usually typical work proposed for performance at a provincial festival, is reported to have said, "Why will people compose when it is so much easier not to compose?" Like all great truths, it bears a general no less than a particular application, and can as readily be asked of the writers of climbing books as of the compilers of cantatas or oratorios. Conceivably a climbing book may be written for the personal satisfaction of its author. Such a reason may thoroughly enough justify its composition; it can, however, in no degree excuse its publication. The motive of gain can hardly be sufficiently compelling, since experience must in innumerable cases have proved its baselessness; and the first fine careless rapture we experience in finding our names in the British Museum catalogue, glowing and gratifying though it be, may often be bought at too dear a price.

It is fast becoming a distinction of the few not to have written a volume of mountain chit-chat, miscalled adventure. The possible topics of such a work have long since been exhausted. The bergschrund no longer affords material for a paragraph. The opening of the inevitable bottle on the inevitable summit leaves us unmoved. The qualities, or the defects, of the common guide have been sufficiently exploited. Our purple patches are worn threadbare. Anything but silence broods amidst the eternal snows. I wonder that you will still be writing, Signor Climber: nobody marks you. Indeed, you have a weightier matter to answer for. You have queered the pitch.

"Every mountaineer... must feel a sense of rage against the pioneers. Their ruthless waste of new ascents, which, properly husbanded, might have provided material for the energy of generations; their reckless exploitation of all the jokes, which, properly preserved, might have kept the club warm far off in 'winters which we shall not see' remind me of the desolating track of an invading army. I should not have asked them to leave us the Matterhorn still untrampled, or the flea unarrided, but they might have kept their feet from, say, the Mettelhorn, or have spared the porter from their mirth."

Thus Mr. Schuster, from whom I have also stolen the quotation that heads this paper. I would take this opportunity of asking his forgiveness, and of pointing those who have not yet read it to one of the most distinguished, fascinating, and compelling books that it has been my good fortune to read, by confessing at once that if in this article there be anywhere found a happy phrase, a delicate turn of words, a notable paragraph, or a subtle suggestion, it is probably taken from the same source.

Climbing books have three excuses for being. They can, as guides, afford information; they can, as accounts of exploration, describe the unknown; they can, as literature, justifiably exist. In the modern instances with which I have to deal are examples of all three categories. If my instances be four, whilst my categories be but three, one of the four works would logically seem to lack excuse, and they who think nobly of the craft will in no way shrink from the conclusion.

Climbing books possess strange properties. There has come to be a conventional climbing humour to which they almost all strive only too successfully to attain — a humour as far as possible removed from the Comic Spirit. No sword of Common Sense, but rather a cumbrous two-handed engine, heavily belabouring, but leaving our withers unwrung. It may take one of two forms. In the one case, an elephantine lumbering after the ridiculous, that can call nothing by its right name, so that a cow becomes a bovine quadruped, or the Parson's Nose an ecclesiastical nasal organ. In the other case, a forced spriteliness, a laboured nimbleness, a devastating gaiety that creates a corruscation, and calls it wit. "At this point," to quote the classical if apocryphal instance, "Smith exhibited a sudden desire to execute some fancy steps in the air, and was only recalled to a proper sense of his position by a vigorous tug from Andermatter; but he remained apparently resentful of this cavalier treatment of his Terpsichorean efforts until we reached the Col, when he revenged himself by annexing more than his proper share of the luscious comestibles with which he had been careful to overload the sack which it would not be his lot to carry."

Another characteristic of such books is their extraordinary employment of inverted commas. Their pages positively dazzle. The proper use of quotation marks would seem a mystery too deep for the ordinary mind to solve. It was once my privilege to be shown a letter of thanks for some small kindness which contained this memorable phrase: "For all that you have done, I hope 'God' will bless you." So far as any principle may be said to direct a use so arbitrary, it would appear that no self-respecting page can be considered complete without at least one pair. Phrases such as this, "and many a disappointed and 'pumped out' craigsman has been forced to give it 'best'," leave one wondering what sign the printer can have left at his disposal to indicate when an actual quotation is intended to be made.

If this be the nature of climbing books, what can be more unaccountable than the desire to possess them? Some men collect stamps, some railway tickets, some postmarks. The object collected seems of little importance. The craving is supplied by the act of collection. And so there be individuals who collect an Alpine library. It is a disease, like measles or any other, to which the flesh would seem inevitably to be heir; and, like measles, it is commonly of no considerable duration. It is, as a rule, suffered young; it leaves, in general, no lasting ill-effects. I have had it, as have my fellows. I was ambitious to possess an Alpine collection. I began my library with *The*

Playground of Europe, and tried each succeeding volume by its standard. My library remained a collection of one volume. It is no longer. Mr Schuster's book has joined it on the shelf.

IN DEFENCE OF POPULAR WRITING.

A REPLY TO MR. MYLES MATTHEWS

(extract)

ARNOLD LUNN

(1913)

The last issue of this *Journal* was enlivened by a witty attack on climbing literature. Like most *ex cathedra* utterances, this indictment seemed to carry its own proof. Mr. Mathews asks, "Why do people write mountain books when it is so much easier not to write them?" He dismisses the hope of gain as improbable, and finds the careless rapture of figuring in the British Museum catalogue inadequate as an explanation.

Let me remark in passing that the masters of language have not always been free from vanity nor indifferent to the gross problem of royalties, but there are other motives which are responsible for Alpine literature. Why, then, do people write mountain books? One obvious answer is that self-expression is an instinct as old as the rude forefather that first carved in some primeval cave the crude image of a mammoth. It is not only the great for whom expression is a necessary function. Even the humblest and most incompetent craftsman feels at times the need for expressing himself in the most natural medium. This perhaps explains rather than excuses much work. Another motive which Mr. Mathews has overlooked is the fact that mere expression of past joys enables the writer very thoroughly to forget the disagreeable present. Idle reflection has not the same power to beget again the golden hours. The labour of crystallising into language the frail hill memories creates an illusion in which the present is forgotten and the past reborn. Mr. Mathews will reply, "Very well. I'm glad your articles give you pleasure. I congratulate you on your sunny disposition. Go on writing by all means, if it amuses you. But don't publish."

But there is another motive, which explains both the matter and its publication. We have seen something that is very good to see. We do not want our friends to miss this pleasure. We can't make them see it with the eyes of the body, but we dare to hope that some chance phrase may bring the hills as we saw them before the eyes of their mind. We are writing for a small, sympathetic circle, and we want to share with them the intimate beauty of high places. And some of our best literature is largely due to the desire to make converts. We feel sure that there are among our readers those who have only to hear the call, and to join us. To some folk, this missionary spirit may be anathema. They climb for themselves alone, and do not wish to vulgarise the Alps by crowds of converts. Such literature smacks of a revival meeting, urges the critic. Let us be courageous, and assert boldly that such literature does give pleasure to the readers. Mr. Mathews tells us that his Alpine shelf consists of two books, *The Playground of Europe* and *Peaks and Pleasant Pastures*. Some of us would not envy Mr. Mathews his esoteric taste. We may admire it, of course, just as we may admire the cultivated person who can only listen with enjoyment to Wagner. But our admiration is unalloyed with envy if we can enjoy not only Wagner but "vulgar and tavern musick."

Good work is too often spoiled by tiresome affectations fashionable in Alpine circles. Certain conventions invaded our literature shortly after the pioneers had done their work. We shall never recover the vigour and sincerity of the older books. The freshness of the early writing was partly due to the romance of unexplored and unknown mountains, but even more to the absence of that pedantic affectation which makes a later and more self-conscious generation ashamed to write as it feels. The pioneers were writing not for an esoteric circle that discounted as "fine writing" any attempt to convey worthily the commonplaces of every climb, the morning tramp, the joy of some windy bivouac. The effectiveness of their work is largely due to the enthusiasm with which they enlarged on the simple issues of the craft, to their delight in their own achievements, and to their unaffected ambition to make converts to a good cause. These men were founding a new sect, and the new creed was on trial. And it is to this that their deliverance owes its vigour.

The pioneers of the Alps were heretics, denounced by Ruskin and by the *Times*. And because they were rebels their writings are still alive. Their successors founded the inevitable Academy, and "the little laws that lacqueys make" became the accepted literary canons. The founders were schismatics; their successors basked in the odour of sanctity. They had a pleasant reputation as being daring beyond the common, and they took good care that those who overstepped the limits of their discreet adventure should be, in turn, discredited.

A protest should be made against the tradition that condemns as "popular" any work that does not conform to critical tastes.

It is much easier to write a dull book than a popular book. That is why the average writer whose work is not popular sets a premium on dull correctness.

Mountaineering has become a science with an appropriate jargon. Mountain literature is too often written only for a select circle that are interested, not in the commonplace glories of every climb, but in technical details that differentiate one route from another. Popular writing makes a wider appeal, and so popular writing is condemned by the few right-minded folk. Worse still is the case of those who write for the magazines. There is something strangely sinful to the average Alpine mind in the thought of a magazine article, and it takes a hardened devil's advocate to defend them. There is a certain type of article which no sane man desires to vindicate. The author who chooses this medium to caricature a fine sport by concentrating on sensational incidents is deserving of severe censure. I do not urge that no man should describe, even in a magazine, some stirring adventure on the heights. It would be pedantic to insist that a magazine article should only consist of a temperate account of a fine-weather ascent unvaried by incident. But those who have seen something of the darker side of the sport will not willingly forgive the man who traffics in the saddest memories of the craft to tickle the ears of the groundlings. A bad article is bad wherever it appears; but good work is good work between the sober covers of the *Alpine Journal* or in the pages of the *Wide World Magazine*. After all, the magazine is the best medium for reaching the unconverted public.

If you feel that the number of mountaineers is large enough, you may criticise this attitude; but it is a churl's part to shut out others from the rewards of the climber. The pioneers who made Alpine literature had none of this contempt for all articles which did not appear in the pages of some climbing journal. Leslie Stephen wrote some of his best work for the *Cornhill;* Whymper wrote frequently in the Press. Mr. Douglas Freshfield, only the other day, contributed a most interesting article on the Himalayas to the *Daily Express*. Sir Martin Conway has written for the *Strand,* and, finally, Mr. Lloyd has sanctified the practice by contributing an account of a climb to the *Morning Post*. Perhaps we may also remind Mr.Mathews that the two Alpine books he condescends to read are largely reprints of articles that delighted the readers of the *Cornhill* and the *Times*.

There is, moreover, a prevalent suspicion that all magazine and "popular" writers are condemned, and that they are supposed to be bent on advertising themselves. There are three things for which the average Briton has a fine nose. He is a regular sleuth-hound at detecting a pose, unconscious that the stupidest of all poses is the affectation of being natural. But he is really happy when he can smell out a financial motive, or accuse his neighbour of advertising himself. Most folk are quite pleased when somebody else advertises them, but are justly indignant with the franker adventurer who acts as his own advertising agent. The situation is intensified in Alpine circles because there is no recognised rivalry. Theoretically, we all climb just for the love of the sport. There are, of course, a number of mountaineers who are unfeignedly modest, and as indifferent as mortal men can be to the credit of achievement. But I have often thought that for the rank and file some recognised rivalry in competition would be better than the bitter jealousies that divide the Alpine world.

It is sincerity that discriminates gush from good writing. The critic implies failure when he uses the phrase, "fine writing." He detects and condemns a conscious effort to write for effect. The greatest masters have perhaps been those who found the statue sleeping in marble, for whom expression has been a spontaneous release, a function as natural as life. But the mere fact that a piece of prose is carefully planned and worked up does not imply that it is not good art. Ruskin and Stevenson and Walter Pater were in a sense highly artificial writers. Art conceals art, and the good craftsman can give to laboured work that appearance of spontaneity which is essential. It is not careful working for effect — if skilfully concealed — but only the appearance of effort that we really dislike. The real touchstone is sincerity. If a man strives to write fine prose and uses for his subject any emotion that seems adaptable, the result will usually be pure wordiness. But if the writer wishes to express some emotion in worthy language, if he wishes to catch in words some echo of the hills, if he honestly tries to write what he feels, and not what he thinks he ought to feel, then, no matter how laboured the graving, or how loose the structure, he deserves something better than hypercriticism. And fortunately there are still some left who refuse to be dull merely to placate British reserve.

One last protest, and I may leave Mr. Mathews to demolish this article at his leisure. I cull the following from his review of a certain book. I make no comments on the context, but as I understand Mr. Mathews to be laying down a general truth I shall criticise it apart from its setting.

"No sane man goes into a dangerous place just because it is a danger-ous place, or would be in a dangerous place if there were any reasonable alternative route. Climbers, like other people, have had accidents or have narrowly escaped them; have been in situations under circumstances which they would have given a good deal to avoid. Such experiences they are not anxious to repeat, and they owe it not only to themselves but to their sport to hide them with a decent reticence. That one should deliberately publish descriptions of such matters is inconceivable."

Mr. Mathews must really fill out that select little library of his. He will then find that it is quite conceivable that men "should deliberately publish descriptions of such matters." In fact, it has been done more than once. Let us appeal only to the two authors whom Mr. Mathews deigns to read. Leslie Stephen wrote "a bad five minutes in the Alps," and a fine account of a party caught in a winter storm. Mr. Schuster, in the best chapter of a notable book, describes "circumstances which he would have given a great deal to avoid," and experiences which I am sure he is "not anxious to repeat." It is easy to multiply classic examples.

As one who has a healthy objection to unnecessary danger, I may be allowed to defend those who are free from "knee-dissolving fear." Come now, Mr. Mathews! When last you carried through some reckless climb in foul weather, did you really slink back into the hotel like a felon detected in the act?

Why in the world should such climbs, once accomplished, not be de-scribed? Mountain literature is dull enough. Let us be thankful if some writer can vary the monotony with a rousing chapter of adventure.

ON FINE WRITING
AN ANSWER TO MR. LUNN

C. MYLES MATHEWS
(1913)

Mr. Lunn, if I rightly understand him, would set us all to writing. An excellent thing in an Editor, and the cause of the conspicuous success of our *Journal* under his direction. Long may he hold to his opinion. So long will our *Journal* flourish and I have no quarrel with him. For nothing in the article that has so finely moved his wrath was concerned with what a man may write for his own club journal. It was wholly directed to what a man may give in books to the unappreciative world at large.

With much that Mr. Lunn has to say I am unconcerned. It does not touch the issue between us, and I have therefore no occasion to follow him into his disquisition upon our national characteristics, or his discourse upon the uses of advertisement. I pause but to remove two misconceptions. He seeks to remind me that parts of a book I liked appeared in the *Times* and the *Cornhill*. The reminder was unnecessary. I was one of the readers who were delighted with the initial publication. He enjoys "vulgar and tavern musick." So, most heartily, do I. In folk songs and drinking catches you have some of the finest tunes in the world. He says that mountaineering has become a science with an appropriate jargon. I agree. A book treating of the scientific aspect of mountaineering rightly employs the appropriate jargon, just as does any text-book dealing with any technical subject, be it surgery, philosophy, chemistry, or what you will. With such books neither Mr. Lunn nor I are for the moment concerned.

Where I differ from Mr. Lunn is this, that, granted a man may have enthusiasm for his mountaineering, granted that be may feel all that Mr. Lunn desires him to feel, when he sets himself to the writing of a book he starts to work at an art, craft or mystery wherein high technical skill is a necessary preliminary to success. I use the word preliminary advisedly, since in this, as in all crafts, in music, in painting, in singing no less than in writing, mere technique and nothing else is an intolerably tedious business. But technique you must have as a basis.

"It is not only the great for whom expression is a necessary function," says Mr. Lunn, and none will gainsay him. But the power and the means of expression are necessary before understandable expression can be made. To speak with the tongue of men and of angels is admittedly not everything, but it at least is an assistance in enabling your hearers to appreciate what you may have to say. "Incoherence," says Mr. Lunn, "is not incompatible with sincerity." But neither does it help to convey your meaning. "Their literary sins are forgiven because they loved the mountains." Here Mr. Lunn and I differ. This reason seems to me to be inadequate and irrelevant. It is as

Peter Biven (belaying) and Trevor Peck climbing Harding's Superdirect (HVS), Stanage.
Photo: Biven Collection.

Pat Littlejohn on Dreadnought (E3), Old Redoubt, Berry Head in 1969. Photo: Peter Biven.

Above: Dave Cook on Scavenger (VS), Three Cliffs, Gower Peninsula in 1976.
Photo: Mike Mortimer.
Left: Peter Biven on the first ascent of The Watchtower, Torbay, Devon in 1968.
Photo: Biven Collection.

Above: The tyrolean from Gannet Rock, Lundy in August 1971. Photo: John Cleare
Below: Alan Blackshaw (left) and Zeke Deacon (right). Photo: Ken Wilson Archive.

though he would listen with pleasure to an execrable violinist, because he was kind to his mother. In each case the characteristic is doubtless admirable and even endearing, but what possible effect it is supposed to have upon the quality of the performance I am quite unable to appreciate. A man may have an intense passion for the mountains, and yet, if he have not the skill, if he be not handy in an exceedingly difficult craft, if he have not served an arduous and often dusty apprenticeship, he may write an intolerably tedious symphony upon them. "The freshness of the early writing" was due, according to Mr. Lunn, to a variety of causes. To my mind, where it exists it was due to one: the fact that the early writers happened to be able to write.

It may well be that a man must love the mountains before he can write adequately of them. But love of the mountains alone will not of itself enable him to write of them at all. Properly to judge of a work it must be judged by the standard of the greatest works of a like nature. One judges a Mass by comparing it with Bach in B minor, not with Stainer in A flat, of an oratorio by comparing it with the Matthew Passion, not with the Elijah, of a book by comparing with the best one knows of the type, not with the stillborn of Paternoster Row.

THE MOUNTAINEER AS ARTIST

(extract)

GEORGE MALLORY
(1914)

In practice I find that few men ever want to discuss mountaineering seriously. I suppose they imagine that a discussion with me would be unprofitable; and I must confess that if anyone does open the question my impulse is to put him off. I can assume a vague disdain for civilisation, and I can make phrases about beautiful surroundings, and puff them out, as one who has a secret and does not care to reveal it because no one would understand — phrases which refer to the divine riot of Nature in her ecstasy of making mountains.

Thus I appeal to the effect of mountain scenery upon my æsthetic sensibility. But, even if I can communicate by words a true feeling, I have explained nothing. Æsthetic delight is vitally connected with our performance, but it neither explains nor excuses it. No one for a moment dreams that our apparently wilful proceedings are determined merely by our desire to see what is beautiful. The mountain railway could cater for such desires. By providing view-points at a number of stations, and by concealing all signs of its own mechanism, it might be so completely organised that all the æsthetic joys of the mountaineer should be offered to its intrepid ticket holders. It would achieve this object with a comparatively small expenditure of time, and would even have, one might suppose, a decisive advantage by affording to all lovers of the mountains the opportunity of sharing their emotions with a large and varied multitude of their fellow-men. And yet the idea of associating this mechanism with a snow mountain is the abomination of every species of mountaineer. To him it appears as a kind of rape. The fact that he so regards it indicates the emphasis with which he rejects the crude æsthetic reasons as his central defence.

I suppose that, in the opinion of many people who have opportunities of judging, mountaineers have no ground for claiming for their pursuit a superiority as regards the natural beauties that attend it. And certainly many huntsmen would resent their making any such claim. We cannot, therefore, remove mountaineering from the plane of hunting by a composite representation of its merits — by asserting that physical and æsthetic joys are blent for us and not for others.

Nevertheless, I am still arrogant, and still confident in the superiority of mountaineering over all other forms of recreation. But what do I mean by this superiority? And in what measure do I claim it? On what level do we place mountaineering? What place in the whole order of experience is occupied by our experience as mountaineers? The answer to these questions must be very nearly connected with the whole explanation of our position; it may actually be found to include in itself a defence of mountaineering.

It must be admitted at the outset that our periodic literature gives little indication that our performance is concerned no less with the spiritual side of us than with the physical. This is, in part, because we require certain practical information of anyone who describes an expedition. Our journals, with one exception, do not pretend to be elevated literature, but aim only at providing useful knowledge for climbers. With this purpose we try to show exactly where upon a mountain our course lay, in what manner the conditions of snow and ice and rocks and weather were or were not favourable to our enterprise, and what were the actual difficulties we had to overcome and the dangers we had to meet. Naturally, if we accept these circumstances, the impulse for literary expression vanishes; not so much because the matter is not suitable as because, for literary expression, it is too difficult to handle. A big expedition in the Alps, say a traverse of Mont Blanc, would be a superb theme for an epic poem. But we are not all even poets, still less Homers or Miltons. We do, indeed, possess lyric poetry that is concerned with mountains, and value it highly for the expression of much that we feel about them. But little of it can be said to suggest that mountaineering in the technical sense offers an emotional experience which cannot otherwise be reached. A few essays and a few descriptions do give some indication that the spiritual part of man is concerned. Most of those who describe expeditions do not even treat them as adventure, still less as being connected with any emotional experience peculiar to mountaineering. Some writers, after the regular careful references to matters of plain fact, insert a paragraph dealing summarily with an æsthetic experience; the greater part make a bare allusion to such feelings or neglect them altogether, and perhaps these are the wisest sort.

And yet it is not so very difficult to write about æsthetic impressions in some way so as to give pleasure. If we do not ask too much, many writers are able to please us in this respect. We may be pleased, without being stirred to the depths, by anyone who can make us believe that he has experienced æsthetically; we may not be able to feel with him what he has felt, but if he talks about it simply we may be quite delighted to perceive that he has felt as we too are capable of feeling. Mountaineers who write do not, as a rule, succeed even in this small degree. If they are so bold as to attempt a sunset or sunrise, we too often feel uncertain as we read that they have felt anything — and this even though we may know quite well that they are accustomed to feel as we feel ourselves.

These observations about our mountain literature are not made by way of censure or in disappointment; they are put forward as phenomena, which have to be explained, not so much by the nature of mountaineers, but rather by the nature of their performance. The explanation which commends itself to me is derived very simply from the conception of mountaineering, which, expressed or unexpressed, is common, I imagine, to all us of the arrogant sort. We do not think that our æsthetic experiences of sunrises and sunsets and clouds and thunder are supremely important facts in mountaineering, but rather that they cannot thus be separated and catalogued and described individually as experiences at all. They are not incidental in mountaineering, but a vital and inseparable part of it; they are not ornamental, but structural; they are not various items causing emotion but parts of an emotional whole; they are the crystal pools perhaps, but they owe their life to a continuous stream.

It is this unity that makes so many attempts to describe æsthetic detail seem futile. Somehow they miss the point and fail to touch us. It is because they are only fragments. If we take one moment and present its emotional quality apart from the whole, it has lost the very essence that gave it a value. If we write about an expedition from the emotional point of view in any part of it, we ought so to write about the whole adventure from beginning to end.

A day well spent in the Alps is like some great symphony. Andante, andantissimo sometimes, is the first movement — the grim, sickening plod up the moraine. But how forgotten when the blue light of dawn flickers over the hard, clean snow! The new *motif* is ushered in, as it were, very gently on the lesser wind instruments, hautboys and flutes, remote but melodious and infinitely hopeful, caught by the violins in the growing light, and torn out by all the bows with quivering chords as the summits, one by one, are enmeshed in the gold web of day, till at last the whole band, in triumphant accord, has seized the air and romps in magnificent frolic, because there you are at last marching, all a-tingle with warm blood, under the sun. And so throughout the day successive moods induce the symphonic whole.

SUNRISE
FROM THE 'THE RELIGION OF A MOUNTAINEER'

ARNOLD LUNN
(1930)

The east was preparing for the sun. In the west a few stars still hesitated like nervous guests who have outstayed their welcome and then went out one by one as if touched by an unseen hand. At noon the sky is a roof, at dawn an infinite emptiness of pure space. The finite and the infinite met where the clear-cut concrete lines of the summit ridges showed against the unplumbed depths beyond. The cold, pure light in the east was the light which Francesca loved to reproduce in tempera. There was colour in the sky and colour in the lake, but it was colour held in solution. The cobalt blues of the water were waiting for the touch of the sovereign alchemist. The solitary chirrup of an impertinent bird was promptly suppressed by an unseen baton, as if the conductor was still holding his choir in suspense.

All Nature was waiting. Hill and lake and bird seemed poised in an expectant mood.

The little wind which goes before the dawn had already changed the steady note of a neighbouring stream into a fitful melody, music interrupted by silence when the wind bore away the fugitive song. Then the wind began to weave its patterns on the lake, covering it with a faint burr, like the lines of a drypoint etching. The water darkened as the breeze touched it and as the wind drove the wavelets forward a shadow seemed to dart across the lake like the shadow of swift-scudding clouds.

Then suddenly the rocky crest of an eastern peak was edged with light. The sun was coming. The grass stirred uneasily to meet the dawn, the flowers opened a little wider, the world was big with hope, and the mountains stood to the salute. As the sun climbed above the hills one rose instinctively to one's feet.

SUNRISE
FROM 'END OF A CLIMB'

J. M. EDWARDS
(1937)

We got up and shook ourselves, for the warmth had left our rock now, and the thin arms of the sun were rising steadily as their burden grew lighter. The colours, however, went still deeper, and then, as if the liquid of the sky became oversaturated with its intensity, it seemed suddenly to sigh and as it did so, it shed a slight, greyish precipitate, that gathered and clung nervously together in a thin strip down the centre of the blue. As it formed, the earth seemed to come out a little and its detail began to rise coldly up the sides of the hill. The arms of the sun, as if driven up into quick motion, lifted their beams clear of the earth, and the particles of their warmth, despairing, concentrated their last effort in a soft rose light along the Western aspect of the strip of cloud. Down on the rocks a squat yew tree, clinging to the face, shivered and drew itself up. The shadows came together and lay cramped stiffly over it.

We turned our backs finally to the hills and began to chatter: setting about to make our minds easy. But behind us, fighting their slow wars, the forces of nature also shifted steadily on.

FROM *SELECTED POEMS ON WEST PENWITH AND REFLECTIONS*

A.W. ANDREWS
(1957)

GRANITE

Granite is not for man's convenience
To chip a block into a human form
And for its shaping there is but one tool,
The alchemy of water etching it
And water born of water fretting it
By constant wearing through the centuries,

A continuity of handing on
That find a worthy setting for the craft
In the long galleries of cliff and sea
Where there is room to show a masterpiece
Some hundred feet or so from base to top.

This is not Lliwedd but a miniature
That Nature made to show what could be done
With granite to her hand on lesser hills,
A fan-shaped ridge whose towers and pinnacles
Lift in a knife edge to the moor above,
Hiding beside its wall a sanctuary
Of bluebells on a hanging garden plot,
And in the cove below a 'battleship'
Of granite on the mirror of the sea.

WICCA

There is a quiet here
Of afternoon,
Where no surprise
To break the monotone
Of even ways
Is or has been.

A quiet that is positive and whole
In a dry June,
When Nature's choice is sober green,
With just a flower or two
To deck a buttonhole
And a few patches where the hay still lies
Against the scarf of water's faded blue.

The ledge on which I sit
Looks on a cave
Where the sea swell
Lifts to a rock and waits
To see if it can find the strength
To get out of the deep well.

And makes a pause and hesitates
And then as climbers do at length
Pulls lazily over the summit
And the last climb is done.

A TRAVERSE

MISLYKETE FORSOG. LOST ENDEAVOUR.
Tide coming in too fast and on our left
A cliff we could not climb and on our right
Nothing but sea, America and night.

ENVOI

UNATTRIBUTED (J. D. MILLS)
(1931)

It was nearly midnight. The Editor sat back in his Editorial chair. He had labelled the plates, corrected the proofs, compiled the index. Volume IV, New Series, was now in the capable hands of those two good friends of the Club, Mr. Jennings, Manager, and Mr. Walker, Foreman Printer, of Messrs. Spottiswoode, Ballantyne & Co., Ltd. The Editorial eyes slowly closed.

It was raining hard. The Editor, suitably clad in Everest cloth and climbing boots, with 100 feet of stout rope, was struggling upwards through the waterfall pitch of a magnificent gully. Above, waiting to receive him, were all the great men of the past, climbers, editors, even presidents. All were clad as he was, though one or two of the oldest were sitting astride chairs with their arms folded on the backs of them. Ice axes hung from the walls, growing longer and longer as they stretched up into antiquity. The Editor struggled out of the waterfall, dropped on to his knee, and presented his Volume. It was condescendingly accepted. Somehow or other a committee of experts got itself together, while the rest, suitably grouped, intoned throughout a solemn chorus, " A natural Cairn is provided, built on Nature's liberal scale." Then the committee got to work. "There are three misprints..." "Not up to the old days of Mallory..." "The justifiable hesitation about printing these dangerous climbs, which we were glad to observe in your first number, seems to have been entirely abandoned in your last." "These young men can't write English..." "... on Nature's liberal scale."

But Chorus and criticism were growing fainter. The gully seemed in some mysterious way to be flattening itself out level with the great slabs which flanked it and which the Editor now saw for the first time gleaming in glorious sunlight. There were no holds, but plenty of bulges and overhangs. The Editor, still clutching his precious Volume, was marooned on a small grassy ledge (stance and belay). He looked fearfully about him. There was no committee of critics, simply one joyful chorus, dancing up and down the slab, waving festoons of the thinnest line and chanting (to the tune of "Here we go round the Mulberry Bush") "Poor old Cloggy's got rickety innards."* Most of them wore rubbers of course, though one could be observed in a pair of light-blue socks, through the end of which protruded a prehensile toe. Their clothes were old, colourless, stained, tattered, they had neither axe nor rucksack. But the sun shone and they were much lighter hearted than their elders of the Gully. The Editor was on the point of offering them his volume when through the rock there swelled once more, like Tannhäuser's

---

* This means that some of the rocks, inside the overhangs on Clogwyn du'r Arddu are insecure.— Ed.

returning pilgrims, the saintly chorale "A natural Cairn is provided on Nature's liberal scale." High rose the opposing bacchanale "Rickety innards... Rickety innards." The Editor hesitated. "A natural Cairn is provided with rickety innards, rickety innards." He was lost. He turned to the folk on the slab; the chorale faded away. "Here," he shouted to the revellers, "would you like the new volume of the *Climbers' Club Journal?*" They swayed towards him, festooning him in their slender coils. His book was seized, thrown from hand to hand, caught, tossed in air and caught again. Covers were soon off, pages flying everywhere. "Steady," cried one, "Steady. It will do to light the Helyg fire with. Don't waste it." "Rickety innards... Rickety innards." With one last great shout they drew tight the festoons. The Editor was jerked into space. As he fell, he was acutely conscious that while his right side was still correctly dressed, there was a large hole in his left elbow, he could feel the wind about his left knee and, horror of horrors, his left foot was wearing a rubber shoe.

'Hiraeth'

"If we could not reach the Himalayas, the Andes, or the Caucasus, the blesssed Alps were within easy reach of us, pure, bracing and invigorating. And if even these were too remote from some of us, remember that Helvellyn and Scawfell were only a day's journey from London, and that God created Great Wales!"
President C. E. Mathews's 'Toast to the Club'
(Vol. 1 No. 4 June 1899)

FIRST ASCENT OF THE EAST GULLY AND BUTTRESS OF LLIWEDD

J. M. A. THOMSON
(Vol. II No. 6 1899)

On April the 5th, 1896, O.Eckenstein, H. Edwards, H. Hughes, W. A. Thomson, and myself left the Pen-y-Gwryd Inn at a fashionably late hour in the morning.

We had no particular *objectif* but a vague impression prevailed that we were to walk up Lliwedd and climb down part of the north face, whereupon someone was to be lowered down a certain series of precipitous crags on a descent of discovery, to place beyond the region of conjecture sundry moot-points which had been much argued to and fro on the previous evening.

A timely reflection that the lightest man of the party might be chosen to carry out this missionary enterprise, while the strong men wrought their will on him from above, had the effect of awakening in me a sense of duty towards my neighbours, and it obviously behoved me to divert their attention from things trivial to the rare beauty and sublime grace of Lliwedd's Eastern Buttress, as soon as its noble outline fairly broke upon our view.

This virtuous desire that the minds of my companions should be edified by a serious contemplation of the beauties of nature, resulted in the enunciation of a theory that a closer inspection of these same beauties, such as might be gained by a climb on the Eastern Buttress, would materially conduce to an aesthetic appreciation of them; whereupon I felt that it would be an unpardonable violation of the altruistic spirit of the age to take exception to the course suggested on the ground of my own decided preference for steep and exhilarating grassy slopes.

An attack on the unclimbed East Gully was decided upon, and this, no doubt, the more readily, because another member of the party, as he subsequently discovered to us in a paulo-post-prandial confession, had long been cherishing a secret affection for the virgin climb proposed — an affection which had lain till then too deep for expression in words.

The rocks at the foot of the gully, through which the water has not yet sawn a defined channel, were surmounted, and the gully proper entered without difficulty. Here it was deemed prudent to leave for a while our novice, whose experience in Wales was limited to having assisted me the day before up the east gully of the Glyder Fawr, and not less so, to appoint two stalwart men to watch his movements, as he chanced to have the lunch of the party in his keeping.

The line of ascent chosen was slightly to the orographical left of the centre of the gully; the rock proved similar in nature to that in the other two couloirs of Lliwedd, being steep, smooth and sound, and offering holds which often slope slightly to the disadvantage of the climber.

We soon reached a water-worn trough, into which it was necessary to squeeze sideways, and work up with the aid of back-pressure. During this process the expansion of the lungs was seriously impeded by the narrowness of the chimney, so that both leaders arrived very well-breathed at the upper end of it. At the height of 150 feet a small flat ledge on the left offered the first "firmus locus," and provided scanty standing room for two. The climb of the next 140 feet from this ledge, though similar in general character, proved somewhat easier until a species of roofless cave, with a steeply-sloping floor, was entered. From this cubicle there was no apparent exit. Eckenstein, who was separated by less than 30 feet, and had a long tail of rope trailing from his waist, joined me here to give me the benefit of his counsel and aid; pressing his back against one wall, and feet against the other, he explained to me the exceptional security of his bridge-like position; it was one in which he could receive me in his embrace, if my attempt to climb out should prove abortive, and, as the next resting-place was obviously the heads of our companions below, I derived much courage and comfort from this assurance. The right wall is some ten feet high, straight and smooth; by utilising a crack in the corner, the climber is able to maintain his balance two feet above the floor; an unseen hand-hold above is thus brought within his reach, and a long draw-up lands him at the top of the difficulty.

"What is it like beyond?" rang out an eager voice from the cubicle. An interval of silence ensued, during which the climber above was ostensibly gathering information — but, in reality, breath — before vouchsafing the reply that the rest of the gully lay back at a relatively easy angle.

Some fifteen feet higher a knob in the bed of the gully forms an excellent belaying-pin, and from here I watched with interest my companion appear —

> "longo cum fune gravatum,
> Prensantemque uncis manibus capita aspera montis."

We had taken 1hr 15m to reach this point, and were now separated by 310 feet from our companions; but, as our party consisted of three originally independent and fully equipped sections, we had just rope enough to reach.

After the arrival of the third man, however, our line of communication became temporarily severed, for the rope, caught by wind, persistently refused to travel down to its intended destination, and when much time had been spent in futile endeavours, the expedient of lowering a flat stone, fastened with the utmost skill and care, was tried; half the descent it accomplished to our entire satisfaction, but then it stuck fast, and for all our coaxing could not be induced to move in any direction whatsoever. Finally, my companions had to "steady" me down to the ledge to remedy the obstruction. In response to a word of warning, the men below shouted that they were in shelter, *so far as the nature of the place permitted;* this important reservation, however, was lost in the wind, and they were in fact fully exposed to anything descending the gully. The stone was thereupon jerked free, but it split in the centre, and the two halves, slipping out of the hitches and splintering in their descent, fairly bombarded our rear-guard below.

That the casualties were nothing worse than an abrasion on one arm seemed little short of marvellous to the witness of an incident, which became, indeed, a subject for much good-humoured banter, but caused at the time some moments of intense anxiety.

From the coign of vantage the line of communication was eventually restored, and in due time the party were re-united around the belaying-pin.

From this point we could either continue in the gully — and a stretch of rock remains before the scree finish — or complete the climb on the Eastern Buttress; the latter alternative was chosen on the ground of its prolonging the climb to the summit, and affording good views of this unexplored part of the mountain.

The climbing at this level on the Eastern Buttress is decidedly superior to that upon the corresponding portion of the Western, the rocks being bolder and far freer from earth and grass. Moving together, we took 50m in ascending it, and struck the summit ridge within arm's length of the cairn.

After a pious halt we walked leisurely down the grassy ridge and back by the Snowdon path, too full of —

"The joy of life in steepness overcome
And victories of ascent,"

to misconstrue the gentle reproaches always in store for those who return to Pen-y-Gwryd late for dinner.

RHYD

G. J. SUTTON

(1954)

Far off stands sea like time, calling its children home.
Nearby, the brown lake sleeps, reaches
streams like arms to cling to the hillside.
And in sky overarching, overmirroring slide
great white flocked clouds regarding
few sights, few sounds but wind, and water carding
heather and gorsefleeced hills of bones and peat ; new lambs
cry to new world that hath such creatures in it as mother and birds
and these small secret people. Peace widens, overflows, laps, fills
these cottages left like morsels in a dish of hills.

WASTDALE HEAD AT EASTER

(extract)

L. J. OPPENHEIMER
(Vol. II No. 5 September 1899)

"You observe that grey-haired old boy making yawning gaps in a leg of mutton? A Liverpool doctor used to come here forty years ago, and knew Will Ritson well Ask him. 'Verily,' he will say, 'the former days were better than these.' 'Foolhardy gymnastics,' he calls our climbing, though he tramps all over the hills to watch us. If you want to know about Wilson and Tyson and Ritson and the olden times, ask *him.*"

"What sort of a man was Ritson ?"

"Behold his portrait at the end of the room, with his clay pipe and mug of beer; the man who boasted that Wastdale had the highest mountain, deepest lake, smallest church, and biggest liar in England."

"Indeed !" remarks the tourist, "I've heard before of the first three, though the third is disputed, but never of the fourth. Who was he?"

"Why, Ritson himself of course, while he lived, and though he is dead, Wastdale still maintains her supremacy. You will be convinced after dinner when you have heard the stories that will be told — climbing with teeth and eyelashes — sticking on to seamless perpendicular cliffs by the mere friction of tweed trousers."

"Well, after looking at the photographs round these walls I am ready to believe almost anything. By the way, you yourself seem to have been trying to stick on to a cliff by the friction of the back of your hand. I hope you haven't injured yourself."

"A mere scrape — I foolishly jammed it in a crack — the smart is trifling, and 'the labour we delight in physics pain'."

"That was not what you said at the time," interrupts the gentleman on the other side of the Bohemian.

"I probably said 'Damn'," he replies.

"I would have respected you more if you had: as far as I remember you said 'Verily my flesh is consume'd away that it cannot be seen, and my bones that were not seen stick out'."

"You probably don't remember how that most apt utterance was followed by a noise as of 'the crackling of thorns under a pot'."

"Oh! I admit that we were not very sympathetic, but it was too ridiculous to watch your pretended indifference to the scrape until you had got out your inevitable quotation."

After this interruption the tourist continues — "How appropriately, from your point of view, this room is decorated. You have photographs of all your

Joe Brown on his first ascent of Suicide Wall Route 1 (E2), Idwal for BBC TV on 27th May 1957. The route had first been climbed in 1945 by Chris Preston. Photo: George Band.

Pete Crew (left) and Al Alvarez (right) about to make the second ascent of Crew's own route, MPP (HVS), on Dinas Mot, photographed for the first climbing story in the new media (the *Observer* Colour Supplement) in June 1965. Photo: John Cleare.

Les and Lawrie Holliwell after the first ascent of Eureka (E1), Craig yr Ogof in 1966. Photo: Ken Wilson.

A young Al Rouse on Erebus (E3) at Tremadog. Photo: Leo Dickinson.

climbs round the walls to refer to, and at the end you have Ritson, whom, I suppose, you would claim as a kindred spirit, to remind you of the days that are past —"

"Yes, and you have a card forbidding smoking in this room at the other end, which reminds you that to-day is not as the days that are past, and is quite inappropriate from my point of view: but you'll see we'll remove the obnoxious document after dinner," the Bohemian adds.

The unsociable elder tourist now hastens to get a word in. "While you are talking of appropriate decorations," he interjects, "don't forget the portrait hanging in the place of honour, looking down between those needles and cliffs and gullies like the corpse at an Egyptian feast: a powerful sermon, but you are all heedless of what it — "

"Sir, will you dare to say that if the Professor could come back to us now he would not approve — "

"No, no, no — I don't want you to take it that way: I know he had the climbing fever like all the rest of you. I spoke with an eye on my friend here: I am afraid he is being seduced by the prevailing enthusiasm, and I wished to remind him that there is 'mountain gloom' as well as 'mountain glory'."

The Bohemian regards him with scorn, saying —

"Cowards die many times before their deaths;
The valiant never taste of death but once."

Dinner over, the company is scattered about the hotel, yet every room seems crowded. Some remain in the dining-room discussing the possibility of new ascents with the aid of the large photographs on the walls. In the smoke-room the sofa and chairs are all occupied, and several men are lying on the floor round the fire, leaning against other people's legs, renewing the adventures of the day and garnishing Swiss experiences of the summer before with lively flights of imagination. The veterans have a stock of stories about their guides, and every exploit recounted suggests to some one else another still more thrilling, humorous or improbable. As coffee is passed round, and the room fills with smoke, criticism slumbers: the narratives become more imaginative, and relate to far off periods: jokes from Leslie Stephen and Mummery pass as original, and raise a laugh for the hundredth time, and gradually the company settles down into a blissful dreamy state, thinking lazily of past victories and defeats that rise and pass and fade with the flickerings of the fire.

Meanwhile, the more energetic may be found in the billiard-room, shouting and laughing as the ball rebounds or flies off the table to the imminent danger of someone's head. "By Jove, what a game! No wonder we couldn't play this afternoon," the bumptious little tourist remarks to his laconic friend, "the ball must be covered with notches." The table is being used for a game of fives, and the partners are rushing wildly backwards and forwards, or into their opponents. The Bohemian stops to take off his coat — " Not that I love warmth less, but freedom more." And now, yet oftener, the ivory ball flies off and adds to its many dinges, until at last a collision between it and an enthusiastic spectator suggests a change. "Let's have the passage of the billiard table leg." All congregate round a corner of the table to watch one after another make the attempt. Only the Gymnast succeeds. He begins by sitting on the table, despite the warning notice above him of a half-crown fine for such an offence ; he lets himself down gently, and, suddenly twisting round, he braces his legs firmly against the cross-bars underneath; from above nothing can now be seen of him but one hand clutching the cushion, but all are watching down below to see that he does not touch the ground. After a struggle, his other hand and his head appear on the opposite side of the table leg, and a moment afterwards he is sitting breathless on the table once more, amidst loud cheers. Then the respective advantages of tall and short men in climbing are discussed, and the heights and reaches of all in the room are marked on the wall.

Next the billiard-room traverse is suggested, but no one responds. After much pressing the Gymnast consents to try. He takes off his coat and shoes, and placing his hands on the edge of the billiard table, he walks backwards up the wall to within a yard of the ceiling. Then he moves along the table and wall simultaneously with hands and feet, avoiding the framed chromolithographs as well as he may. With an enormous stride he reaches from one wall to another at the corner of the room, and is just saved from upsetting some half emptied glasses of whisky on the mantleshelf by the terrified shouts of the owners. The next corner is easier, and in the middle of the third wall he can rest his legs awhile on the window ledge. The fourth wall is more difficult again : it contains a large recess, too deep to reach from the billiard table, and only a foot lower than the ceiling. All round the angle of this he must pass before he arrives at the door, which is set diagonally across the corner of the room. This is the *mauvais pas* of the performance. The Gymnast cautiously brings one foot down until his toe rests on the latch hold; then, supporting himself from the corner of the billiard table with one hand, he reaches the top of the door lintel with the other, lets go with the first, swings round in the opening, and catches the lintel on the opposite side also. Here he gets the first rest for his arms by jamming himself tightly in the opening with his back and legs. To complete the traverse in the orthodox way he has still to work along the passage as far as to the smoke room, and this, after an uncomfortable rest, he quickly does with back against one wall and feet against the other, finally opening the smoke room door and descending to *terra firma*. The tales and visions of the company there assembled are interrupted by cheers, and those who have missed the performance unreasonably clamour for a repetition. An old hand insidiously suggests that there are three variations of the move into the doorway, and the Gymnast is dragged back once more to try them. Then there are tests of balance, of wriggling through narrow chair backs, of hanging on the rope and lifting people with it, and the evening wears away in attempting or watching all kinds of mad antics.

Outside, in the cold clear starlight, the literary tourist, having deserted his two companions, is walking up and down with the Oxford man, looking up in reverent silence at the dark silhouette of Great Gable, or discussing how best to enter into the spirit of the mountains.

"My own experience," the undergraduate says, "leads me to think that only by spending the night alone on the fell tops can you fully enjoy the grandeur and solemnity and the weird mystery of the mountains."

"If you feel so, why do you desecrate them by climbing about in their most secret recesses with those noisy fellows inside? I myself have at times felt a very strong inclination to climb amongst the rocks, but I have always been deterred by the thought of approaching them in such company - and perhaps by the danger that everyone talks about. I would like to go alone, but I am too afraid of getting into a fix."

"Well, do you know, you cannot have every kind of pleasure at once: there are joys of exertion and victory and of jovial company as well as of meditation amongst the lonely hills. As to the danger, I am afraid a very exaggerated idea of it prevails. Many people have certainly been killed on these fells, and I would not advise you to go rock climbing alone, but no serious accident has yet happened in the Lake District to any properly roped party, and a great amount of climbing is done here. I remember when I was a boy hearing that not half-a-dozen people had ever reached the top of the famous Pillar in Ennerdale; that there was only one way, and it was necessary to start with a particular foot first, for if you failed to do this you arrived at a difficult corner in such a position as not to be able to advance or retire. Well, of course this was all nonsense: there were at least six routes known even then, and plenty of people climbed it. Now there are nine principal ways and many variations: I should think over a hundred ascents are made every year, many of them by the long and difficult routes on the north face, so you may feel that the danger is not so considerable. Will you come there with us to-morrow? I am sure you would enjoy it. The views are grand; every muscle will be called into action; ingenuity has to be exercised continually to overcome obstacles, and I promise it will make you feel alive in every fibre But my enthusiasm for climbing is running away with me. You see I'm a believer in Scott —

'Sound, sound the clarion, fill the fife!
To all the sensual world proclaim,
One crowded hour of glorious life
Is worth an age without a name'."

"Well, many thanks for your invitation: if my companions will allow me to desert them, I will go with you gladly. Merely as a lover of Wordsworth, I would like to see the Pillar."

"Yes, but don't come in a Wordsworthian frame of mind: if your brain is pre-occupicd with that 'something far more deeply interfused', you won't do your share of looking after the rope. But I see candle flickerings in some of the upper rooms, which means bed-time, I suppose. I warn you, by the way, that you won't find the clothes you sent to be dried, outside your door in the morning. You'll have to hunt for your stockings amongst some four dozen pairs hanging over the stair rail, and someone else is sure to have run off with your underclothing by mistake — it's one of the amusements of the place. Good night, and good luck on the morrow!"

While writing these notes of my impressions of a Wastdale Easter, the joy of many visits to the place returned to me, and lightened the dreariness of Manchester for a while, but, in an evil hour, I shewed them to those who know, and they have rudely disturbed my tranquil enjoyment. My tall friend reminds me that my climbs with him were in the broiling heat of summer; asks me if I don't remember how we tramped over from Keswick; how some Oldham trippers rattled past us in a waggonette, shouting out as they caught sight of our ropes - "Eh, sithee! They're goin' a 'angin' sumbody"; how elated we were when one of our heroes, who has taken part in half the ascents in the district, also overtook us on his bicycle, and got off to shake hands, and to wish he were free.

THE WALL

BILL MCKEE
(1989/90)

Among the many days of adventurous escapades which it has been my good fortune to partake of on our lofty peaks and crags, there is one which remains uppermost in my memory. It is with no little pleasure that I would like to relate to you our activities on that particular day.

My companion on this occasion was none other than that character of sterling worth, E. Harrison Forbes, of whom some of you will no doubt have heard. Now 'Harry' was a fine friend: amiable, considerate, and above all dependable. He had the rare gift of being able to impart a feeling of safety even on the trickiest of passages. This latter virtue was one to which I attached especial importance on this day, for I planned to attempt an ascent of the fearsome wall right of 'The Corner'. For such an arduous undertaking I deemed that Harry's support might indeed be of great significance in promoting the likelihood of a successful conclusion to the venture.

We were up with the dawn, and what a dawn it was. I have always maintained that a dawn in the mountains is like no other dawn. We breakfasted heartily in the bracing morning sun, feelings of considerable trepidation on my part being dispelled by Harry's relaxed but confident approach to the whole affair. "Just crack on up and give it a damned good go", he would say, happily oblivious to any doubts I had concerning my meagre ability to cope against such Titanic odds.

We decided on the precaution of taking a few line slings in case I should reach a rugosity in the wall around which such an implement might be secured in order to afford a degree of protection, a controversial step, as we were well aware, and one which did not endear our plan to some of the old guard in the hut. We nonetheless reasoned that our daring would not be equal to the task without the assistance of such modern appendages. I had also been fortunate enough to be the recipient of a somewhat antiquated snap-link donated by B.J. Farquharson on his hearing of my plan to attempt the wall. "Take it, my boy", he had spluttered, "the damned thing's no use to me." Armed with this paraphenalia, we felt satisfactorily prepared for the undoubted severity of the ascent.

Leaving the road at the stone bridge we shouldered our packs and struck off up the scree towards the looming cliff. The precipitous walls frowned menacingly upon us as we toiled, ant-like, to their centre. Harry, being a fine and accomplished fellrunner besides an able mountaineer, was soon striding far ahead of my snail's pace. Apart from pausing momentarily to admire the breathtaking panorama now revealing itself and to remove our woollen breeches, which were found to be exceedingly uncomfortable in the prevailing weather conditions, our ascent to the base of the bastion was uninterrupted.

Perched on a comfortable heather terrace under the sheer face we regained our breath and took in the surroundings. Below us lay a commodious theatre within which we assumed would soon assemble a sizeable group of fellows, for the wall had long been regarded a last great problem. To our left lay The Corner, Harry's tale of a glorious epic struggle on this classic climb sprang to mind, told many times with a twinkle in his eye during fireside conversation in the hut.

Taking my worthy companion's advice, I decided to 'crack on up and give it a go'. I settled on a hundred and twenty foot length of stout hemp, judging this to be sufficient to reach a tiny ledge running across the wall at approximately two-thirds height. My boots had recently been re-shod so I was at least able to expect little trouble on that score. With an encouraging pat on the back and a hearty, "Do your best, old man," I set off alone, for we were both in agreement that to climb simultaneously on a course such as this would be folly of the utmost order.

Inching up I gained a definite toe hold at 15 feet. The rock was most sharp and the pulls fierce, quite unlike anything I had encountered before, and most unsettling. Soon I became aware of a strange sensation of pain in my forearms and to my great consternation discovered that they were beginning to swell, not an encouraging prospect when one is clad in rather tight tweed. Spotting a poor spike to the left I draped a length of No.2 line around it and pressed on, hoping my route might take me past a friendlier spot where some semblance of a rest could be obtained. To my great surprise, such a spot was gained in a further 15 feet of stiff climbing. It was a delectable haven of repose and quite unexpected for such a precipitous face. I have to admit I was most thankful to grasp the firm holds which were in abundance here, for my arms were tiring remarkably rapidly, the bizarre pain not having subsided, and my feet having at one point momentarily scrabbled for a purchase. Carefully assuming a rather peculiar attitude on the ledge, which consisted of sitting facing out, with one leg astride it — an operation which might only be performed with great difficulty by a fellow more clumsy than myself — I was able to bring Harry up to my perch. He managed without undue bother, employing a judicious use of the left knee to ease the most difficult step of the passage, and was soon beside me enthusing over the intricacies of the rock we had climbed.

After my good friend had lashed himself to a tiny thread belay which was anything but stout, I began to work my way leftwards towards a large shallow pocket. Halfway to this destination I reached a *mauvais pas* which was to prove a source of no little anxiety. The problem was, I could not see how to pass the obstacle while maintaining the obligatory four points of contact, as Layton-Smithers observed in his commendable text on rockcraft. After several minutes to-ing and fro-ing, Harry suggested in a laconic and tongue-in-cheek manner that I should regard each digit as a point of contact, which I suppose it was, logically speaking. After convincing myself of the value of this apparently dubious advice, the impasse was no more and a further delicate posture enabled me to stand on the smallest of projections in the aforementioned pocket. The pain in my forearms had recommenced but seeing no option other than to press on, I did so. With nails biting firmly into small indentations in the rock's smooth surface I was able to raise my body a little. Then, by means of a side pressure hold in a small fissure and a downward motion of the hands in relation to the body, I gained a precarious stance beneath some sound-looking holds which apparently led to the ledge we had spotted earlier. Careful to avoid rash movement, for a fall from my present position would not be an attractive proposition, I proceeded steadily to the ledge whereupon I belayed to a comforting spike and announced my safety to Harry.

On his joining me at the ledge we noticed a gaggle of spectators beneath, somewhat spoiling the solitude we sought with their unseemly and boisterous antics. They seemed friendly enough however, and some encouraging remarks were heard to drift up from time to time.

A fierce move enabled me to leave the safety of the ledge. A gymnast would have been more suited to that wall than a rock climber. With the benefit of hindsight, I think I owed a lot to the strange exercises we had practised on the walls of the hut. A small spike appeared a little higher — the climb was certainly yielding ample opportunity to protect an ascent — and I was soon virtually dangling from my arms at a strange porthole in the face, a feature the like of which I was hitherto unaware. If offered a fairly good purchase for the hands although a rather strenuous upward movement was then necessitated by the distribution of the holds. On reaching these, again with no little relief, I traversed some 15 feet to the right into a cleft splitting the wall. It immediately became clear to me that we would be able to complete the ascent, so, bringing Harry up to where I stood, I began to ponder over the choice of name.

The final cleft went with a minimum of difficulty but the course we had taken was, in its entirety, undoubtedly a severe problem. Had there not been such a large group of witnesses I think we would have considered the ascent unjustifiable. Ever witty, Harry imaginatively suggested the name 'The Wall', being a fitting companion to 'The Corner'. I agreed.

After coiling the hawser with the customary difficulty, we lingered awhile, dwelling on the innermost feelings our experience had laid bare, before turning to the valley, the comfort of the hut, and welcome rest.

ENTITY

C. J. MORTLOCK
(1961)

Easter 1960. A crowded campsite at Dale Bottom Farm near Keswick. The Rock and Ice were there in force, with numerous hangers-on like myself. The 'Boys' were doing a few routes of top quality and a large number of pubs of low quality. Easter Sunday — after hangovers — Don Whillans and I messed about on Castle Rock. I felt like doing something hard but Don just laughed (he'd done all the routes many times, though only one or two in snow and ice!). We stayed on the classic routes and in the pubs.

The next day at 8 a.m., I was rudely awakened with, "Hey up, yer ready?" I woke fully as we shot round to Dove Crag on Don's bike. It was a perfect day, even if ruddy cold at that hour on a bike. An hour's walk, and the little cliff I had seen from the road loomed fierce and black.

I hastily gave Don the end of the rope. He expected it, thank goodness. His aim was the obvious central corner — the main feature of the cliff — between Hangover and Dovedale Grooves. Others, including Don, had tried the corner, but with scant success.

The first pitch looked deceptively easy: one hundred and forty feet, up a steep crack and easily across to the first stance of Hangover. Don found a couple of runners and took about twenty minutes. I took the mickey as he was slow (for him). He said nowt. When I climbed I said a lot — mostly purple in colour. The crack was very greasy and awkward, movement often largely by reptation. At the stance we took stock over a quick smoke. I was not a little overawed: a large, black, sunless corner containing a hundred feet of nearly vertical rock and steep slab, topped by about forty to fifty feet of mostly overhanging rock. It was rather like a double-sized Cenotaph Corner topped by overhangs and without a crack in the corner. There were no escape lines and no place for a stance below the top.

It took Don two and a half hours to climb this pitch. It must be the finest piece of rock climbing I have ever seen. I sang 'rock' to relieve the tension (mine as well as his). Don smoked incessantly in extraordinary resting positions. Two climbers passed the foot of the cliff and the following ensued:

"What route's that?" (looks of disbelief from below Don's overhanging positions);

"It ain't... yet" (from above).

"Who are you?" (from below).

"Whillans" ... pause as a big grass ledge narrowly misses the amazed ones below (premeditated?).

"Yer must be mad" (parting shot from those below, who were not seen again).

This final pitch turned out to be just as long as our rope (150 feet). It began well with a short vertical traverse which revealed good holds, then a steep forty-foot wall where holds and grass sods were again adequate. A runner here protected the next fifteen feet. It needed to (Don fell off here on a previous attempt). The slab was not only steep but greasy and minute ripples accounted for all holds. Don cracked it by patience and magnificent skill. Despite being second and having a long reach I found it similar in difficulty to the crux of the Great Slab on Froggat Edge, though with greasy holds thrown in.

Above this, another runner, and straightforward slab and groove climbing for thirty feet. Then the corner overhangs forced one diagonally right towards a small overhang forty feet above. Progress at this point was made by small flakes which were so situated that all the handholds were on the left and all the footholds on the right. The result was a sideways progress — itself out of balance and accentuated by the vertical to overhanging rock. Don had climbed this out of my sight. I found one runner. Trying to climb too fast I grabbed a flake which reciprocated by breaking off. Tired and out of balance I came on the rope — in space. By swinging I grabbed the runner and rested (or tried to). After five minutes I moved up, still finding it very hard. Just above the overhang, in a shallow groove, was a peg (for protection only, said Don). I said something else, grabbed the peg, swung clear and pulled up. Of course even the last twenty feet up the groove were pretty holdless. By now, however, I was not worried, for there were Don and the top a few feet away.

We called the route 'Entity' for obvious reasons. If it's had a second clean ascent I shall be surprised.

SONNET

WILL WATERPROOF
(1929)

Lord of Lancastrian fells, thou proud Old Man!
I long to gaze on thee, but long in vain,
All on account of this infernal rain
Which shrouds the dripping landscape that I scan,
As fast and fierce as when it first began
To pour in torrents down my window-pane
At early morn. How futile to complain!
Let's triumph o'er the weather if we can
And see if we can't have a bit of fun,
Keeping our spirits up with spirits down
(Ah, please forgive the execrable pun!);
But something I must really have to drown
My weariness. It may be at The Sun,
The Black Bull, or The Waterhead, or Crown.

A WET DAY AT WASDALE
(extract)

C. B.
(Vol. III No. 9 September 1900)

Last September a merry party was gathered at the Inn, though the Fates were unpropitious, and in three weeks we were only allowed the same number of fine days on which any serious climbing could be attempted — hence, we had plenty of time to explore the diversions in the Inn, invented from time to time by well-known climbers in search of exercise, as an outlet to their superfluous energy.

As an example of the shocking weather, it may be mentioned that a party of four enterprising climbers, being disgusted at the fickleness of Nature, determined to reverse the order of things, and climb by night if not by day. A start was accordingly made from the Inn at 3 a.m., headed by a frequenter of the Alps, the possessor of a folding lantern, and the Pillar being safely reached by sunrise, the party were rewarded by a splendid climb on the North Face, bathed in sunshine all the while, returning to the Inn in time for breakfast.

To their inward satisfaction — an outward display of it not receiving much enthusiasm — the rain came down soon after breakfast, and continued in the usual fashion of Lakes rain all day, preventing everyone from leaving the shelter of the Inn!

A LONGING FOR WALES

S. GONZALES (BAZ INGLE AND PETER CREW)
(1963)

He was sick of walking up to Cloggy so I reckoned it was time to tell him about this new line I had seen on Dove Crag in the Lakes. He was derogatory as usual, but I pointed out that we might escape the Whitsun crowds, so he consented to go.

Now whenever I see a line I get really nervous and jittery in case someone else should swipe it and so we expected Oliver and Brown, L or Ross to come rushing round in the night to steal a march. Even though they didn't come we got up early just in case they crept over from Dunmail.

Flogging up to the crag he kept moaning about the b——y long walks up to Lake District crags, even though this one was only half as far as Cloggy. And then we were there and he was impressed ("nearly as good as the East") and I was even more impressed because I would get the first pitch since it was my idea. Anyway there was no one else around so I talked him into doing this Dovedale Grooves route which hadn't been repeated for 10 years.

So we went over to the climb but the idiot fell off straight away trying to shift a loose block. I swear he's only the clumsiest bloke in all the world. Not to be defeated and determined not to let me have a go he leapt up again and pushed the block off and some more lurching and swearing and he crept into this hole under the overhanging chimney and tied onto some cranky chocks. And I tried to look nonchalant on the hard bit, because I never admit that anything he does is hard and vice-versa, but this was hard so I said "good un, youth" and left it at that.

So I grabbed his spare slings and climbed over him and stood on his head. And he started moaning so I said the block above his head was loose to make him moan more. Then I rushed up and grabbed the block and there was this big thrutch and a long step onto a slab on the left. But one of the ropes got jammed so I had to untie it and I was dead chuffed because it's always him that messes the rope up and leaves me in desperates. And he came up the chimney with the rope pulling him off but he didn't fall off so I was dead sick. There was a lot of spare rock above for a direct finish but we reckoned we would just make a dinner-time pint so we leapt past this raven's nest and rushed off down the valley.

But we couldn't get in for the tourists so we went back to camp and he moaned about drunkard tourists and threatened to smash the loudspeaker which blared out music all day for the spartan campers in their Richard-Ill-type tents across the river. We could even hear the b —— y thing on the crag.

Next morning we got up later but burnt up to the crag in record time determined to smash this new route into the deck. It was my idea so I got first go. A crafty thread and a queer mantelshelf led to the first hard bit. He said traverse right, so I went straight up and nearly fell off and as usual he was right but he got gripped following so that made us even. The stance was a sloping grass ledge that was sliding off, especially with him on as well so I sent him up this steep wall and he lurched round the corner and muttered something sick. But he was at the stance in no time so I let him off, seeing as he hadn't used a peg either. The next bit started off with two loose blocks which he kicked off later saying "that'll sort 'em out" and they hit the deck like an H bomb and shifted a tree and half a ton of grass and scared the wits out of these two birds who had come up to watch us. I got lost on the bit after and he was jeering so I leapt up this green groove that was hard and unprotected and I was really chuffed when he had a tight rope. Evens again.

The wall above was full of overhanging grooves but he couldn't do any of them so he traversed right and descended to a stance about 5 feet above me and several feet out and passed the buck. But the overhang was easy for me but I got gripped on this queer slab that would be even harder in normal damp conditions. We looked down the top bit of Extol and I persuaded him to save it for tomorrow and we got down dead on opening time. We decided to call it Hiraeth because we were longing to get back home again to Wales.

Black clouds were rolling over on Monday but we reckoned we might do Extol before it started raining so we rushed up even faster than ever. The first pitch was a rotten narrow chimney that he couldn't get into so I had to give him a tight rope again. But he got his finger out on the big pitch and was up in under an hour which seemed good going considering its reputation (see *CCJ* 1961). The last overhang was a bit dicy and he kept the ropes slack to get his own back for Dovedale Grooves. If I had come off I would have ended up in Ullswater but I didn't and we were dead chuffed and got back to camp with the black clouds chasing us hard.

It rained so we went to Keswick and they were all dead sick because we had swiped their routes but they bought us some beer and we bought plenty more for a party. But the clumsy fool dropped the case in Lake Road and broke half the bottles. Still, the empties made good missiles to throw at the tents in the next field.

THE SHEAF CLIMB

A. D. M. COX
(1948)

"Armchair" used adjectivally of mountaineering is a term to which I give a wide interpretation. It implies any form of climbing in which it is not merely unnecessary, but positively out of order, for the climber to leave the ground; and, while it can be indulged in with perhaps the greatest degree of comfort at home, it is perfectly legitimate, though rather more dangerous, to practise it elsewhere. Indeed the most realistic form of armchair mountaineering demands that the climber should be physically present at the scene of the climb, where he can trace his route, not in imagination or from a photograph, but up the actual cliff itself. Undeniably this demands care; there is sometimes a real risk that the enjoyment of doing the climb two or three times from the ground may so disturb the judgment as to produce an attempt to translate the imaginary into the actual, and it is at this point that the sport becomes unjustifiable. So it was in the instance I am about to describe.

During the palmy days at Llanberis in 1945, described in last year's *Journal*, there were many occasions on which the near side of Llyn du'r Arddu had suggested itself as a place of repose and, as anyone will agree who has ever sat there for an hour or two on a sunny day, it is impossible from that magnificent viewpoint not to do a good deal of armchair work on the twin cliffs across the lake. In certain lights the climbs go very easily. We found that conditions were best soon after dawn, when we were seldom there, or just before sunset, when there was sometimes a half hour in which the various routes, old and new, went with very little difficulty. Personally I was never very happy on the girdle traverse of the East Buttress, and the face of the Pinnacle above the Green Gallery had a few feet which were always troublesome. But there were two particular routes on the West Buttress which gave interesting climbing of no excessive severity. One of them, the Central Rib, in the following year doubtless gave Carsten and Macphee more trouble than had been experienced on earlier ascents; the other was the most conspicuous of the long slanting slabs between Longland's Climb and the Narrow Slab, a route whose light colour caused us to christen it the White Slab.

I had indeed done this climb from the same vantage point a number of times before the war and considered it a perfectly safe armchair route, since practical experience of its left-hand neighbour had on more than one occasion given me a very high respect for that part of the cliff. But the weather of the late summer of 1945, combined with the extraordinary chance which had endowed me with powers of a commanding officer over a number of first-rate leaders, created a situation very dangerous to the armchair mountaineer. The danger was heightened by a visit, in the middle of a strong rope, to the Narrow Slab, the approach to which involved actually crossing the lower reaches of the White Slab. Curiously enough, I do not remember giving it a thought at the time, possibly because my attention was exclusively occupied with other things, but Jock Campbell's leadership on the thin bits of the Narrow Slab had the certainty of touch to give confidence to the most apprehensive; and it was undoubtedly this which afterwards put into my mind that feeling of tremulous resolution which is the sure sign that the canons of armchair mountaineering are about to be overstepped. So it came about — no powers of command were called for — that a few days later Campbell and I started onto the Buttress to try and see whether or not there really was a route on the White Slab.

We took the start of the Bow Shaped Slab, partly because that seemed in the line of our route, partly because we did not seriously expect our route to go, in which case we hoped to be able to finish by the Bow Shaped Slab itself. Campbell's leadership of the first three pitches wasted little time. The belay which we lassoed for the rope move was discovered on arrival on the other side to be the wrong one; mechanically sound though it must have been, it was much better at the bottom of the cliff. The big bollard beyond it was perfectly safe, but the combination of loose rock and steepness on the long pitch which follows gave, I thought, a very difficult piece of climbing This brought us to the point where the Narrow Slab and Bow Shaped Slab entries reunite, and to the base of the White Slab itself. It was a most impressive stretch of rock, whose obvious firmness at least contrasted favourably with the unpleasant rotten ness of the lower defences of the Buttress. Its appearance however, did not encourage any idea that it could be climbed. My recollection is that, apart from a few feet of easy climbing in the corner, not on the slab itself and leading nowhere, it gave a very strong impression to the contrary. Round to the right, however, between it and the foot of the Narrow Slab, were some rocks which looked much more amenable. They form, I suppose, another layer in the sheaf of slabs on the left side of the West Buttress, though their structure was not so obviously slabby as that of most of the other slabs in that area. We had no great hopes that they would lead anywhere, but it was possible that they might allow us to look over onto the White Slab higher up, and perhaps afford a route onto it at a point where the chances were more encouraging.

To our surprise these rocks were perfectly straightforward, and, with two excellent stances at not very long intervals, we found ourselves making height without serious difficulty. Above the second stance Campbell moved up to the left and disappeared over an edge, and I presently joined him, tightly ensconced in a curious nook in a small chimney close beside the White Slab. This opening up of a new foreground was a noteworthy moment. Up till this point optimism as to our chances had played a most negative part, and neither of us had seriously believed that there was the least likelihood of the route developing. The unexpectedly easy progress so far was clearly too good to last, and had done nothing to dispel the feeling that it was only a matter of time before the bubble was pricked. With little expectation of success, there had been little excitement; nor had the detail of the climbing left much definite impression. This was now altered. Although appearances from the nook certainly gave no positive assurance, they did suggest the possibility of a future to our route, even to the extent of allowing some latitude in our speculations as to the line it might take. The result was an exhilarating change of mood. Nothing, I suppose, could be more childish or more completely exciting than the intensifying state of suspense in which I, at least, found myself for the next couple of hours. It was not so much the difficulty of the climbing, which except for a single move was not, for a good leader, outstanding, nor the quality of the route, which impartial judges may well find less excellent than that of the other climbs on the West Buttress. Mainly it was the vivid uncertainty of whether there was a route at all, combined with the fascination of watching a favourite armchair climb of long standing gradually working itself out in practice.

The view up and down the White Slab from the neighbourhood of the nook was impressive, but what was of more immediate interest was the obvious accessibility of the thin but prominent crack running up the centre of the White Slab itself. Campbell moved across to the left into it, up it for a short distance and out again to a splendid little perch and serviceable belay on the right. On the way to join him, I looked over the outer edge of the slab, and discovered there an improbable line of ample ledges, from the last of which it looked as though one might be able to rope down to somewhere in the vicinity of Faith and Friction Slab. We took note of this as a possible emergency exit. The Slab itself at this point was discouraging. Its roughness and not impossibly steep angle gave a faint suggestion that it might be just climbable, but there was no apparent resting place for at least fifty feet, and after about fifteen feet of extremely delicate climbing Campbell decided not to persist with it. But up to the right of the perch was a possible alternative, a very pronounced black-looking corner where one facet of the slab abutted against the supporting wall of the next slab to the right. This straight and sinister groove could obviously be entered without much difficulty. If it could be climbed, it was clear that it would emerge eventually through the cannon hole in the large ledge below the final pitch of Longland's Climb; but this was a point of purely academic interest for us, since it was equally clear that there was no chance of climbing it. Campbell, however, moved up for twenty feet as far as the groove would reasonably go, and found himself a running belay. The right wall of the groove overhung, as the right walls of the grooves on that part of the cliff usually do, in generous measure, and I could see no likelihood of our being able to break out over it. There seemed to be some sort of ledge with handholds over the top, but the heavily undercut wall gave no foothold, and this meant that the pull-up which any such move would involve would have to be a most extraordinary contortion. This proved to be the case. So far as I remember, the position from which the manoeuvre had to be started involved placing the feet far out to the left on the slab, the hands far out to the right on the wall, and suspending the body almost horizontally between them; an attitude ill-suited for the execution of a straight arm-pull. To my surprise and undying admiration, Campbell after a brief preliminary survey made this remarkable unpleasant move without hesitation; the landing was good, and a stance and belay immediately to hand. This was news of the first importance to me, the place being astonishingly airy and not one on which to be particular about ways and means; I have never had less hesitation about asking for a haul at full strength. Whether or not it was a move of great technical difficulty to anyone with really strong arms I am not in a position to judge, but without them, or a good rope ahead in lieu, I had no doubts at all at the time that it would have been impossible.

We were now to some extent committed, since the move could only have been reversed by an abseil; on the other hand the new, but limited, horizon which was opened up was not without encouraging features. The new groove immediately ahead, while it did not appear easy, was at least an unqualified improvement on the one we had just left, and the next twenty or thirty feet went well enough up the corner, partly by a sort of layback. We now found ourselves on a comfortable little grass ledge, two or three feet square, tucked in under the retaining right wall of the groove. Straight up the groove appeared to be the only possible line. For the first few feet the right wall boasted an irregularity which allowed some purchase for the feet; thereafter it looked as if the friction of the slab would be the main support until some kind of a grass landing could be reached at about thirty five feet. It looked extremely difficult, but not as downright hopeless as the first groove we had encountered. If it did not go, it was hard to see how the climb could be completed, and we should have to use the remaining hour and a half of daylight to good advantage in order to let down. On the other hand, although we did not know exactly where we were, there was not much doubt that this would be the cliff's last kick before the top. At the first attempt it was obvious that it was extremely hard, even at the bottom; Campbell returned to the ledge after a few feet. At the second attempt he made his way a good deal higher, and came down again with some difficulty. He decided to try it facing outwards so as to get better purchase against the wall, but got no further than before. Each descent was a tiring business, and on this occasion to save strength he jumped the last few inches down onto the ledge. As bad luck would have it, there was some kind of a lump concealed under the grass, and he twisted his ankle sharply in landing.

This was the point at which the suspense became quite agonising. We sat down for Campbell to rest and to examine the damage, which was clearly going to be a considerable handicap. Like the mechanically sound belay lower down, the ankle seemed only good for stresses in certain directions, and although Campbell was still hopeful that the groove could be climbed, the awful possibility began to dawn on me that I might be called on to try and climb it. A drowning man clutches at a straw, and under the stimulus of the alternative prospect I was roused to make my one contribution to the day's success. The retaining wall on our right overhung, not in the uncompromising fashion of the groove we had earlier escaped from, but with a general configuration that had not suggested that there was any possibility

Brian Crofts on Llithrig (HVS 1pt. aid), East Buttress, Cloggy 1961. Photo: Ken Wilson.

Jim Rubery on Tennis Shoe Direct (HVS), Idwal Slabs. Photo: Chris Craggs.

Left: Lew Brown, who made the first ascent in 1966 of The Crucifix (E2), Dinas Cromlech, 'a bold outing at the top of its grade'. Photographed in the winter of 1972. Photo: Bob Allen.
Below: Left to right, Al Harris, Jancis Baldock (Allison), Baz Ingle and Pete Crew below Gogarth in 1966.
Photo: Ken Wilson.

Left: Bob Conway below the Black Ladders in February 1985. Photo: Chris Jackson.

Right: Bob Conway climbing on Gallt yr Ogof in February 1985. Photo: Chris Jackson.

of repeating our previous tactics and breaking out over it. In point of fact, I think there was no chance of a straight arm-pull over the wall but low down, at about the level at which we were sitting, far out on the edge of the wall I suddenly noticed a small foothold. It looked as though, by an enormous straddle, it might be just possible to get a foot to it from the ledge, more particularly as the stride would be made with complete protection from the immediately adjacent belay. A tentative experiment while the ankle was still undergoing treatment showed that it was indeed possible, and that the edge of the wall gave a good grip on which to swing out; but I was not able without committing myself (which I was reluctant to do) to see where the move would lead or whether there was any landing.

Campbell was reluctant to abandon the groove, and thought his ankle was good enough for one more attempt, but the injury obviously handicapped his efforts, and he came down again without attempting to force it. He then tested the ankle gingerly on the long straddle, found it good for that particular pressure, and in a moment had pulled out onto the foothold. His terse "This is it" brought a sudden end to the tension, for a single balancing move round the corner was all that was needed to land us on the easy upper rocks of the Narrow Slab, about a hundred feet below the top. It was a curiously abrupt ending to our uncertainties, and one which came as a surprise, for we had not, for some reason, realised that we had been forced over so far in that direction. Rapid scrambling brought us out on the top of the cliff with three-quarters of an hour of daylight in hand.

Nothing is harder than to form a fair appreciation of the standard and quality of a climb on which one's critical faculties have been dulled at the time by the absorption of finding the route, and by the inordinate importance one attached, for those few hours, to getting up it. It was quite clear that it needed a leader of exceptional judgment, and that it contained one move which, if only for lack of arm strength — but not only for that! — it would have been entirely beyond me to follow unassisted. Apart from this, I doubt whether the Sheaf is as difficult as the other routes on that buttress. Only the one move seemed harder than the pitches of the Bow Shaped Slab entry, and the rest very considerably easier. The route shares with Longland's Climb the enormous merit of short pitches, small but good stances and excellent belays. As regards its general character, this again, while showing the typical West Buttress qualities of good rock and exhilarating situations, seemed different from that of the other routes; and this was probably due to the fact that it is the only one of them which is forced to disregard the natural slab structure of the Buttress and on two occasions to cross the retaining walls of the grooves. This gives it a certain directness of line, for, with the Bow Shaped Slab start, it takes a roughly straight course up the cliff; but because of the slant of the rock structure it is in fact going not with the grain, but across it, and its difficult moves are mostly in, or out of, grooves, rather than up slabs. Hence it lacks the delicacy of either of its neighbours, and derives much of its interest from surprise situations. Artistically it would have been a better climb had it been possible to finish independently of the Narrow Slab, but it may be that the climbing of the final groove will eventually give it a cleaner and much harder finish.

The White Slab itself, of course, was hardly touched except for a short stretch half way up; so the White Slab Climb not only retains the old attraction, but has now become the most completely safe route I am ever likely to do from an armchair.

IF I CAN THINK OF A TITLE I'LL SEND IT ON LATER

PETER EVANS
(1968)

Like many men I become generous in my cups and, I think it was at the Annual Dinner that I, in my unaccustomed Day Clothes, hired for the occasion, promised another dormouse in the same cup who thought he was the Editor a "frothy little piece" (his phrase) that I had thrown off (not over) previously. Like frothy little pieces the world over, it proved not to be there when I wanted it. Soooo, que faire? The Editor's a nice chap and who am I to add to his burdens and, besides, we're in the same racket, the academic racket as those revolting students call it. The trouble with the climbing world, sorry, Climbing World, to a forty year old Dad, as Mac the Telli insists on calling me, rot him and him thirty-nine or maybe that's his waist, the trouble is that it seems to be full of Hard Men and I'm about as hard as yesterday's ice cream. O, I could regale you with tales of Mods led in appalling conditions of bright sun without dark glasses (a grading I originally suggested for Diffs-done-with-a-hangover, known as VS-in-dark-glasses) but I feel that the place for them is in the guidebook as laconic little accounts that only fool people like me with their 'move up the 30 foot vertical wall using any combination of the two available holds'. However, it's a far cry that has no echo and...

Well now, I have had a traumatic experience since writing the foregoing going clang. I am the proud possessor of a field in Llanberis. The definition of a field in Llanberis is, for present purposes (being seized in fee simple), a collection of other people's septic tanks entirely surrounded by hedges. Anyway, dizzy from my brush with destiny at The Great Auction (a fete worse than death as the Tory member said to the vicar) I went boldering with Joe the Handjam and Mac the Telli (name dropping). Trouble is I wasn't bold enough. Wasn't it Dr. Thomas Patey who said, "In P.A.'s you just step up on the discolourations in the rock?" He's bluddy wrong. While you heave and puff in your new P.A.s, all feeling fled from those pedal extremities and your chewing gum arms getting visibly longer as your body sags nearer and nearer the ground, they have girdled the travesty. O Playtex! O Youthform! As impregnable a girdle as ever one came across in Grantchester meadows all those years ago; one needed the belay of a sported oak to cope with those, but I digress.

That night, up to my neck in the Padarn Lake (somboolically enough), a scheme for regaining face slowly took shape. As every dart plunked unerr-

ingly home in the scarred wood surrounding the board I didn't let the faint-
est flicker of a muscle in the firm line of my chin betray my emotion (well my
chin sort of looks firm if I throw my head back so that it becomes less reced-
ing; trouble is I can't see very clearly what I'm doing and I get a stiff neck
after a while, so I have to keep rushing to the Gents to get the crick out, still
it's not a thing to be noticed when you've been putting away all those halves,
is it). By closing time I was pretty sure I was on to something good but just
to make certain I went back and slept on it.

Next morning I said to the Herr Direktor, "Sehr geehrter Her Direktor
Professor Doktor Honoris Causa I.G.McN-D, wot abaht a climb then mate."
He fell for it. I hadn't counted on that. "My dear Yates-Weinstube," he replied
in his urbane manner, "you can go and — ." Throwing caution to the winds,
as my Mr. Banerjee used to say, I gently pointed out the implausible nature
of his suggestion. His frank countenance clouded for a moment then cleared
as the mists will clear suddenly from the summit of Little Tryfan showing
the climber the smiling world of the Great Tops. "Orlrite," he said, with what
in anyone less lupine would be described as a wolfish grin, "you're on." I
naturally took this to mean that I was on form and thought that perhaps my
struggles with the bolder the previous evening had not gone unremarked,
though personally I was wishing by then that I had struggled with the shy
one instead. However, it was too late now. He should have been sporting
with his family at the seaside or delving in the rich ground of his newly
acquired estate. Instead he chose to take me climbing. I was strangely
touched.

"Something easy in the Pass," he muttered, an inner glow lighting his
handsome equine features the while. Now I have climbed in the Pass before
(that surprises you, I'll wager) and now that my blood was up (I am not
insensitive) I thought that with him leading we might attempt something
like Spiral Stairs. I threw my head to the ceiling hoping he would notice the
firm line my chin made then and mentioned the climb through clenched
teeth. Again that wolfish (?) grin. "Just come with me," he said. I looked
wildly for a way out but the Baron barred the door. "Better go quietly," he
said. "Yes," I said, weakly, seeing that the game was up and my bluff called.

To think that I might have spent the day at Caernarvon imagining the
glory of the Investiture, with the Sovereign holding aloft the Young Prince to
the acclaim of the assembled populace, or sitting in my field eyeing the septic tanks, planning to be worthy of their trust, instead of toiling up this
weary hillside. He was well ahead of me now. I dodged as another stream of
merry quips was flung over his shoulder. Perhaps I ought to put my helmet
on. Slowly his boots, to which my eyes were glued, receded until they were
no bigger than a man's hand. And still we trudged upwards. Then the rock.
A wall rose shear before us. He paused and I got out of the way just in time.
"That," he said, "is better." I knew what he meant. An unspoken something
was beginning between us.

He was halfway up the first pitch and I was too diffident to tell him that
I had unaccountably forgotten how to tie a bowfell. Thinking furiously I did

the only thing possible. "That hold looks loose," I shouted, and gave the rope a gentle tweak. He was beside me in a flash, puzzled wrinkles creasing his helmet. I said something about not jumping for holds, but he just glared at me, muttering under his breath, so I remembered how to tie it.

How will I ever forget the hours of agony that followed? The rock leaned. It nudged you gently, almost surreptitiously, off balance. It sloped out and sideways in unsporting fashion. The rope stretched for miles into the clouds, the leader nowhere in sight. Silence, save for the chink, chink, chink, as his runners came off. "Your runners are off," I shout, helpfully, but all I get is a torrent of invective for my pains. My turn to move. The hard traverse. Feet jerking over the misty void I edge my way on. Suddenly I see a small spike and knotting a loop in my beard with my teeth I slip it over for a moment's rest (I should explain about my beard. It's a false one that I mostly wear on campus so that the younger generation won't automatically mark me down as a square. It does so help to break down the barriers between the generations, don't you think? I usually climb in it too, warmer, and somehow 'with it', don't you think?). The elastic was beginning to give over the years (next time I'll buy one from Joe's) so I had to move on, on to a tiny ledge scarcely a yard wide. I edge myself over it. The strain is beginning to tell. I tap my barometer anxiously. Thank heavens! It still functions. He's moved on again now. Hope I'll be able to untie myself this time. He does get so bad tempered if he has to come all the way back to free me from my belay.

How I overcame the crux I shall never know, but after a couple of hours I pulled myself together and cried, "I **will** do it." Then it was as though something tightened round me and I just ascended, as though drawn from above, to his cries of, "You great big knit" (a strange time to notice my sweater, I thought, but then he's a strange man, but alright when you've proved your worth on the rocks. I mean he very decently let me pay for the whisky later).

PUNCH-UP AT THE PADARN LAKE

HAROLD DRASDO
(1988)

One weekend Dixon brought a group from London up to Wales. It was a first visit for a number of them and some had not climbed before. On the Saturday evening I was in the Padarn Lake Hotel, the clearing-house for information on recent climbing, with one of these last standing beside me when in the generalised noise and disorder I found him pulling at my elbow and whispering seriously in my ear. It was a moment before I could catch his words and a moment again before I understood them. The urgent message was:

"Will there be trouble later?"

He misinterpreted those beards and ragged clothes. He thought that two parties might at any second start smashing chairs or tables upon each other's heads; and he was afraid that the whole company would exuberantly join in. I tried to allay his anxiety. Them old men might look rough and talk dirty but they don't mean nobody no harm. It needed several such assurances before he was persuaded that violence was unlikely and a certain wariness showed in his sidelong glances all that night.

The punch-up did not take place, but he was not to know that after some years of climbing many of us find that our activities fit more often into the realm of the Absurd than into that of the Heroic; at any rate, we have to treat our epics as comic epics. This article is about a crag which came off the secret list quite recently — the apparent irrelevance of the title and introduction, which may have misled the sensation-seeking reader, will be reverted to unless the editor's fifth reminder prevents the completion of these notes. The cliff is the quarry at Cae Coch, a mile north of Trefriw. It looks east over the Conway flood-plain and it is not seen from the road beneath, the quarry floor being flat and broad and the whole steep hillside afforested. I saw it from the other side of the valley in 1965 and thought to walk up to it a year or so later; but I had not located it carefully enough and to my fury I spent over an hour in the trees before darkness came. A few weeks later I tried again and found a steep and well-built wall; but I did not know that I had not yet entered the main quarry. It required another visit before we discovered the incline which leads directly from the roadside to the top level and from then our quarry could elude us no longer.

The amphitheatre proved to be an interesting place. Nature was locked in isometric exercises on the floor with a mob of healthy young birches pressing an assortment of taller conifers. (An informer in the Forestry School slipped us a more prosaic note on ownership and on the surrounding hill-

side: "Compartment 26: planted in 1953 with beech and Japanese larch...")
Three sheep and a huge orange dog lay rotting in the trees and we had to
steer tortuous lines through these obstacles. Later, with a correct compassion,
Swallow removed the dog's collar and read the inscription aloud. I have
forgotten what it said. In every sod and behind each loose flake a worm was
coiled; the whole place stank of death and rebirth. Evan Roberts was astonished when I described it to him and his old head nodded. He had been
working there as a quarry-man when operations were abandoned just after
the war and there was not a blade of grass to be seen then.

One wet week I persuaded Tony Moulam to come to look at it and so we
laid hands on it at last. The first day we broke through the undergrowth and
climbed the most cowardly line: Owydir Gully, not easy in the rain to start or
finish. A day or two later we got onto the slabby buttress on the right and
climbed it in three pitches: Transect. (He says it happened the other way
round and he's usually right.) Next I came back with Soper and Swallow.
Jack did well to lead the first pitch which was a bit thin and was further
defended from mid-height by a short but menacing shower. I went a fair
distance up the second pitch but I could see that the finish was really dangerous so I came back and proposed Jim. Jack seconded and I went third —
it seemed a characteristic situation and I believe the words have a familiar
ring: but then they made me lead the last pitch. Eventually I found an easy
way out, though I was told afterwards that at one point Swallow bent his
head downwards and slightly sideways and called, "Speed, speed," with
emphasis but without malice, so showing consideration for everyone's feelings. That route tended rightwards and we called it Tendency. Later I did a
more direct route to the same finish with Holroyd: Embargo. There was more
excitement in these climbs than this paragraph gives away.

This brings me to the climb we called The Nave. It is *the* line of the cliff.
It is the junction between the main slab on the right — two hundred feet
high, three hundred long, and still unclimbed — and the cracked buttress
left of it, giving the routes already named. The line is evidently inescapable:
diagonally left up the steep, nearly featureless slab to the corner of the big
overlap; along and up beneath the overlap to get into the main fault; and up
that Garden of Eden to the top.

We were a party of three. Trevor Jones, full of enthusiasm and drive,
and kept saying so. Mouly, quietly keen and confident, kept egging Jones on
but prepared to step in if things didn't go ahead as intended. The writer,
sceptical but fascinated, wanting to combine irreconcilables by climbing a
desperate new route without doing anything risky.

Jones led off in fine style but came to a halt after thirty feet just above
a shallow niche. Said it was impossible but would only come down if someone else would go up. Mouly went up, put a nut into its proper place, and
came down. I went up, stood in the sling in the nut, cleaned out a hold to
allow further progress; and came down.

Round two. Jones went up, got onto the hold, lurched upwards, knocked
a peg in and came down. While he was up there he reported several times

that he was buggered; but when he found himself safely back on the ground his strength and optimism were miraculously restored. A change of order then and I went up to the peg and moved fractionally higher. It was barely fifteen feet to the overlap where a crack with vacancies for every sort of piton had been teasing us for a long time; but there was no wrinkle anywhere in that gap on which hands or feet or hopes might rest. Since no movement in the right direction was possible it was necessary to stand still or descend; since we wanted the climb very badly it was inexcusable to go down; and since standing still for a long time looks foolish I had to find something to do.

Well, what happened was this. Only eighteen inches to my right there was a projecting penny-sized tuft of grass — we wanted to go leftwards. To make the place tidier I pulled it off. And it proved to be securely attached to a perfect core of earth a foot long, revealing a bore-hole into which the shaft of a hammer slotted perfectly. It was set at just that angle to give confidence and I was surprised to notice then that the weather was magnificent. With tension from a sling round the hammer I was able to precariously lay away and with the reach gained I could inspect a hairline crack marking the back of a small flake. So I forced the blade of a second hammer into it — a degree of brutality is admitted here — and so split it as barbarously as the last infinitive. This done, a perfect hold for the archetypal steep mantelshelf was produced. It looked good. By this time Jones was extremely excited so I excused myself from a rather committing move, went down, tied him on, and had him hoisted halfway up before he realised I was taking advantage.

Well, he did the pitch. First he got to the overhang and supplied the crack with its peg. Then, with the determination of which he had spoken earlier, he slowly followed the stepped overlap upwards, removing what was temporary and leaving behind a briefly spaced series of runners on which the eye was able to rest with some satisfaction. From time to time he called out that he was finished and at times we feared this might be true. But there was little that we could do to help him and as you know it gets to the point on a long and arduous pitch like this at which going on is desolately exhausting, but at which the mere thought of trying to get back without leaving your gear or honour behind drains you completely. Your throat gets so dry. With a hundred feet out he reached a sturdy little tree with a neat little ledge underneath it and without stopping to get his breath he lashed himself hard on to every possible point of attachment. Powerful stuff, boy. We tried to encourage him along the remaining thirty feet of overlap but it is impossible to pass a stance like that after such effort.

Mouly went steadily up to join him and set out immediately on the remaining traverse. Again this proved difficult, the sort of irreducibly awkward passage that may be taken by two or three methods but no way easily. It needed cleaning and it was greasy and insecure. Mouly crossed it in his crabbed and painful but unfailingly effective style. Jones and I were both rather unhappy on it. It was a real bit of Moulamite. Coming last I allowed myself the luxury of a back rope round the little tree.

I caught up with them at the foot of the huge corner attached to two much bigger trees. These were ostensibly healthy but I suspected that their roots lay on stony ground. Everything seemed ready to peel off and I was forcibly restrained from setting a magic circle of pegs around the whole party. The corner was filled with grass and other matter for its whole distance and it was steeper than we had expected. It proved deceptive at a couple of points and we thought that not all the decoration was there to stay. You dig your fingers in, make some sort of foothold, move up, and the stuff starts to pull away before your eyes. Gripping. I will show you fear in a handful of dust. But there was no stopping now and a typically gruesome quarry exit was avoided for a pleasant nose on the left.

We were all pleased at this result. Jones, who had led the crucial pitch and had incidentally snatched first place in an eventual list of first ascents; Mouly, who had directed the ascent and had used his authority to allow no one to chicken out; the writer, who had shown the way up a good eight or nine feet of difficult rock but who was easily able to persuade himself that his contribution had been a significant one.

And now we have another communication from the editor — "a final despairing reminder!"... "certainly before I go to the Alps" and so on. An embarrassing thought strikes me. He asked me to write an account of how I wrote the new guide to Lliwedd. Alas, some six hundred inches of rain has wet that cliff since first I started work there; and I could still only present an Interim Report. But I comfort myself without difficulty. Only a half-dozen routes left to do. And this experience has not been of so digestible a kind as to lend itself to summary in the *Climbers' Club Journal* — it deserves a book; and this, I hope, will appear shortly.

A note in conclusion to set the record straight about Cae Coch. Jones' description of The Nave in the Ynys Ettws log sites it in "the quarry at Trefriw". Certainly the quarry at Trefriw offers some remarkable lines but The Nave is not amongst them. In any case exploration in the Trefriw quarry should be discouraged since the intervals between blasting would allow only the very fastest parties to complete a climb.

WELSH RAREBITS

BALDWIN SHAW
(1939)

I. LAZARUS, A PARABLE.

A certain man took with him his friend and his friend's wife, and led them to the Slabs which lie beyond Idwal. And they girt them about with ropes and went up the rocks by the way which men call the way of Hope. And it was wet and the sun shone not upon them. And seeing upon the left hand other climbers, that went upon the common road, they were themselves puffed up with pride. For were they not upon the way of Hope? And upon the common way there walked with difficulty a Headmaster and a Headmaster's wife and one who rowed boats at Oxford and another, whose name we knew not, a tall man, comely and gentle withal.

And after a while they came to a resting place and did eat the food which they had brought in their sacks. And they looked at the high rocks above them and considered amongst themselves what they should do. And the man said we will go by the way which is called Lazarus. Truly men say that it is very difficult, but there is no severity. Many times have I gone by ways which men call very difficult and found them in no wise beyond my strength. And straightway his friend and his friend's wife did agree to go with him.

And they discussed one with another and said, Why is this way called the way of Lazarus? And one said it was because in past time Abraham did make a path there, but now the secret of that journeying was locked, even as Lazarus was locked, in Abraham's bosom. But the man laughed and said, Nay, it is because the dogs will lick our sores, when we shall fall like crumbs beneath the table at which we now sit at meat together.

And after they had taken one or two steps in the gully which goes before the rocks which are named Lazarus, the tall man, comely and gentle withal, stood below them and called unto them and said, Go ye upon the way which is called Lazarus? And they answered him, Yea. Tell us, we pray thee, of what sort is this way? And he answered and said, Of a truth it is as one which leadeth another up a pathway in a garden. So they did continue on their way, in no wise comforted.

And it came to pass that when the man came to the place where once had been a piton, that the rain beat upon his head and the waters flowed round about him and he was at a loss how he might get him any further. And he called to his friend and said, I cannot go forward; verily I must come back to thee. And his friend and his friend's wife still tarried in the gully. And they cried to the man with one voice, Return unto us quickly while there is yet time. And the man began to come down unto them but liked it not, so that he stretched out first one foot and then another and found no resting place for either of them. And he cried with a low voice and said, What shall I do? I can go neither forward not backward and ye cannot help me.

And while they communed thus one with another, one saying cannot thy right hand find lodgment in yonder crevice and another cannot thy right foot rest upon yonder bollard? of a sudden there came a cry from above. And a voice said, Wouldest thou that I lowered a rope unto thee? And behold it was the tall man, comely and gentle withal. And the man and his friend and his friend's wife were humbled and said, Yea, we pray thee, send us a rope. Of a truth thou art a good Samaritan and thy place is not in this parable of Lazarus but in another; but that is of small account in this place. So he lowered a rope and they were drawn up and were thankful.

And they that cannot understand this parable, let them in no wise set foot upon the mountain, for they be men of weak understanding.

IV. THE TRYFAEN GULLY GAME.

This game is frequently played by any number of players from two to six. Unlike all other games; the players are unaware that they are playing it. The more players, the greater the confusion. It is, however, difficult for more than six to talk at the same time. The only requirement is thick weather on the Heather Terrace. For old hands it is best to have very thick weather. Novices have been known to play well, even in clear weather. There are no rules.

The game is best explained by describing a few typical "hands" played by a party of four.

First Round.
At the foot of Bastow Gully.

Smith. Hullo. Nor-Nor Gully already?

Jones. Already? Why, we passed it yards back. This is the North Gully.

Smith. Rot. It can't be the North yet. I'll show you that cross cut in the rock. *(Goes to look for it.)*

Jones. He won't find it, because this isn't the Nor-Nor.

Brown. I believe you're both wrong. It's Bastow.

Jones and Robinson (together). It's certainly not that.

Jones. It's too deep cut for Bastow.

Robinson. It's too shallow for Bastow. Perhaps it's No Gully.

Smith (returning). It's odd. I can't see the cross. But the rock's there on which it used to be. I'm still sure this is the Nor-Nor.

Jones. Well, let's go on. It's no use arguing here. We shall come to something definite soon.

Second Round.
At foot of Nor-Nor Gully. (Five minutes later.)

Smith. Ah! This is Nor-Nor Gully. I'm sorry, you chaps, I was wrong. That last must have been Bastow after all.

Jones. No. You were right. I was wrong. This is the North Gully. Look at all that water coming down. There's no waterfall in Nor-Nor Gully.

Smith. You've never been here in such wet weather, to say nothing of melting snow. Look, there are the rocks you stand on to see that cross. I'll show you. *(Goes to look for it.)*

Brown. Smith's right.

Robinson. Jones is right.

Jones. We can't both be right. Well, Smith, found that cross?

Smith (returning). It's very odd. I can't find it. But I'm sure those are the right rocks. It must have been cracked off by the frost.

Jones. Well, let's get on. It's no use arguing here. We shall come to something definite soon.

Third Round.

At foot of Green Gully. (One minute later.)

Smith (passing without noticing). I can't make it...

Jones. What's that gully there?

Smith. That must be Green Gully and the last *was* Nor-Nor; but it can't have been. There was no cross.

Jones. Well, if it's Green, it can't be far to the North Gully. Let's go on and find it. We can't mistake that when we get to it.

Brown. Listen. I heard voices just above. There's a party climbing there. Let's ask them what climb they're on.

Jones. Hullo, up there. What are you climbing?

Two Voices (together).   Gashed Crag.

Grooved Arete.

One Voice. Well, we thought we were doing the Gashed Crag, but it seems to be turning into the Grooved Arete. Are you at the foot of a Gully? If so, can you tell us which it is?

Enter along Heather Terrace a party of three with competent and determined leader.

Leader of New Party (to his friends). We're getting on fast. This is Grassy Gully all right. *(To Smith, Jones, etc.)* Morning! Pretty thick, isn't it? Almost lost just now. Got the gullies muddled. All right now, though. This is Grassy Gully.

Smith, Jones, Brown, Robinson, and Voices above. ????.

Game continues at foot of North and South Gullies, and at selected intervals between these.

N.B.— Cheating. Last time that I was on the Heather Terrace, the words Nor-Nor Gully were deeply scratched in the pure white snow at the foot of Bastow Gully. This is cheating.

HAMLET AT HELYG

R. L. PLACKETT
(1945-46)

II B, or not II B - that is the question:
Whether 'tis safer on the whole to risk
The bitter scorn of outclassed climbing skill,
Or else deceive the cragsman's feeble mind:
By overgrading, fool him? To grade, to brood
No more, and by this subtle means to end
The blasphemous remarks in certain logs
That I could mention — 'tis a supposition
Too frenzied to be true. To grade, to doubt —
To doubt perchance to think — ay, there's the rub;
For in that dubious mood what thoughts may come,
When we have classed some frightful climb as mild,
Should make us pause: this is the time
The youthful pioneer may quickly age;
For who would bear the stigma consequent
Upon such deeds, the editor's delay
In publishing the journal, and the spurns
Received from fellow-members of his club.
0, what a rogue and peasant-slave is he!
When he himself might his quietus make
By piton hammer. Who would rucksack bear,
To grunt and sweat along the Idwal path,
But that the dread of those who write our guides,
Those satirising jesters, from whose cracks
Few Lakeland climbs escape, defeats him still,
And makes him rather do his climbs in Wales,
Than fly to regions that he knows not of?
Thus criticism cows us, every one,
And thus the pallid hue of city life
Is crusted o'er with Gallt yr Ogof sludge;
And expeditions of importance great,
That nightly gull him with intelligence,
Are made to Capel Curig.

'The spirit of the age'

'The patches on his jacket have been so carefully sewn on as to be inconspicuous. His watch is carried for safety in a small leathern pouch fastened to his belt, but he does not take the same care of an exquisite Greek cameo which he wears set in a gold ring of Venetian workmanship, for the scars on the back of his hands shew that it has been often in peril of a too close acquaintance with the rocks'.

from 'Wastdale Head at Easter' by Lehmann J. Oppenheimer
(Vol. II No. 5 September 1899)

WHARNCLIFFE CRAGS

(extract)

C. F. CAMERON
(Vol. IV No.15 March 1902)

The great chimney is a large wedge-shaped gap in the rock face; at the inner end of the wedge the rocks do not quite meet at the foot, and beyond this incomplete apex there is an inner chimney. To the left of this is an interesting face climb with a dramatic situation which involves steady balancing in a very cramped attitude. To the right is a crack which is exceedingly hard work, for half the ascent at any rate. The next notable group has for its centre-piece a large square-shaped cavern, about twenty feet high, with a perpendicular slab of rock above. On the right side of the cave is a gallery — a partly enclosed ledge, with a small entrance about a dozen feet above the ground. The attack upon this entrance by a novice is accompanied by prolonged and violent kicking at the atmosphere. Having struggled into the gallery, you walk along it, and step boldly into utter darkness. If you step boldly enough, you find a foothold; thence you make your way upwards to a hole which brings you to the top of the crags. The great climb in this group, however, is the hand-traverse across the rock-face above the cavern's mouth. I am told that it is bad form to name climbs after individuals; but I am unwilling to relinquish the title of 'Puttrell's Progress' that has been bestowed on this particular piece of work. Mr. J. W. Puttrell, as every reader of this journal knows, is a capable and daring cragsman. It is more to the point here to mention that he is the discoverer of Wharncliffe Crags as a climb-ing-ground, and that he has not only wrought mighty deeds there himself, but has been the preceptor of various pupils, good, bad and indifferent. This hand-traverse is at present his monopoly, and is one of the most sensational climbs to be found at the Crags. The difficulties do not end with the traverse, for the ascent to the top of the rock involves some awkward balancing on small ledges that slope downwards.

The aim of this article is not to convey that in the Don Valley there exists a rival to Wastdale Head. Sheffield climbers know the limitations of their play-ground as well as they know its advantages. It is true that, in an article which recently appeared in an enterprising halfpenny morning journal, it was sug-gested that Sheffield might in course of time become an English Zermatt; but this was an astonishing flight of imagination of a kind of which only an enter-prising halfpenny morning journal is capable in these days. Wharncliffe Crags do not provide giddy precipices or towering pinnacles; but they do provide a feast of short climbs on hard, rough, firm-set rock, and by experience on them the climber may acquire a skill which will give him valuable aid in his endeav-ours after greater achievements. Cragsmen who dwell in other towns have good reason to envy Sheffield her possession of a well-equipped training-ground so close to the city's boundaries.

FIRST ASCENT OF THE GREAT GULLY OF CRAIG YR YSFA

(extract)

J. M. A. THOMSON
(Vol. IV No. 15 March 1902)

We tried a chimney on the right, but mindful of the scriptural warning — "He that removeth stones shall be hurt by them" — finally resorted to strategy, and traversed to a small pinnacle, from the top of which the slabs of the face were reached.

After gaining much valuable experience in step-cutting with a penknife, we reached an ample grass ledge about 70 feet above the pinnacle, and followed it to its abrupt termination at a point where a partly detached slab facilitates descent to a small platform in the gully. A line of advance is here afforded by a black chimney, and into its damp recesses the leader must squeeze in order to allow room for the third man of the party to alight upon the platform.

The chimney was liberally supplied with tempting holds, most of which, being undercut and treacherous, have now gone to their own place upon the scree. On leaving the chimney, we have merely to walk up a rushy slope to the next pitch, where a cave, surmounted by four wedged blocks, presents a very imposing obstacle. The vertical side-walls are set at a convenient distance for backing up, and a weathered crack on the right offers some foothold, but at the top a difficulty is experienced, for, while it is necessary to transfer the weight in order to land upon the right wall, the hand-hold much needed for the process does not come within the reach of a climber of average stature. The leader spent much time here, "gratis anhelans, multa agendo nihil agens," before effecting a lodgment upon the landing place. His companions showed how skilfully a height of 6 ft. 2 in. could be turned to account in places of the kind.

Chris Craggs climbing Western Front (E3), Almscliff. Photo: Craggs Collection.

Peter Biven (climbing) and Trevor Peck on Valkyrie (HVS), Froggatt Edge. Photo: Biven Collection.

Paul Nunn giving Wuthering a look, Stanage Edge. Photo: Ian Smith.

Keith Sharples climbing Saucius Digitalis (E4 6a), Shining Clough, Bleaklow. Photo: Ian Smith.

ALMES CLIFF CRAGS

(extract)

C. E. BENSON.

(BY PERMISSION OF THE EDITOR OF THE *YORKSHIRE POST.*)
(Vol. VIII No.31 March 1906)

[About twenty minutes from Weeton Station, between Harrogate and Leeds. By road from Leeds 12 miles; from Harrogate about 6.]

Many strange beasts came out of Noah's Ark; and out of Noah's Ark (a farm-house close to Almes Cliff) on Saturdays and Sundays, and even Wednesdays, issue a modern development of the *familia homo,* to wit *the Scansor Eboraciensis,* with kindred scansores from other counties, on scrambling intent. (N.B. It is contrary to custom to go through gates; the correct procedure is to climb the wall.)

Almes Cliff Crags ("Great Almias Cliff" of the Guide Books) are a happy hunting ground for lunatics, nuisances, and qualified nuisances, *i.e.,* climbers, tourists, and trippers who throw about glass bottles. The tourist regards the scrambler as a lunatic, the bashful scrambler looks on the curious tourist as a nuisance; for a terse and comprehensive expression of opinion as to the third species, you are referred to the scrambler who has just met with a good, satisfying handhold in the shape of a broken lemonade bottle. I write as a scrambler.

Lunatic though the scrambler may seem, there is method in his madness. To the uninstructed and unenterprising Almes Cliff Crags appear two insignificant outcrops of millstone grit, at no point exceeding sixty feet in height, standing on the brow of a small hill overlooking Weeton. To the climber they are full of interest. He wants practice to keep himself fit for more serious mountaineering, and, if he knows how to look for it, he can get all he needs on Almes Cliff. Without effort, I can recall more than fifty problems, all offering sport, and some calculated to tax, and indeed to overtax, even the very best.

About the stiffest thing on the High Man (the upper outcrop), and possibly the hardest climb on the Crags, is a double chimney, shaped something like the section of two overgrown extinguishers, one on the top of another. It is on the side that looks towards Wharfedale (the south-west, I fancy), and cannot possibly be mistaken, and, so far as most men are concerned, cannot possibly be climbed. Indeed, I believe it has only been done twice, its original conqueror being Mr. William Parsons, of the Yorkshire Ramblers, who is reputed to have accomplished everything possible and impossible on the Crags. In my opinion, Parsons' Climb, as it is called, is the most impossible of all the possible gritstone climbs I have ever seen.

I was present at the second ascent the year before last, on a day when

I was very much off colour. Last year I happened to be singularly fit. "The lunatic, the lover, and the poet, Are of imagination all compact," and I was lunatic enough to imagine I was equal to tackling the problem. I mentioned my intention to a wise man, who very rightly pointed out that, without a rope from above, the climb was unjustifiable for anyone, and that therefore, from a mountaineering point of view, the ascent was merely a useless gymnastic feat. For two days I preserved my sanity. Then I yielded. I had just conquered, as I conceived, the first difficulty, when I came off; and, but for the rope, in another second I should have been on the ground "in a fine phrensy rolling."

That is the worst of gritstone; you never know when it is not going to let you down or throw you off Ordinarily a gritstone Edge is merely a great chunk of glorified, petrified sandpaper. Of course, such material plays mischief with one's skin and clothes, but, as compensation, there are few other kinds of rock you can hang on to by your waistcoat and the seat of your breeches whilst you are feeling about for hand and foot-hold. Then, all of a sudden, without decency or warning, the roughness changes to an absolutely smooth bevel; of course, entirely to your disadvantage, affording no possibilities for either grip or friction. Or else the rock bulges out unexpectedly and knocks you backwards. It has a vicious habit of doing this just at the end of the climb. Three inches will suffice. There is a humorous little problem of this kind on the low rocks at the Rigton* end of the High Man. It is not more than ten feet high. Its aspect is mild, but its disposition ferocious. There is a splendid right hand-hold, a pocket you can grip with all your fingers and as much of your palm as you wish, a left toescrape, and in a moment you are up; that is, you have both hands over the top. True, there are no holds, except a sprinkling of broken glass, which is not generally commended, but you friction up on your palms and forearms until your head and shoulders are above the edge. Then the "shameless rock" maliciously bulges out, hits you in the chest, and throws you on the back of your head; and, unless you are safeguarded by a rope, you will hurt yourself.

Close beyond this, on the proper left of the wall with a small gate in it, is one of the best climbs for a lady the Cliff affords, the South Chimney. It is a nice, straightforward climb of 40 or 50 feet, with a resting place half-way up. The finish is a tight squeeze, and beginners are reminded that in chimneys it is advisable to wear the knot of the rope on one side and not plumb centre. The pressure of a lump of rope the size of a child's fist on that region of the body known as the "mark" is not conducive to comfort, and does your wind no good.

The patter of rain on the window reminds me that gritstone, like all rocks, becomes more or less beastly when wet. Almes Cliff is peculiarly abominable in this respect. It would seem that the rocks are covered with a minute

---

* Tea, ham and eggs, milk, &c., may be obtained at the farms, but the nearest "house of call" is at Rigton, and far enough off at that. Like all other houses in that detestable — I mean estimable — estate, it has only a six-day licence, so that total abstainers will do well to take their whisky with them on Sundays.

vegetation, invisible in dry weather, but, in the wet, execrably in evidence in the shape of a nasty, mossy slime. This may seem strong language, but it is nothing to the expressions I have heard applied to the stuff.

The most genuine climb on the whole cliff is on the southwest face of the High Man, to the left of Parsons' Climb. It is some fifty feet of genuine back, knee, and foot work, and consequently is called the Sixty Foot Chimney. All you have to do is walk into the cleft right shoulder first, and wriggle up till you get to the top, a process not so simple as it sounds. About fifteen feet up the work becomes severe for some six feet, and often drives the exhausted climber to an exit, thoughtfully provided half-way up the back of the chimney.

After the difficulties have been passed, the simplest plan is to scramble up some rounded boulders and walk out at the other side of the Crags. This, however, is not "playing the game," and the containing walls of the gallery kindly provide plenty of sport. First, on your left, comes a nice little crack; next, a pocket climb, short but severe — when a gale is blowing it is as well to finish this climb without thinking about the wind — and next, a balancing problem. My own attempts on this have hitherto been confined to stepping on to a small ledge with extreme deliberation, and off again with extreme rapidity, the minute interval between the two movements being filled by frantic gropings for holds. I once met a wasp there. A wasp is no earthly use as a hand-hold.* I have never seen this bit ascended, though one man I know has managed to get down.

Since writing these lines, the problem has been solved by the Rev. Harold Firth, Y.R. I gather that the method is simplicity itself. You merely throw your thigh round a buttress that isn't there, and so friction up till a respectable hand-hold comes within reach.

---

* On page 131, Vol. III. *C.C.J.* Mr. H. V. Reade writes of these crags — "A curious feature of the place is that several of the chimneys have been carefully filled up with masonry at the bottom, as though to prevent the sides from falling in." The real object of the masonry is to keep badgers, foxes, &c., from using these rock recesses as "bolts." I am glad of it. I conceive a badger might provide an even less satisfactory hand-hold than a wasp.

EARLY DAYS IN SKYE
(extract)

L. G. SHADBOLT
(1956)

We had rain on each day of this holiday (1911) and the morning of our last day was not promising, so we thought to obtain some shelter and took Archer Thomson and (H.O.) Jones up the North Chimney of the Bhasteir Tooth. I think we all enjoyed the climb but Thomson was a little uncomplimentary about the amount of shelter it afforded. He wrote afterwards that although he could see nothing of the upper part of the climb, he never failed to feel

"How Bhasteir's blessed river ran
In culverts through the clothes of man
Down to the sunless scree!"

We descended by Naismith's Crack and so ended a memorable and delightful holiday. As far as I was concerned it was the end of exploration in the Coolin before the bow and arrow war. We little thought that both Archer Thomson and Jones would be gone before two years had passed.

PRELUDE

A. W. BRIDGE
(1949)

To all the Manchester gritstoners of my generation the words "9.15 a.m. to Chinley from Central" or "7.50 a.m. to Marsden from Exchange" were a clarion call to Derbyshire days, and to me they bring nostalgic memories. Actually on most occasions it was "6.40 a.m. from London Road," and that to most of us meant a walk into Manchester from the suburbs, to the music of our nailed boots beating a happy tune on the hard pavements. The four or five miles we had to walk slipped along as we planned our gritstone day; now and then we would suddenly be brought back from the rocks to our immediate surroundings of dirty pavements and grimy warehouses by a cheerful greeting from a policeman or the newspaper men returning home from their night duties.

These early climbing days become more golden to me as time passes along, and I look back with sympathy and understanding on these gallant efforts to become a mountaineer; so much precious time seems to have been lost in finding one's way around, and yet the help was really very near at hand. But in those early mountain days of mine a man had to achieve a certain level and prove himself a hill lover before his guardian spirit came from his stance on cumulus clouds and took him by the hand as an accepted apprentice to the craft. How very different it is now when there is too much talk of training the youngsters in the principles of our craft and too little done, beyond a somewhat dehydrated system of impersonal, and often immature, training schemes en bloc. I am not, of course, speaking of such training schemes as those promoted by the F.R.C.C. for their younger members, for which I have admiration.

My first tutor on gritstone climbing was Bobbie Burns of the Rucksack Club, and I believe my first lesson under my maestro was at the Roaches. From the moment I first roped up I had the urge to lead, and it was with a great thrill that I led my first gritstone climb, the Via Dolorosa. In my eyes the climb was grossly libelled in its name, for to me, that day, it was a route of perfection.

It was about this time (1926) that I first met Eddie Holliday — a staunch and loyal companion if ever there was one. One Sunday morning on the 9.15 I looked with longing at the obviously experienced climbers wearing the then popular corduroy plus fours. One of the climbers was in a flat spin because his companion had not arrived. Now was my opportunity to go climbing; I begged him to take me along, and well remember how crushed I felt when he turned me down "because I had never climbed on Stanage." (At a later date I was to have the pleasure of rescuing him on the Idwal Slabs.) But it was that same day that I met Eddie who suffered my enthusiasm when he could most justifiably have refused. Nothing ever dismayed him; and he and C. I. Ward were with me when I led two new gritstone routes we named Fairbrook Buttress and Pavlova, both climbs being on the Fairbrook Edge of Kinder Scout — the shaping of things to come.

How useful is gritstone climbing in the development of one's mountaineering values? It is of little usefulness *unless* one adds to the week-end's work a strong dose and large quantities of bog-trotting. Gritstone climbing, even less than rock climbing, will not develop stamina, and Eddie and I arranged a fine series of climbing-cum-bivvy-cum-bog-trotting week-ends with that brilliant fell-walking Club, the Bog-trotters. In 1927 I was made President of this Club, an honour I shall always regard in the highest sense. Our heroes were Eustace Thomas, Fred Heardman and Harry Gilliat. We used them as our yardstick and what a mighty yard-stick

These were halcyon days of great personalities in the climbing and fell-walking world, and the Bog-trotters as a Club looked towards these great names; we did our best to follow the example of getting every inch and minute out of our mountain days. There is no doubt that the Bog-trotters were fell-walkers of the very highest grade; and of the members Ben Bennet was — and is — really brilliant. It was he who asked me to walk(!) the full length, north to south (Penistone-Ashbourne) of the 1" Ordnance Peak District Map, and we covered this distance in the remarkable time of 10 hours 20 mins. The Marsden-Edale walk I used to do in well under 4 hours, and *not* via Wessenden Valley in lieu of Black and White Moss. Many were the fell-walking feats of this Manchester Club; I think I can justly claim to have walked the fells with the best men in the country, but never have I met the equal of the Bog-trotters as a fell-walking Club.

These early days were invaluable training, together with our gritstone climbing on Stanage, Cratcliffe, Laddow, Castle Naze and Black Rocks.

It was in 1928 that I listened in awe to the accounts of gritstone climbs done by the " 3 H's," namely, H. K. Hartley, Roy Horsman and A. T. Hargreaves. These climbers did brilliant work in the development of gritstone climbing; I doubt if this fact is fully realised. To see Herbert Hartley at work on Laddow was, indeed, an exposition, in a superb class, of the technique of balance; and it was equally good to see Roy Horsman and 'A. T.' working out their brilliant new routes on Stanage Edge. And I also heard whispers of one, Maurice Linnell, who was in Hartley's year at Manchester University; but at this time it was only a name and I could not foresee how much the name Maurice Linnell would mean to me in later days.

I carried on my climbing under the guidance of Bobbie Burns and with Eddie Holliday as my very trusty second. How often Bobbie used to say to me, "I know you can do Tower Face (Laddow) in boots, and maybe Priscilla also, but it is just not done. Leave the rocks tidy; and how can you do that if you score the grit with your nails? Remember that 20 years from now climbers will want to come to these rocks." Sound advice, but we need not have worried. Today we find our gritstone edges scored and bleeding — on them, mock heroics, and, at their foot, gaping tins and bruised rocks.

It was at Cratcliffe that I first met Maurice Linnell, in 1929, as I was making a solo descent of Giant's Staircase at the close of a summer's day. We introduced ourselves and our climbing partnership was given birth on gritstone. Little did we know of the adventures which were before us; the Girdle Traverse of Pillar, Clogwyn du'r Arddu and a magnificent day on Ben Nevis in Easter of 1932, when, under really great Alpine conditions, we did the Douglas Boulder and Tower Ridge in the day.

I remember that as we arrived at the Tower it was to find a group of our leading climbers on the point of retreat with the information that they could not follow Jack Longland and Paul Sinker who had forced the route; and the great thrill which was mine as I also forced the *mauvais pas* and led the route to the finish, to be greeted by Ivan Waller who came dashing along from the top of the Ben with his congratulations. The Tower Ridge is a tough proposition when tackled under truly Alpine conditions such as we had in 1932, but to include the Douglas Boulder as well, in the same day, is a day's climbing to be long remembered.

But I have wandered from Derbyshire and gritstone. It was at Castle Naze that I first met Ivan Waller, and we soon roped up together — or did we climb solo? We probably did. I remember that Ivan bundled me into the Alvis and off we went to Black Rocks, Cromford, where Ivan reigned as Chief Inquisitor. Black Rocks is to the Climbers' Club as Laddow is to the Ruck-sack Club, and Ivan was truly *the* expert of his day on Black Rocks. Jack Longland, in 1928, made a typical J.L.L. route named Birch Tree Wall which finished with a very delightful traverse — pure balance work — to the pine tree just above Chancery Slab. A later visit by Jack, Ivan and myself led to an escapade which resulted in a very severe and exposed climb which Ivan had forced me to lead and which even to this day is looked upon with respect by Peter Harding — a worthy successor to Ivan as the present day Chief Inquisitor of Black Rocks.

The Cratcliffe weekends arranged by Eustace Thomas were in a class by themselves and to me most enjoyable, for I knew that prior to the climb-ing I was assured of a top-notch fell walk with Eustace — and no mercy shown. It was on one of these Meets that I managed to force a greasy ascent of the groove at the left of Hermitage Crack on Cratcliffe, and I seem to remember Eustace taking a pictorial record of that ascent and also the Gi-ant's Staircase.

It was about this time that Eddie and I arranged to go to Chinley one Saturday afternoon ; we planned to walk to Stanage (climb), Cratcliffe (climb), Robin Hood's Stride (climb) and Castle Naze (climb), returning, of course, from Chinley on the Sunday late afternoon. It was a grand show and a good trial for me, for I was only just recovering from a very badly sprained ankle and I did this round in gym-shoes and a very heavily bandaged ankle. At a later date, I made a jolly little round of Greenfield to Chinley, including climbs on Laddow, Stanage (High Neb and Robin Hood end), Robin Hood's Stride, Cratcliffe and Castle Naze — with no less than two Very Severes to be done on each gritstone edge. We left Greenfield on the Saturday afternoon, straight from work, and in point of fact we did four V.S.s on Laddow, with two, as planned, on each of the other edges.

But the prelude was drawing to a close. I had met Maurice and much time was being spent in Wales and the Lakes. Bobbie Burns and Eddie had taught the fundamentals to me and I was well prepared for greater adventures.

The Cuillin Ridge in Skye was completed, and the Welsh Three Thousands" — but for this latter round we started from Llandudno Junction and finished at Beddgelert. Records never entered into our minds, yet I make bold to say that we could have more than held our own with the so-called record times of later parties.

Before breakfast I would do the Great Gully on Craig yr Ysfa (particulars in the Rucksack Club Log Book) and then, after some breakfast, on to Idwal Slabs — Holly Tree Wall — Central Arête — Glyders — Bristly Ridge — Tryfan — down Grooved Arête and back to Helyg. Every precious moment was squeezed out of our week-ends—youth, vigour, ambition and the joy of living in our mountains meant so much to us.

Gritstone climbing in itself could not possibly have prepared us in the stamina required for sterner adventures, in the Alps and at home; but Derbyshire days well spent, can be of enormous value in preparing the body and the mind for the greater demands made upon it by higher places. Let those of us who live near the Peak be thankful for our opportunities; and I suggest to the real gritstone climber (I have no fear that the acrobats will take note) that to know Bleaklow and Kinder on a black, stormy winter's night is to experience a worthy test of courage, stamina and the exercise of good, sound mountaineering principles.

My Prelude is completed and the stage is set for mountain days with Colin Kirkus, Maurice Linnell, Jack Longland, A. B. Hargreaves and other well-known names of my generation. The Epilogue belongs to a more worthy pen than mine.

"I'M A SICK MAN, FITZGERALD"
A STROLL WITH ALAN HARGREAVES

KEVIN FITZGERALD
(1960)

In the early spring of 1951, or it may have been 1952, my doctors thought I needed a rest. "Go to a place where you can potter about on your own," they said. "But nothing strenuous, mind: take a book into the open air and sit down often if you go for a walk." I knew just the place for all that and I sent a telegram to Mr. Christopher Briggs. He met me at Colwyn Bay, smiled grimly at the hundred feet of alpine hemp Lorimer Richardson had asked me to carry up for him, and put me into a room labelled 'Tryfan'.

I was having a drink after dinner with Tony Moulam, at that time theoretically engaged in a one-man reading party for his degree, when there was a minor disturbance in the hall. "That will be Alan," Tony said. "I don't think you've met him?"

I was introduced to Mr. Hargreaves who thought he could manage half a pint. "I must be careful," he said. "My days for all that drinking and larking about are very much over. I'm a sick man, FitzGerald."

I took a close look at this famous character. I had heard him called 'The Little Man', and that was what we had called the chief cowpoke in our outfit in Western Canada in 1926/7. I remembered that our little man had dealt rather more than adequately one afternoon with fourteen and a half stone of angry Red Indian called Bulling George. I also remembered a night in Devonshire in 1921 when half a dozen six-footers like me had failed to control a young man who, when sober, rather liked his nickname of 'Tiny Mac'. Finally, as I looked at Mr. Hargreaves I recalled a dreadful affair in a Derbyshire public house in 1930. The police reserves from Sheffield arrived too late to save the bar from my friend 'Little Jimmy' and it took eight of them to get him into their van. It is clear then that I had met some other little men in my time, but one is never too old to refuse to learn. I could easily have run away but instead I talked happily with Mr. Hargreaves as the night brought various wet unshaven persons in from the surrounding countryside. I observed that he knew them all. "No," he said to each individual greeting. "I'm afraid not. I'm a pretty sick man; only here for twenty-four hours or so to get a breather. I simply must rest." He said much the same thing while we were washing up about two in the morning. He had just demonstrated to an unbeliever that it was quite easy, given what he called 'some general sense of balance', to eat a cheese and onion sandwich while standing on one's head in the middle of a room. "Damn silly, really," he remarked as we said good-night. "Shouldn't do that kind of thing when I'm as ill as this. May see you tomorrow if I feel better."

About ten o'clock next day I was sitting outside on the little white bench and wondering if I could perhaps get as far as the causeway and back before dark when Mr. Hargreaves stood before me. "What about a stroll?" he asked. I told him that I was not well enough for more than the gentlest exercise and he laughed. "Look at me," he said. "I don't think I could get a mile from this hotel if I tried. I'm not just off-colour like you, FitzGerald, I'm a sick man. Get your boots on and let's see what we can do. I've asked young Moulam to come along; we need someone fit to take care of us."

I got very wet crossing the river. It was full and the stones were a foot or so under water. "You want to remember what I was saying last night about balance," Hargreaves said as he and Tony pulled me out. "It's never any use blundering about at random. Always leads to trouble sooner or later."

I caught up with them about an hour later. Moulam was on something he called a 'problem crack' and Hargreaves was about six feet up on a large boulder nearby. As I lay down he climbed with extreme care to the heather and joined me. He pointed with a piece of meat from his haversack at some long scratches in a slate outcrop at the foot of the boulder. "See those," he said. "Some ignorant fool must have jumped off. I bet he hit the mountain twenty or thirty feet down after that." I remembered a day with Hilton-Jones and his happy cry of "Your first real fall; are you all right?" "Yes," I said to Hargreaves. "He was an ignorant fool, that's for sure."

They were waiting for me and looking at a wild goat when I had found my way off that wet plateau at the top of the miners' track and had begun stumbling about on the screes at the other side. "You make a lot of noise with your feet, FitzGerald," Hargreaves said, getting up as I sat down. "I'm afraid we haven't time to hang about if we're to get to the top."

"Top of what?" I asked. "I shan't be able to go much further; I'm all in now."

"Top of Tryfan," Hargreaves said. "It's no distance from here and a pity to come as far as this and do nothing." He looked down at me as I lay at his feet. "I don't believe you eat enough," he said. He put his hand into his haversack and dredged out a bit of cold bacon. I can still see it. There were raisins adhering to it and it was smeared with chocolate. "Have a bit of this," he said.

It was as Dr. Bridges aptly observed in his 'Testament of Beauty': "Late in my long journey when I had clomb to where the path was narrowing and the company few." Three feet above me stood Hargreaves and Moulam. I lay in a little trough of rock. "Look," Hargreaves said. "That's the summit forty feet from here. You can ease out of there and walk up, you know you can." He moved a foot to his left and stood looking down at something. "Just get to where I am, FitzGerald, and you can hang over the finest precipice in Wales." I went on clinging to the sides of my trough.

About ten minutes later I heard boots on rock and two men, strangers to me, joined Moulam and Hargreaves. The committee of four stood at the

head of my trough and considered my situation. One of the newcomers offered a solution. He smiled and waved. "Don't think about anything," he
said. "Make your mind a blank and flow up to me." The proprieties had been
outraged. "I don't think you've met, have you?" Hargreaves said. "Mr. Geoffrey
Sutton, Mr. Kevin FitzGerald."

"How do you do," I said.

Time passed and I made my proposition. "If I move out of here and go
to the top will you promise I can sit down. Will you promise that?"

Hargreaves seemed astonished. "Good Lord, Yes. As long as you like.
Need a rest myself. Not at all fit."

On the summit we looked for mice and put sardine tins out of sight. I
declined an invitation to try the jump from Adam to Eve. I also declined to sit
on top of either. I thought that in perhaps an hour I might be able to think
about another move.

"Good thing you had that rest in that little trough," Hargreaves said.
"We don't want to be up here in the dark."

We started on down, as the mountaineering books say, and that was
something I could do in those days. The hope of perhaps crashing to uncon-
sciousness lent wings to my feet, and I was still with the party when we
arrived back at the path across the screes.

I saw them, every now and again, until we reached the top of the miners' track. It was dark then and cold. I had not been able to breathe properly
for some time. They were sitting waiting for me.

"Well, here we are," Hargreaves said, getting up as I arrived. "Safely
back after a nice quiet day. Just keep to the wall and you can't go wrong." He
peered at his watch. "Tony," he said, "they're open. I'll race you down." They
crashed into the dark.

They beat me to the hotel, but dinner had only just finished when I
arrived. It was not having anyone to pull me out of the river which really
delayed me. I fell in three times before I got the sense to wade about feeling
with my hands for a place where I could cross and drag out on my own.

Mr. Briggs was kind to me in the morning and put me into the fresh air
with some brandy while breakfast was being served. He had ordered a car
and asked Blodwen to pack for me as soon as I came down. I don't think I
can have looked half as ill as I felt all the same.

Hargreaves came to say good-bye about half past ten. He looked relaxed in a dark suit and a rather nice hat. "You want to keep away from
places like this, FitzGerald," he said. "You really aren't fit enough for it."

I was allowed to get up two or three weeks later and I came back to P-
y-G to finish my convalescence. The first evening someone said: "The Little
Man was here ten days ago. He was asking for you, Kevin. He was sorry to
hear you were ill again and said to tell you that he still wasn't awfully fit
himself."

FIRST AND SECOND

A. J. J. MOULAM
(1956)

Recently I made my second ascent of Mur y Niwhl this time at the other end of the rope. It was a pleasant ascent, with time to enjoy the route, the knowledge that it had been climbed before leaving my mind free to wander and so it did, back to the days when I first desired to climb this face.

Alan Hargreaves was really to blame; he had mentioned the wall as a magnificent possibility in his article, 'More of Arfon', which reviewed the future of Welsh climbing. For some reason, although I had not seen this amphitheatre wall, the idea stayed with me. Later, every time I climbed Amphitheatre Buttress I saw the wall, boldly present over the screes. Somehow no opportunity came as I did the field work for the Carneddau guide, possibly because that was schemed to do the existing routes, and new ones were made only incidentally. Mur y Niwhl was an undertaking not to be approached in that lighthearted way.

Three years passed, and I looked at the wall many times. At first it seemed impossible that a way could be found up it, but each view added a little to my knowledge of its topography. The grass pedestal, the steep wall to the foot of the V-groove were obvious enough; but then, where? Perhaps a traverse; there seemed to be a line, over to the right. Anyway, the eye can ignore obstacles, and there seemed to be enough holds at least to justify a try. Three years were long enough to wait for the fulfilment of such a wish as mine. I was fit, after a series of week-ends in Wales and the Lakes and so, arbitrarily, a day was chosen.

John Disley, Alan Francis, and I walked over to Craig yr Ysfa, laden down with ropes, slings, pitons and other paraphernalia. We must have looked a determined party, but we passed others on the path who accepted our statement that we were going to do Amphitheatre Buttress without comment. Perhaps they thought that this was the modern way. There was a tongue of old snow up to my projected start, and none of us seemed keen, or able, to leave it. It started to spit with rain, so I hid my disappointment and agreed to the others' suggestion that we climb Great Gully. Never had I found it easier; encumbered though we were, we completed the climb in under an hour, and returned to P-y-G. Sitting in the bar there my determination returned. Might our default have been cowardly, just due to nerves? The threatened rain had not materialised; the next time I would not so easily be dissuaded.

Not so long after, and before the snow had gone, another large party sat in the Amphitheatre. We delayed setting off as long as we could, by eating sandwiches and looking at the great wall. I felt small and frightened as I looked up at it, at the line I intended to take curving out over space, up

into the sky. Eventually no more excuses could be found and Johnny Church-
ill and I moved reluctantly over to the side of the gully, below my wall. This
was it; my prolonged wait was maybe about to be rewarded. My theories,
and incidentally Johnny and myself, were to be put to the test.

The still present snow was quite an obstacle in rubbers, and the wall
beyond was immediately steep. There were good small holds though, and I
climbed quickly up to a horizontal crack with an unsatisfying edge. I chose
the lower of two possible ways to reach the long grass-topped pedestal on
my right and made a landing on the ledge with aching arms. As I brought
Johnny up, I scanned the rocks above; we had at least made a start, but
things looked uncompromising now. Our traverse had presented us with
quite a lot of exposure, but now we had to go up. Three times I tried the wall
before I gained a niche about 20 feet higher, which a loose rock flake shared
with me. Clutching it with one hand, as much to keep it in place as anything, I searched over the overhang with the other, and found a good hold.
Warning Johnny of the flake I pulled myself up, stepped out onto the right
wall and followed grassy holds to the foot of the big V-groove. Immediately I
was disappointed; it seemed unclimbable. Gloom: there seemed nothing to
do but descend. I did not wish to withdraw so soon, and idly pulled some
turf off a ledge, and then some more. I stepped onto the revealed hold, and
the turf hit the ground with a thump.

Suddenly I realised what a fine position I was in, standing above a
tremendous drop, in the middle of a rough bare rock face. Looking down to
enjoy the exposure before retreat, I noticed a small hold, and beyond it the
scree. Then the upturned faces of Fred and Emlyn brought my mind back to
the problem that faced me. I had decided to go on.

Plucking up courage, from myself and the presence of my friends, I
made a complicated move down from the red edge of my ledge, and hanging
at arm's length my foot just touched the hold. I relaxed again now. The die
was cast. I could go on... to what? Little quartz holds led over to an open
groove of steps, on the edge of all things. Nothing mattered but the odd few
feet of rock around me, as the groove 'went', not too hard, and I tied myself
on as well as possible when I reached the stance. Johnny came up with a
few pulls on the rope and a lot of encouragement. " How do you expect to get
out of *this* place?" he asked as he arrived, looking rather frightened, but I
didn't answer as I didn't know!

This place was an awe-inspiring one, a sort of rock pulpit with a sound-
ing board formed by the overhanging roof, a place to heckle climbers congre-
gated on the opposite buttress or in the hollow beneath! Mist had descended.
It filled the cwm and swirled around the top of the cliffs forming picturesque
wreaths, perhaps for us! Emlyn shouted up that he wouldn't come, it was
getting late; and all the time my confidence and courage were going. The
nervous energy expended had left me weak, and now it seemed the real test
was yet to come.

A thin crack led out right beneath the overhang. I hoped I looked confident as I tried to swing out on my hands, along its now greasy edge, but I

had to move back to the perch for a moment's rest. Again I tried, and found myself at the far end, held above the abyss by my fingers. A last desperate pull and I stood up shakily on the tiny ledge beyond. Even now the outlook was uncertain and I knew that we should fail if there were any pitches more difficult than the last.

Johnny found the hand traverse quite difficult to start, but easy to finish. We followed slabs and a steep groove to a grassy glacis and a ledge only 15 feet below Emlyn's smiling face. He had walked round to the top and told me that the finishing holds were good.

And now, back to the present. Again I stood beneath that final wall. The thin white rope went up, and disappeared over the edge to David. Something seemed wrong; there were no holds — or was I being stupid? Before, I had found the final wall easy, but now it took me three attempts before I joined the others on the bilberry terrace. The climb is still the best I've done in Wales, and all I want is a future supply of leaders to take me up, on the end of their ropes, Mur y Niwhl.

CRAIG YR YSFA MEMORY

A. B. HARGREAVES
(1944)

Reading the most excellent Craig Yr Ysfa Guide, published in the 1943 *Journal*, brought back to me a number of sudden, clear-cut memories, particularly of an old adventure, one of many experienced during the period 1927-1934 when I had the good fortune to be in at some of the major proceedings of the Welsh revival in the matter of rock climbing. The Guide says " Pinnacle Wall, Direct Start—C. F. Kirkus and A. B. Hargreaves — 1932" and describes this item as "Standard VI" (which, being put back into the old nomenclature means, I understand, "very severe"). Well, it certainly was very "VI."

As I was constrained to "retire" from serious climbing a couple of years after that, I think it would probably be the last time I climbed on Craig Yr Ysfa and the day dug itself into my memory, not only because this new thing was done but because of a little bit of "fun and games " — as a happening "not according to plan" used then to be called. I had always had fun on my occasional visits to the place because they were usually to do the Great Gully, which is hardly a small man's climb. For instance, I remember, very early on, being introduced to the place by those *maestros* of a previous generation, J. M. Davidson and W. R. Reade. I believe my language, when trying to back up the Big Pitch with one ear on one wall and my toes scratting on the other wall, was considered shocking and there was also some little trouble over my going to ground in a hole under the Capstone and refusing to move until towed out on the rope though I believe I got a bit of my own back on that nice little penultimate pitch. Later on, when I had acquired cunning and the habit of not taking much notice of how sixfooters did things, I used to go up the right-hand crack of this Cave Pitch — most interesting, certainly "stiff," as per Guide! I also remember a winter ascent when our party of three got so wet and cold that we had to walk all the way back to Helyg *roped,* the knots having somehow got seized...

But this day with Colin was much "funnier." The previous year he had made the Pinnacle Wall climb — solo — and he proposed that we should go there to do it *(a)* so that he could get my opinion for classification purposes, and *(b)* (a) turned out to be only a blind so that he could have a go at a little thing he had tried the day he did the climb and which he thought might go if he had a bit of moral support... I suppose I ought to have detected that there was something out of the ordinary in the lad's mind because he not only piled a lot more food than usual into the sack (that is, about a war-time week's ration of body-builders and energisers) but also a little bag which jingled, and the Helyg poker. This latter was quite a normal item of our equipment in winter because funds did not run to ice axes — but we did not usually borrow it in summer time — though the hearth brush was sometimes requisitioned then. Well, it was a nice fine day, not too hot, and we talked a lot on the way over about Clogwyn du'r Arddu, and gardening, and about Menlove and *his* gardening activities on Idwal East Wall (blast him!), and about a certain young woman who had recently changed ownership and about the Pinnacle Wall, of course, but no information was given me about the "little thing" we were going to try. We began by doing the Amphitheatre Rib (very good climb) just to warm up, and from there I had pointed out to me the run of the Pinnacle Wall climb ("It's a pity one has to go right along that Bilberry Terrace to get on to it instead of straight up the corner") and then my attention was drawn to the wall below the said Bilberry Terrace ("What about that crack, that would straighten it out a bit, wouldn't it? ") I was cocky enough to second this proposal but I did jib at Colin trying to do the thing unseen, because it looked a perfectly horrible place and I insisted that we commence operations by my going to the top of the crack and fetching him up it on a rope. This turned out to have been a wise move; it took about an hour, several pulls and a lot of Colin's energy to get him up. He then reported that it would probably go if thoroughly gardened (he had already removed quite a lot of stuff) so I was sent down with the poker and spent another hour preparing the pitch for the lead. Then Colin led it, having very great difficulty, especially at the start and the finish (which would have been quite impossible as it was before it was cleaned up). I remember very well the "poor belay" near the top and the difficult traverse out to finish; that was about the hardest bit. It was just the sort of pitch to justify Menlove's famous description — "very annoying."

We were both pretty exhausted after this and were glad to fall to on the sardines wrapped in sliced tongue, and the jam sandwiches laced with Nestle's milk; we also opened a tin of bully which, with Carlsbad plums, was to constitute a final *bonne bouche*... But before we had got to that stage the aforesaid little bag was produced and I was surprised and rather shocked to see that it contained a little hammer and a couple of flat pitons. I say shocked because we two were generally agreed that steeplejack's ironmongery was out of place on crags, British crags at any rate, *unless* there was something that could not possibly be led safely without such aids and which, if it could be done, would result in the completion of a climb such as on the Overhanging Wall climb on the East Buttress of Scafell, made by Linnell and my namesake. Anyway, this was the first time to my knowledge that C.F.K. had thought of using the things and the place where he thought they might be required was directly above us where we sat on the Bilberry Terrace at the top of the Direct Start crack. This was a nasty-looking V groove of perhaps 30 feet, approximately perpendicular to start with and definitely overhanging at the top where it gave on to the Quartz Ledge of the Pinnacle Wall climb. I again proposed to go round to the top of the pitch and drop a rope so that Colin could try it that way first, but he said he had already been some way up it when he had done the Pinnacle Wall climb and he thought it would certainly go if he could get a piton fixed below the top overhang; also, time was getting on, so he decided to try it "clean." With some difficulty my leader got himself

Neil Foster on the bold Great Arête (E5 5c), Millstone Edge. Photo: Ian Smith.

Peter Biven on Quietus (E2), Stanage. Photo: Biven Collection.

Morty Smith on Elder Crack (E2), Curbar Edge. Photo: Nat Allen Collection.

Martin Boysen, obviously at home on Coronation Crack (5c), High Rocks, Southern Sandstone.
Photo: Ken Wilson.

lodged in a sort of saint's niche about 20-25 feet up and then proceeded to fix the piton in a crack at the back. This was not so easy because he had to hold himself into the niche with one hand while hammering the piton with the other. However, he eventually got it in to his satisfaction, then he ran his rope through the ring and climbed down for a rest. We both pulled hard on the rope and the piton was O.K'd as firm. Then Colin went at the pitch. His idea was to use the rope running through the piton to hold him in (à la Leo Maduschka, *vide British Mountaineering Journal* of about that time) while he leaned back and reached upwards for the holds which he hoped existed above the overhang. He tried once — and came back into the niche — he tried again (harder) with me holding the rope taut — and then — (a loud "ping" and a "whirr") — the piton was out and Colin was in mid-air

Fortunately, although the Bilberry Terrace from which we were operating was quite broad at that point, I had a belay, though rather a small one, and was able to get some rope in during his gracefully parabolic descent, because he landed on his stomach at the very edge of the Terrace and just as the rope came tight on him he bounced over the top of the Direct Start crack... The brakes held, but only after I had been dragged several feet with the belay rope (line) stretching like elastic. I can still see his legs waving in the air... But although the leader was saved (it was a fairly soft landing) — at the usual cost in second man's hand-skin — a disaster had occurred; the bully tin had got kicked overboard during the proceedings so we had to eat the Carlsbad plums neat.

We did *not* do the Pinnacle Wall climb (ordinary way) just to preserve our nerve, according to the old prescription, although we did try — dithering down the Quartz Ledge into the corner and then back, even more ditheringly — in fact, as the sun fell we crept silently up one of the Amphitheatre gulleys (roped — short run outs) and slunk, chastened, down to Helyg where nothing was said about the day's doings — in fact I don't think even the Direct Start was logged.

As I did not try the pitch myself I cannot say whether or not it seemed climbable, with or without artificial aid, but it does seem worth commending it to the attention of post-war "tigers " because if it would "go" the combination of it with the Direct Start and the upper and difficult part of the original Pinnacle Wall climb, would obviously form a superb route worthy to rank with the best on Clogwyn du'r Arddu. It may be identified in the illustration facing page 143 of the *Journal* (25 of the Guide reprint) by reference to the bottom end of the Quartz Ledge where there is a bit of turf (see also illustration of Quartz Ledge) with a black V slot just below it; the attempt was either by way of the V slot (I think it was) or a little further to the right, facing in, where on the photographs the angle appears to be easier.

At the beginning I referred briefly to the new Guide to Craig Yr Ysfa and I must say that it seems to me a very fine job of work, particularly because it must have been a most boring business combing the uninteresting sections which form the major part of the cliff. However, the authors evidently had the satisfaction not only of making several new routes but of breaking new ground where there are further possibilities. Being one of the last generation to regard the rest of Craig Yr Ysfa as useful merely to hold up the walls of the Great Gully I should certainly like to be taken on a conducted tour, secured by competent tugs fore and aft, of the Cirque and the Dancing Floor.

THE NOSE OF DINAS MOT

A DIAGONAL SOLILOQUY

H. G. NICOL
(1953)

Rope tight, glance at guide-book, everything set.

"Ready, Andrew?"

"Ready."

The first pitch won't be too hard anyway, though it is difficult to see where it goes. Let's try the crack: it seems to lead to the partly detached block they talk about.

"Am I right, Ted?"

Ted is on the ground taking photographs. He mutters something affirmative without leaving his shutter.

The crack goes alright and I can put an enormous runner on the block up here — which is very satisfactory.

Now for the traverse.

Not much to hang on to, but a curious move with an outward swivel of the left knee lands me on a commodious ledge with a somewhat unconvincing belay low on the left.

"Can't you do better than this, Ted?"

Ted has been here before and he can't he assures me. Without wasting much time Andrew comes up, leaving Ted below for the moment — to his camera, and some mild gymnastics to dispel the cold.

Back on the ledge the atmosphere is obviously strained, for the crucial pitch is above and this inhibits conversation.

Now Andrew has belayed and drawn on his gloves — silently but with emphasis.

"Have a good time."

I say nothing. After all, one is supposed to be enjoying oneself. Useless to put it off any longer, though an initial feint up an obviously unpromising line gains some time.

"Try farther left." This from Ted, unfeelingly.

I do and it goes. Curious tiny flakes and great heaves and pauses for breath. And now I am alone with the rock — no rope — no second — no sky, future, past, regrets, ambitions, fears... space. Nothing but an utter concentration on rock: the holds on it, small and firm, each one a jewel seized with desire, relinquished with infinite regret: the belays on it, which end one agony only to usher in the next.

At 40 feet I knew I should find an esoteric type of running belay, a shaky pebble which by manipulation can be jammed in a slot. And yet I sought it as ardently as a lover his mate.

This must be it.

The stone smirked at me from its little groove, conscious of the advances which, by the scratches on the surrounding rock, had clearly been made on it.

I made the rope firm, and left my pegs and hammer to be collected, for they could be of no help above.

Now back to the mid-line for the overhang, the crucial overhang below which on holds of faith, so they say, one moves to easier ground.

The rock was slightly greasy after a fortnight of rain. And I could see no holds: the jewelled casket firmly closed.

First I'll dry my rubbers and have a rest.

"I think this lot's wet."

Absolutely no comment from below: no help either.

And then the first move, and then the next, up from one toe-scrape to another, hands and feet brimful of air. Now bend down because the overhang is directly above, grinning at the nape of your neck.

Don't like this at all. Have to traverse right. Can't see how to do it. Wait now, this must be the key — see up there, under the overhang, firm little beaded knobs of quartz. Pull on them, sweat-shining palm-sinews standing out. Try to tear them away! Now for it. Make a long stride (watch out for that obvious foothold; people have come off on it) and plant the right foot well enough. Too stretched out for comfort. What to pull over on ? Yes, there are definite holds. Can't understand it. Must be a trick somewhere. Left foot shaking. Over you go — and up!

"Well done, Hamish." Ted still there.

"Not up yet, damn you."

And as if to prove this I have to perform some ridiculous antics far out on the right.

The overhang is bounded by an undercut chimney, and up this you must go.

Wonder if I can jam my shoulders in it?

It seems possible, but what a funny situation — leant back in an armchair of rock, before some atmospheric hearth.

But the flames below are leaping impatiently. I belay and bring them up.

The next pitch looks interesting. It seems I have to go over that way, to the right. First a long low traverse into a groove, flutter hands and friction feet.

"Bad bit there, Andrew."

Here's a pocket hold for my right foot at waist level. Too high. Have to stand in it. What has the book to say?

"... groove ascended on widely spaced holds." Widely spaced, yes, I see their point.

The move is as obvious, however, as it is repellent, and presently I am

standing in the pocket, slightly incredulous. Up on the right is another resting place, a mantelshelf well protected by smooth walls. At one point, however, its defences are at fault, for a two-finger hold for the left hand — the
kind of feature one remembers for years — makes possible a determined foot
progress in a vertical groove, and a gasping lodgement.

Still the future does not look brilliant, but in the book again is a glim-
mer of hope. Take a jug handle on the right at full stretch and swing up into
a groove and respite.

"Definitely harder than the crux."

" Cheerful blighter."

And so I sat down and took in Andrew, and then Ted, who had by this
time forsaken his camera and more athletic pursuits.

At this point it is possible to traverse off onto Western Slabs, and so
avoid the final direct chimney pitch. At least one member of our party was
willing to do so.

"It's an over'angin' 'and jam all the way, lad"... knowing my ineptitude
at this sort of manoeuvre.

However, Purism triumphed, and again I started off, with a layback
and a jug handle or two into a large recess below the hardest part.

First, take a jam in the left crack from where you can just seize with
both hands a promising spike, and hang there in a rather futile and self-
conscious way until exhaustion enjoins retreat.

Clearly I have to stand on the spike, an impossible feat while still suspended from it. However, on the second or third cycle of ascent and failure I
succeed in fitting a sling on, which forms a poor, if gratifying, return for the
effort involved.

But on the left there is a pocket-sized underhold which gains a few
inches. Now detach a hand and look for something higher, quickly though —
not much time. Right foot still waiting for something to do. Have this tuft of
grass out of the way. A hold! Pull quickly up on it and slap the right foot on
the spike. Missed it by two inches... foot caught in sling... can't lift it... do
something quick... knee on spike.

And so I gained a painful, though safe, release. The worst is over now,
and a few more finger jams bring holds within reach.

Pull up and over.

Done it!

THE LATE FIFTIES
A PERSONAL ACCOUNT
(extract)

C. T. JONES
(1973/4)

In the late forties in Derbyshire. the youthful Joe Brown and his friends were hardening their already considerable muscles on the overhanging Derbyshire gritstone outcrops and laid the physical foundation for the most tremendous increase in technique and élan that rock-climbing had ever known.

The Welsh exploits of the flinty-faced Manchester Sherpas who constituted the Rock and Ice Club resulted in their taking over the leadership of rock-climbing there as well as in Derbyshire. They charted ways up rock thought before their time to be quite inaccessible. It was felt it was impossible to repeat them unless the aspirant was a fully paid up superhuman union member of the Manchester building trade.

Stories were heard on the bush telegraph in the Welsh public houses of a horror-climb on the Far East Buttress (wherever that was) on which Joe Brown had forced a way. No one had been able to follow him. After overcoming its ferocious difficulty Brown had been forced to rest in a darkened bedroom with a dampened towel over his forehead for three days. The gullible general climbing public lapped up nonsense like this avidly, because there was no-one outside the Rock and Ice to question the validity of the story.

In 1958 I made one of the few repetitions of Cenotaph since Joe's ascent. Seven ascents in seven years did not imply it was an easy day for a lady. I was the first non-desperate man to make its ascent and the seven leaders who had done it before were all spoken about in the Welsh public bars in hushed reverential tones.

The climb was hard, but not too desperate, in fact three quarters of the way up there had been a sloping shelf on which I was able to wedge half one cheek of a backside; with one foot bridged out at ear-level it was surprisingly restful. But apart from the one resting place it had needed a new concept in muscular tension. No move was very hard, just a tendon-sapping strain of staying to the smooth rock. For the first time there was terrible neck-ache due to the need to force my head back to plan the next sequence of moves up the relenting verticality.

Urged on by the ascent of Cenotaph which had been physically and mentally exacting, but not at the ultimate limit, I decided to attempt the girdle traverse which had only been repeated once by a Scottish team led by John Cunningham, the scintillating star of the Glasgow Creag Dhu, who were a Scottish equivalent in many ways of the Rock and Ice.

Mike Harris of the Climbers' Club and I decided to try to make the third ascent.

Things had gone quite smoothly on the easier left-hand part of the cliff until we came up against it as we reached the edge of the great open granite book. Everything had gone quite smoothly in the couple of hours that we had been climbing. It was my turn to lead and I was half-way along the left-hand wall. I had been there some time and was clinging to a thin vertical crack with a very poor finger jam while I tried to thread a running belay round a small jammed stone. There were gravelly voices from below and looking down I recognized with a start the ultimate heavy mob, forty feet below me — Joe Brown, Don Whillans and Mortimer, their gifted apprentice. A few seconds later the stone shot out of the crack as I jerked at the nylon loop. The surprise of this caused me to slip and fall about fifteen feet, gyrating slowly at the end of the rope as Mike expertly stopped me.

Broad grins from the hardmen; cigarette ash happily tapped into the heather as I spun round. "Excellent, what's yer next trick?" shouted Brown.

This was my first experience of the Joe Brown deflation phenomenon. Although he means no harm, as soon as he appears at the foot of the crag, violent vibrations affect the limbs of most of the climbers at work. They dither, fall off or retreat. If you happen to be climbing with him, this, of course, is worse and in nine cases out of ten a muscular paralysis sets in as you watch the Rolls-Royce climbing machine sliding effortlessly upwards. When it is their turn to follow the rest of the team gasp, struggle, stare hypnotically at the inadequate hold and often end up rotating like a turkey on Christmas Day on the end of the rope.

Later on that summer I got to know the Rock and Ice members quite well and I started going out with Barbara Bennett who lived in Manchester and who was Joe's wife's best friend. I used to travel up to Manchester to see Barbara and also took part in the climbing activities at week-ends and became a part-time Birmingham advanced rock-climbing apprentice. Winter week-ends were usually devoted to gritstone outcrops, the furnace of painful difficulty in which all the Rock and Ice members had been fired.

One particular week-end was spent at Ramshaw Rocks high on the moors near Leek in Staffordshire. These crags have a reputation for difficult cracks lined with needle-sharp millstone grit crystals. The cliff itself is of a split level formation, on the lower tier was a massive overhanging roof split with a three-inch wide crack, which seemed to grin venomously at any prospective climber. It was an obvious challenge to Joe as he tried again and again to climb over the prow of the overhang, hanging completely from painful hand-jams. But ruthless determination made Joe give one final great muscular effort and he pulled over the final bulge. He lay gasping at the top with the blood pouring from the tattered strips of flesh which before had been part of the backs of his hands. Two or three people including myself had a go, but it proved to be another climb up which no-one could follow him.

The greatest contributions to Wales by the Rock and Ice had been on Clogwyn du'r Arddu, a steep forbidding north-facing cliff on the side of Snowdon which only receives the sun early in the morning or late in the evening.

One of Whillans's great innovations was Slanting Slab on the West Buttress. The major difficulty which had repelled all the pioneers from the very foot of the climb were great overhangs shaped like the inside of half the arch of a railway bridge. Loose Sword of Damocles-type stalactites were wedged precariously in the trickiest part. Whillans nonchalantly climbed the enormous roof despite shifting pegs and tottering rock and got on to the superb-looking slanting slab from which the climb got its name. One of the pitches was an incredible 180 feet in length — the longest pitch at that time in the whole of the British Isles. Don's companion was Vin Betts, a well-known raconteur and humourist of the period. In one place there was a nasty overhang which Vin couldn't seem to climb. He shouted to the distant Whillans who yelled to him to reach up very high for the enormous hold. Betts did as he was told, reached up as far as he could and found a nail scrape. His anguished, surprised shout at its smallness brought the wry Whillans reply that "That was it."

One week-end, instead of going to gritstone, Joe and I went to Wales and walked up to Cloggy to attempt to repeat the product of Whillans' masterly slab climbing. The overhang looked absolutely awful and despite knocking in peg after peg, all of which rattled in their imprecise slots and clefts, Joe was unable to reach to the firmer rock on the slab above the overhang and so had to retreat. I had a go as well but could make no impression either. A very rare defeat for Joe on his old friend's climb, it enhanced the reputation of the route enormously.

All my gritstone and free Welsh week-ends were interrupted by the Ogwen Cottage traumatic sabbatical year. Back in Birmingham the atmosphere felt completely alien, although it was nice to be back with my family. Nearly everyone I climbed with either lived in Wales or in the Manchester area. I'd had enough of living in Wales for the time and as Barbara too lived in Manchester decided to move up there and so applied for a job with a large electronics firm in the research and development department. Eight jobs already and an abortive attempt at a business didn't look too good when written out on the application form. I had some difficulty in convincing the head of department that I really was going to settle down. The continuous glass windows of the interview room with the hot sunlight streaming through them made the sweat pour off my face more than had many a hard climb. Despite my unpromising background he took me on and I moved to Manchester.

Just about the time that I decided to stop climbing with Joe, I got to know Hugh Banner quite well. I was used to the rippling power-house muscles of the Rock and Ice as they surged up the cliff. Banner was much slighter in build and moved more delicately, but his results were just as positive. He too lived in Manchester and started to climb a lot on the sandstone outcrops of Helsby which rise out of the River Mersey flood plain near Chester. No really modern climbing had been done there and nearly all the sandstone overhangs were still virgin. Banner relentlessly worked at this outcrop with the same enthusiasm that he had applied to the Avon Gorge while he was at university. The overhangs were gradually conquered as Banner forced his lithe form over the most difficult parts. Impressive names spewed forth: Gallows, Gorilla Wall, Illegitimate. Heisby had a late coming-of-age and it was nearly all due to Banner.

There was an unfortunate incident on a route called The Steep Band. This is on a buttress below the western part of the cliff. Hugh and I had noticed the possibility of climbing a slab which led into a groove system. It looked hard but feasible. Hugh led the first pitch which was a slab with an awkward step in it half-way. No matter how I tried, I couldn't do it. Finally after an hour's dithering I gave up and Hugh had to return. I said I would come back and try it with him another time when I was in better form. Our joint arrangements never resulted in another attempt and I eventually had a go at it with Les Brown as my partner. This time I led the slabby first pitch which I had been unable to do and Les and I completed the route.

After his spectacular career crowned with his Cloggy triumphs, Hugh set himself the enormous personal task of trying to deflate the mystical aura that surrounded the Rock and Ice Club and its climbs. There was still plenty of uncharted rock left on the Welsh crags as the young explorers of the sixties were to prove. But the shadow of Joe Brown lay heavily across Banner's later climbing career.

He did repeat route after route of Joe's, taking all day to do some of them. But second ascents are not recorded in the backs of climbing guide books and twenty years afterwards their memory will fade. Fortunately not everything that Banner did was in the shadow of the Rock and Ice colossi.

A new climb of his to the right of Curving Crack on the East Buttress of Clogwyn du'r Arddu charted a new standard for rock climbs of the time.

The East Buttress is almost vertical and all the climbs including the new ones of Joe's had followed natural cracks or grooves. Between two of the features, Curving Crack and Pedestal Crack, was a smooth wall of rock with no obvious features on it which could be climbed. The odd ledge, a tuft of grass, but nothing seeming to connect them.

Banner's solution of this improbable-looking piece of rock with very poor protection proved to be the next really great step forward after the Rock and Ice era. He called it The Troach and it still retains its very serious reputation a dozen years after it was done.

It is interesting to look back at the Rock and Ice exploits of the fifties as well. Joe had done nearly all the major exploration in Wales and gritstone. Hundreds of new routes had submitted to his twinkling feet. His perceptive eye evolved climbs of the ultimate difficulty and his immense strength had allowed him to protect the climb with running belays.

Whillans hadn't even done a tenth of the new routes that Joe had done, but his inventions — Slanting Slab, Taurus on Cloggy and Erosion Grooves Direct Finish in the Llanberis Pass were the ultimate in difficulty and poorly protected as well.

Joe had failed to lead Slanting Slab when I was with him and had needed a tight rope from Don during the first ascent of Taurus.

This, of course, was unknown to the general climbing world at the time. They just knew of the existence of yet another overhanging impossible-looking climb and that the superhuman climbing race from the Northern mists had struck again.

It was a pity that the finest partnership in British rock-climbing eventually foundered. Good luck statistically should break evenly, but in the case of Joe and Don it all seemed to go Joe's way. In the Himalayas as well the same pattern was repeated. Joe triumphed on Kangchenjunga, Mustagh Tower and Pic Communism.

The Masherbrum expedition of which Don was a member was marred by the death of Bob Downes. Terrible ice conditions defeated Don and Joe Walmsley within a stone's throw of the summit. On Trivor Don was laid low by a mild attack of polio at the critical time when the summit was climbed. The polio vaccine only brought back the use of his legs some days after the successful bid for the top. Just before the Nuptse expedition he was knocked off his motor-cycle by a lorry and his kneecap fractured.

These disappointments, together with Joe's flair for commercial exploitation of his ability, combined with his easy-going likeable manner, contrasted with Don's abrasive Northern conversational manner which probably repelled the Southern English holders of the purse-strings.

Happily Don has now had his Himalayan reward with the conquest in 1970 of the South Face of Annapurna.

WHITE HELL PURSUING CENTRE

(extract)

K. I. MELDRUM
(1966)

... We have tried to introduce various educational climbing gimmicks. Many of these were the product of Joe's fertile imagination and just before he left to open his shop in Llanberis we had reached what was, I suspect, his ultimate objective of being able to teach all the techniques and skills of climbing without actually having to endure the discomfort of walking to a crag and touching proper rock. This all started when Joe devised the Chapel traverse. Nothing was more humiliating than getting dressed up in P.A.s and then being overtaken three times by Joe as he rushed round in bedroom slippers. The next stage was the development of a falling machine. For two days Joe hung in slings thirty feet up a tree drilling holes through the trunk. From the platform that eventually appeared we all played about, dropping weights to simulate falling leaders. We did this mainly to test Joe's advocacy of the shoulder belay. Pete Crew was beguiled into an argument over the relative merits of waist and shoulder belays and was persuaded to try the machine. The man-weight falling stone left both of them writhing on the platform: Pete in surprise and pain, and Joe in hysterical laughter. The machine has fallen into disuse rather since John damaged his knee at a time when Joe had his bad back and Alan had his ankle.

In spite of these sorts of advanced training methods, accidents still occur. Recently I had to write an accident report on a student who fell:

'... he fell and landed on the ground. He sustained a serious fracture to his right malleolus. At the time he was unroped. As he fell the instructor tried to grab him...'

I fully expected the authority to make an issue over this and was looking forward to quoting the Kinder and Roaches Guide which describes the Quarry traverse at Windgather as 'a 200-foot route never exceeding jumping distance from the ground' but was surprised that it went through without question.

Competition seems to be almost irresistible to the young lads on our courses and a favourite trick of Joe's was to tell them that they would die if they hung from their waists on a climbing rope for more than a few minutes unless they knew what to do. It says much for their determination that in the long evenings in the mountain huts which we use there would always be a line of red and purple faced lads hanging like bats from the rafters.

In all outdoor centres competition is inevitably tempered with a very large margin of safety and the incidents which provide such good copy for epic mountaineering articles are almost non-existent. It's during the off periods, when instructors go off to Wales, the Lakes and Scotland that the most entertaining incidents happen. Like the odd trips that I had to Wales with Joe. I should have learnt that each time would turn out to be full of the unexpected. We left White Hall last winter and arrived in the Pass at about lunch time. The idea was to do some winter climbing on Lliwedd. We got to the lake at about 2 p.m. and I fully expected to just have a look at the conditions or to pick out a line for the next day. We plodded on at the bottom of West Gully. Joe stopped and unslung his sack.

"I'm putting my crampons on here."

"I think I'll wait till we get above the rock and..."

"Put them on now."

"... and onto the snow above and then..."

"Get the ——s on now."

He knew all the rock was thick with verglas. With two hours of daylight left it was a race against the clock and we just managed to get up before dark. This was a first winter ascent. The next day was supposed to be Central Gully but, like most of my trips with him, plans changed and we just lay about. The next time in Wales it was Pellagra on Craig y Castell. The name came from a Kellogg's packet, the only reading material available in the Cromlech hut. My most vivid recollection of this climb was the traverse on the last pitch. The hand jams are like getting hold of barbed wire or gripping a sea urchin. Even so, or perhaps because of this, I penduled across to the crux of Wasp; by contrast it might have been a V Diff. Climbing in the Lakes with him is just as unexpected. He always moans about the weather and has developed an interesting meteorological philosophy. He seldom makes a move before midday; this is to give the rain a chance to clear up or alternatively to wait and see whether it will stay fine. This time rain came with no chance of letting up but we still drove out to Castle Rock with Frank Davies. Again I thought just to have a look. But no. In the driving rain we plodded up to May-Day Cracks. The first pitch was a real waterfall and would have done credit to any pothole. Even with a caving ladder I would have found some difficulty on it. Above, all the ledges were waterlogged and as Frank, who was wearing his inevitable flat hat, got to a taxing section, a mud avalanche slithered down the crack. Under a pyramid of mud two startled white eyes started from a black face, his mouth working, at first uncontrollably and silent and then equally uncontrollably but voluble.

Not all our time without a course in is spent like this, much of it being devoted to maintenance. Most of the routine maintenance is pretty dull and Joe was an expert at thinking up interesting schemes which usually worked. Probably the biggest thing that he started was a programme of glass-fibre canoe building which has occupied all the instructors for many hours. At first the novelty was exciting, but stippling for hours at a time can wear anyone down. One of the problems is to prevent the canoe sticking to the mould. Brian Fuller produced one day an aerosol spray of PTFE with strict instructions not to use it when smoking. Joe at this time had succumbed to the weed again, having passed through the familiar phases of withdrawal symptoms, and cigars. He was, in fact, rolling his own. Some PTFE dust must have been rolled in with one and after the first deep draw he was flat on his back unable to breathe and thinking that he was going to die. Our doctor, who was unfamiliar with PTFE poisoning, told us not to worry and that it was probably just flu symptoms. Once having started in glass fibre we all started to realise its potential, but again it was Joe who took the initiative and started making crash hats. These started off as canoeing crash hats and we decided that they could quite well be climbing hats. Within a few weeks we had the first ones produced. It was a slow and tedious job. So instead of making hats, he made moulds, and in the end he was making batches of twelve hats simultaneously. We never have more than a dozen students climbing at a time but by this time Joe had become a compulsive crash hat manufacturer. It was soon after he discovered that we had fifty hats that he decided to open his shop.

THE SUMMIT
RETROSPECTIVELY IN ENGlAND

WILFRID NOYCE
(1955)

There the wind has been a long time calling;
There the ice glints blue from the banished snow;
There, ten thousand years before there were voices
From hill forms growing crazy as mushrooms grow.
Ten thousand years from now there will be thunder
Over the rock steep, groaning to snow-drift tears;
Ten thousand years from now grey cliffs will shudder
At avalanche rage roaring in ice-wind's spears.
Here a May morning all the blasts were weary,
Took their rest in a breeze, and men, the small,
Cut their fine path in the huge breast of mountains,
Timid turned back, went home with their tale to tell.
Soon the winds wipe the slate clean of man-marks;
Soon their etching, not his, imprints the snow.
They were proud, who once climbed the mountain;
They went away, ten thousand years ago.

'A very distant prospect'

'To be crossing of the Channel with your luggage
labelled "Bern"
And regarding your profession with a lordly
unconcern!'
A. Godley
(Vol. II No. 5 September 1899)

THE ACCIDENT ON THE DENT BLANCHE

W. M. CROOK
(Vol. II No.6 December 1899)

The Editor has asked me to write a brief account of the terrible accident on the Dent Blanche, by which Owen Glynne Jones and the guides Furrer, Zurbriggen and Vuignier lost their lives. On Monday, August 28th, presumably because, like so many of those who will read these lines, I was a friend of Jones, and because by one of those accidental meetings which so often occur among the mountains, both at home and abroad, I saw Jones off on his last expedition, I met his body when it was brought back by the search party, and I had the melancholy satisfaction, with others of his friends, of paying the last possible respect to his mortal remains.

We met at the Kurhaus at Arolla on the night of Saturday, August 27th. Circumstances compelled me to go down the valley to Evolena immediately after breakfast on Sunday morning. Jones and Hill were starting about the same time, and the former suggested that we should walk down together, to which, of course, our party gladly agreed. At Haudères we parted, and Jones and Hill, with their three guides, Furrer of Stalden, Zurbriggen (Clemens) of Saas-im-Grund, and Vuignier of Evolena, went up to Ferpècle, intending to spend the night under a rock on the west arête of the Dent Blanche, which they proposed to climb the following day. I heard on Monday that they had altered their plans and slept at the Bricolla Alp.

I remained at Evolena, and heard nothing more of them till Wednesday, August 30th. Just before dinner on that night our landlord told us that a terrible accident had happened on the Dent Blanche, by which one tourist and three guides had lost their lives; but he knew no names, and did not know the day on which the accident had happened. A telegram to Dr. Seiler soon set any doubt at rest. At eleven o'clock that night a strong search party, composed of fifteen guides and porters from the Evolena Valley, accompanied by Mr. Harold Spender, of the Alpine Club and of the Climbers' Club, set out to recover the bodies. By the evening of Thursday, they were carried down to Haudères. On Friday, Mr. Hill came round from Zermatt for the funeral, which was arranged to take place at nine on Saturday morning, and from him I heard a full account of the accident, which I reproduce here as fully and as accurately as I can.

Mr. Hill states that up till the time of the accident the climb had been a most interesting and enjoyable one. At the moment of the fatal slip the whole party were on a traverse. They were in the following order — Furrer, Zurbriggen, Jones, Vuignier, and Hill. Stopped by a difficult rock, Zurbriggen attempted to give Furrer a foothold on the top of his ice-axe, but the axe

John Wilkinson on the East Face of the Aiguille du Plan, August 1979. Photo: Mike Mortimer.

Tom Patey and Martin Boysen below the Diedre Brown-Patey during the first ascent of the West Face Direct of the Aiguille du Plan. Photo: John Cleare.

Eric 'Beardie' Beard photographed in July 1965, five years before he was killed in a car crash, *en route* to the Boccalette Hut. Photo: John Cleare.

The Central Tower of Paine Expedition 1962-63. Left to right: back, Vic Bray, Derek Walker, Chris Bonington and two Chileans; front: John Streetly, Barrie Page, Don Whillans, Ian Clough. Photo: Bonington Collection.

shook under his weight, and Jones scrambled up to them and held the axe close to the head to steady it. Furrer then stood on it, and feeling on the rock above, got what he evidently thought were two good handholds. He was mistaken, for when he tried to swing himself up on them, his hands slipped, and he fell backwards on Zurbriggen and Jones, knocking both down. They slid down the awful rock face, the rope slowly uncoiling between them and Vuignier. Mr. Hill did not see him fall, though he heard him go. He felt it was his turn next and waited his fate, clinging on to such indifferent handholds and footholds that the slightest chuck would have pulled him off The chuck never came. Why, he does not know. To his great surprise he found himself with some thirty feet of loose rope hanging from his waist.

The rope had broken close to Vuignier. How, will never be certainly known. Most probably it caught in a crack between two rocks, and when the dead weight of the four bodies came the rope gave, and the rocks took off the force of the pull, which would otherwise certainly have killed Mr. Hill. I have seen the rope. I should describe it as burst, rather than as broken.

For a few moments Mr. Hill watched his unfortunate comrades sliding down the west face of the Dent Blanche. Soon he could look no longer, and turned from the sickening sight. He thinks they were killed instantaneously, as they made no effort to grasp at anything and showed no sign of life. They rolled over and over helplessly with arms outspread. None of them uttered a sound.

Then began a struggle for life carried to a successful issue with a cour-age, coolness, and an amount of physical endurance unparalleled, so far as my knowledge goes, in the history of mountaineering. Save five raisins, Hill had neither food nor drink. He had not his watch with him, and therefore all his times are fixed by the position of the sun during the daylight hours. He thinks the accident took place about 10 a.m., as Jones had looked at his watch shortly before and remarked that it was twenty minutes to ten.

He had noticed a little earlier that there was another party on the moun-tain which had come up by the ordinary route on the south arête. He there-fore determined to get to the top as quickly as possible and try to join them. He did not attempt the place which had proved fatal to his four companions, but turned it, and gained the top, he thinks, in about an hour. He had heard someone (probably the party on the top) "cooey," and he "cooeyed" and shouted in return, but got no reply. So he hurried to descend by the ordinary route to Zermatt in the track of the party he had seen. He successfully reached the lowest gendarme on that arête when bad weather came on, making further descent impossible — first a mist and then snow. It was then about two p.m.

Mr. Hill found a hole in the rock gendarme and crushed himself into it to shelter from the snow and wait for fine weather. He wound the remainder of his rope round a projecting piece of rock, and jammed his ice-axe in two clefts of the rock in front of him to prevent him from falling out. Then he fell asleep. When he awoke it was night, and the stars were out. He was stiff and cold, and new-fallen snow rested on his sleeves, his knees, and his boots, which projected outside the hole in which he sat, and which was his sole shelter from the storm. Having beaten his hands and knees and stamped his feet to warm them, he went to sleep again. He estimates that he spent twenty-two hours on that gendarme.

At last, however, Tuesday morning dawned, and later the storm ceased. He resumed the descent, but with increased difficulty. The snow had partially obliterated the steps cut by the preceding party in the ice and snow of the south arête. So his progress was very cautious and slow.

At last he got on to the Wandfluh, or great ice-clad rock-wall that projects to the south of the Dent Blanche. But he had forgotten the way down to the Schönbühl glacier. He tried several — he does not know how many — couloirs, but all ended in precipices, and he had to make his way back again, a terrible ordeal for a man who had gone through what he had so far endured. On one occasion he had the misfortune to drop his ice-axe, and had to make a difficult climb down the mountain-side for about an hour, in order to recover it.

It was late on Tuesday afternoon when he succeeded at length in finding a way from the Wandfluh to the Schönbühl glacier. He soon got on to the Zmutt, and made comparatively rapid progress.

But the end was not yet. His strength was nearly gone. As darkness fell, he wandered over grass slopes, through low bushes, and over stones, tripping, stumbling, once falling down a deep hole. He imagined his companions were still with him, and he kept talking to them. Sometimes he fell asleep. He awakened, thinking he was asleep in a chalet, and called to them that it was cold and time to go on. He tried to go on, fell, and went to sleep again.

When he finally wakened on Wednesday morning the sun was already high in the blue heavens. He quickly made his way to the nearest house, which was the little beer chalet about an hour above Zermatt on the way to the Staffel Alp, which he appears to have passed in the darkness. He had only 60 centimes in his pocket, which he spent on bread and milk, and then walked on to Zermatt. Between 11.30 and noon on Wednesday — fifty hours after the accident — he walked into the Monte Rosa Hotel and told the awful news.

That is, as far as I can remember, the plain, unvarnished tale of the sole survivor of one of the greatest of Alpine accidents, which will make the year 1899 memorable in mountaineering annals.

For the sake of completeness, I append an extract from Mr. Spender's account of the search party, which appeared in the *Daily Chronicle* early in September.

After describing the tramp up in the darkness from Evolena to the moraine above the Bricolla Alp, Mr. Spender proceeds:

"But the pace soon slackened. We halted on the edge of the glacier, roped in fours, and began to search gingerly for a way through the terrific ice-fall of the glacier. We were mounting by the old approach to the Dent Blanche, up the ice-fall, now long since abandoned. The glacier was, of course, quite changed since any of these guides had last visited it. The ice was split and rent into every conceivable shape. We were surrounded with leaning towers of ice, threatening at any moment to fall on us and crush us. A great pile of seracs on the northern ice-fall, across the ridge, fell with a mighty crash. Away to the right we could hear the thunder of avalanches. But never for a moment did the guides hesitate. Steadily and unflinchingly they threaded their way between the menacing seracs, crossing broken fragments of ice, balancing between profound crevasses, now thwarted, but ever searching for a way. At last we suddenly struck upon the tracks of Jones' party, away to the north side of the glacier, close to the rocks. Here we scrambled up, half by the rocks and half by the ice, and then at last, after many hours, found ourselves on the great plateau beneath the long snow-couloir running down from the West Ridge. There, if anywhere, they were likely to be.

It was now ten o'clock, and the sky had cleared. A party was formed and mounted the rocks to fetch the bodies. As they climbed, suddenly another army of men appeared below us above the ice-fall, advancing swiftly. They were the party of the Zermatt guides. They came on unroped, climbing fast. It was a magnificent sight to see this troop of giants in their own element, a troop of equals, masters of peril. They halted below the rocks, and sent up another small band to join the Evolena guides. There was a long pause, and then they all began to descend, bringing the bodies.

Below the glacier we were met by men with a sledge, and then the work grew easier. But it was four o'clock before the Bricolla hut was reached, and darkness had fallen before the bodies came to Haudères. The Zermatt guides were out for twenty-four hours, and the Evolena guides over twenty."

The accident happened through no fault of Owen Jones. An excellent guide slipped, and the destruction of four of the party was the inevitable and awful consequence. In difficult mountaineering, such accidents must occasionally happen. Jones was a daring, but, at the same time, a very careful climber. Of his wonderful ability as a rock-climber it would be almost an impertinence for me to speak. To his courage and resourcefulness on the mountains he loved so well, to his intellectual power and charming companionship, I wish to pay my humble tribute. He will be long missed by many members of the Climbers' Club; he will be long remembered for his climbing exploits by many of those who had not the privilege of knowing him while alive.

ODE ON A VERY DISTANT PROSPECT

A. GODLEY
(Vol. II No.5 September 1899)

In the steamy, stuffy Midlands, 'neath an English summer sky,
When the holidays are nearing with the closing of July,
And experienced Alpine stagers and impetuous recruits
Are renewing with the season their continual disputes —
      Those inveterate disputes
      On the newest Alpine routes —
And inspecting the condition of their mountaineering boots:

You may stifle your reflections, you may banish them afar,
You may try to draw a solace from the thought of "Nächstes Jahr" —
But your heart is with those climbers, and you'll feverishly yearn
To be crossing of the Channel with your luggage labelled "Bern,"
      Leaving England far astern
      With a ticket through to Bern,
And regarding your profession with a lordly unconcern!

They will lie beside the torrent, just as you were wont to do,
With the woodland green around them and a snowfield shining through:
They will tread the higher pastures, where celestial breezes blow,
While the valley lies in shadow and the peaks are all aglow —
      Where the airs of heaven blow
      'Twixt the pine woods and the snow,
And the shades of evening deepen in the valley far below:

They will scale the mountain strongholds that in days of old you won,
They will plod behind a lantern ere the rising of the sun,
On a "grat" or in a chimney, on the steep and dizzy slope,
For a foothold or a handhold they will diligently grope —
      On the rocky, icy slope
      (Where we'll charitably hope
That the aid they get is Moral from the presence of a rope):

They will dine on mule and marmot, and on mutton made of goats,
They will face the various horrors of Helvetian table d'hôtes:
But whate'er the paths that lead them, and the food whereon they fare,
They will taste the joy of living, as you only taste it there,
      As you taste it Only There

In the higher, purer air,
Unapproachable by worries and oblivious quite of care!

Place me somewhere in the Valais, 'mid the mountains west of Binn,
West of Binn and east of Savoy, in a decent kind of inn,
With a peak or two for climbing, and a glacier to explore —
Any mountains will content me, though they've all been climbed before —
  Yes! I care not any more
  Though they've all been done before,
And the names they keep in bottles may be numbered by the score!

Though the hand of Time be heavy: though your ancient comrades fail:
Though the mountains you ascended be accessible by rail:
Though your nerve begin to weaken, and you're gouty grown and fat,
And prefer to walk in places which are reasonably flat —
  Though you grow so very fat
  That you climb the Gorner Grat
Or perhaps the Little Scheideck — and are rather proud of that:
  Yet I hope that till you die
  You will annually sigh
For a vision of the Valais with the coming of July,
For the Oberland or Valais and the higher, purer air,
And the true delight of living, as you taste it only there!

THE MIDDLE DISTANCE

(extract)

SIR CLAUD SCHUSTER
(1926)

Here the other party moistened their lips and pressed on. My companion sat down in the stream. The guides hovered round and urged him on. "Dear sir," they said, "here it is very dangerous. The stones fall from the Aiguille du Midi." "How many people have been killed here?" he enquired. "None, dear sir, that we know of; but you can see that it is very dangerous." "And for how many years have people gone up and down this path?" "We do not know, dear sir, but..." "Then here I stop until I am rested." And there he did stop for ten mortal minutes — all three of us being so overcome by his logic that we could prevail by no argument.

At 8 we came to the little restaurant of the Pierre Pointue, whose open door gave out a flood of golden light. We found our friends waiting for us. "I waited," said our leader, "because, when studying the wine card the night before last, I observed some G. H. Mumm (and he named the vintage — alas, I have forgotten the year). If you approve, I will send — here to run down to Chamonix to have it put in ice, and to order the baths, while we follow at leisure."

The project was approved. The others, preceded by their fleet-footed guide, moved on. We followed, and both groups were swallowed up in the blackness of the night, intensified soon by that of the forest, so that, during the whole descent neither party caught a glimpse of the others' light. The path was thick in dust, which rose as our feet moved; catching the rays of the moving lantern it made for me, coming last, a strange luminosity in the track. We became conscious of some object moving in front of us, and in a few minutes we overtook it, or, rather, them, and found a man following two mules. I suppose that the mules were tired; they went very slowly, but they could not be passed on the narrow path, and we asked the man to stop and let us go by. He did his best, but the mules would not be persuaded. At last our leading man lost patience, and himself addressed them in the language of the Zermatt Valley. What he said I do not know, nor has he ever since been persuaded to disclose. But the effect was instantaneous and remarkable. The second mule stopped dead and let us pass. But the first gave a squeal and shot off at a gallop. He disappeared, but the sound of his hoofs came back to us through the night. The man and the second mule resumed their equable course behind us.

Many hours afterwards, as it still seems to me, though, in fact, it was about an hour, we stumbled into the light of a lamp at the first house at Les Praz-Conduits. Several excited men sprang at us, and a lively dialogue ensued, conducted on our side in the *patois* of Zermatt, and on theirs in that of

Chamonix. As neither side could understand the tongue of the other, I do not know how the guides made out and interpreted to me that the infuriated inhabitants accused us of murdering the muleteer and stealing the second mule, the first having reached home in a muck sweat, the sole survivor and eye-witness of the slaughter. We pacified them as best we could and passed on. A few minutes later we were laying down our knapsacks in Couttets Hall and shouting for the other party.

They, however, had not arrived. We had just time to lament that we should be obliged to sacrifice dinner in friendship's name when they appeared, their vexation at having taken a wrong turn in the forest mitigated by the fact that the bath-water was hot and the champagne cold.

THE ASCENT OF THE BEISPIELSPITZ

B. H. KEMBALL-COOK
(1947)

(Editor's Note : All readers of that classic of climbing manuals, the Badminton Library volume *Mountaineering,* are familiar with the noble and flowing lines of the Beispielspitz. This peak presents the most fascinating enigma in mountaineering literature. On pages 143 to 156 of the Badminton book (third edition, 1901) methods of ascent are exhaustively discussed. Yet nowhere had survived any record of the first ascent of a peak which must early have attracted, and not for ever withstood, the ambitions of British mountaineers.

At last the enigma is, in part at least, resolved. On a pavement in South Audley Street, a member of this Club found a tattered sheet of manuscript, of provenance unknown. Though but a fragment and partly illegible, it is clearly a page from the original climbing diary of a member of this Club. The conquerors of the Beispielspitz must, alas, be known to us by initials only, until a further happy find enables us to complete the narrative which follows. The authenticity of the document is, however, guaranteed by the presence in one corner of a stain caused by Bouvier of the vintage of 1890, tested by our Honorary Analyst.

This lucky find sheds light incidentally upon another problem which has teased Alpine scholars, namely the origin of the illustrations in the Badminton volume. It has long been thought that these graphic and masterly pictures represented scenes of actual experience. The sombre gloom of "British Hill-Weather" (page 356); the extraordinary antics of the "Crack-Climbers" (page 242), all moving together to get the difficult part over quickly; the pitiless realism of "Serve Him Right" (page 110), in which members of the Alpine Club moodily abandon the straw-hatted tourist to his fate in a snow-concealed crevasse; all these bear the stamp of truth. What was long suspected is now certain, and that gripping picture "Backing-Up" (page 184) undoubtedly represents the most critical moment in the victorious ascent of the Beispielspitz, which brought imperishable laurels to this Club.

We cannot too strongly condemn any attempt to explore the origin of this document, or to enquire why it has remained so long unpublished. We deplore above all certain malicious reports that have gained currency, suggesting that it might have been suppressed by a fellow body, whose long roll of Alpine victories need not grudge this one triumph to a younger rival.

We give this fragmentary document in its entirety, and with its opening words find ourselves engaged on the first rocks of the North-West Ridge. (End of *Editor's Note.)*

... "Verglas!" Old Kaspar Abendessen rapped out the dread word in his rough patois, and Zum Fruhstuck blanched beneath his tan. This was serious! The real business of the day still lay before us (B., sturdiest trencherman of the Climbers' Club, had but lately finished his third breakfast) and already the grand old Beispielspitz was weighting the scales against those hardy mortals who were presuming to
"molest his ancient, solitary reign."
I knew well that at the first sign of irresolution on my part the guides would finish the Bouvier and counsel retreat, convinced, like all natives of the Kartoffelthal, that the Beispielspitz was inhabited by malicious demons of a terrifying power and very touchy disposition.
"Vorwärts!" I cried therefore, lifting my stout baton and prodding Zum Fruhstuck firmly in the back...

... a desperate situation! Between us and the further rocks the wide and ice-glazed couloir plunged at an angle of seventy-five degrees to where, 2,000 feet below, the gaping bergschrund awaited impious mortals who would tamper with the ice-fringed solitudes of the Beispielspitz.
Old Kaspar shrugged his shoulders. "Es geht nichts," he muttered. "I have a wife and twelve children whom I have a fancy to see again. If we set foot there we are all dead men. Let us drink the Bouvier and turn back, before it is too late."
Such words from the cock of the Kartoffelthal were an eloquent proof of the terror inspired by our peak. But I was determined that we would not be foiled by the superstitious spell which had for so long thwarted the best efforts of the Alpine Club. I turned to see what B. thought of it. Old B., stoutest scientist of the Climbers' Club, had already set up his boiling-water apparatus and was timing an egg with his stopwatch. The sight gave me confidence.
"Vorwärts!" I cried, prodding Abendessen in the back with my baton...

... Kaspar was half over, plying his axe with dogged haste, when I heard a horrified whisper in my ear. It was B.
"Look, J. ! *The fleas are deserting Kaspar!*"
It was true. Even as he spoke, a little group of those persistent ministers to the discomfort of the Kartoffelthaler gathered on the snow and hopped off purposively *(heu pietas! heu prisca fides !)* down the couloir. Fearful of the effect which this portent might have upon Zum Fruhstuck's superstitious soul, I turned. Fortunately he had not seen, for, infected no doubt with B.'s scientific zeal, he was engaged in testing the specific gravity of a bottle of Bouvier, and, finding it, I should say, less every minute. I turned back. Kaspar was over!
"Vorwärts !" I cried, and advanced in my turn...

... a most desperate situation! My slip had been arrested, but not until I was extended at full length on the nearly vertical slope, my pick driven firmly into the ice above my head. But the rope — and my comrades — held! That moment is graven on my memory.[1] As I lay there, in the cold shadow of the rocks, my glance travelled from good old Kaspar, poised lightly on the further edge of the couloir, and belaying firmly beneath his right thumb the rope which held me: to good old B., backing up staunchly in his ice-steps, with the sunlight gilding his grand white beard and the ancient and decrepit hat which he dare not sport below the tree-line lest Mrs. B. behold it and consign it to instant destruction...

... I hope that I shall not be accused of unmanliness when I confess that it was with a momentary pang of regret that I planted on the summit of the Beispielspitz the new standard of the Climbers' Club, with its noble design of two purists, rampant, gules, upon a field of pitons...[2]

(Editor's Note: Here the fragment ends. It is certain that B. at least got down safely, and lived to cry "Vorwarts!" another day.)

[1] This is the scene illustrated on page 184 of the Badminton volume. Zum Fruhstuck can have been of little help at this crisis. He is precariously placed and appears the worse for drink.

[2] It is a pity this flag has fallen into desuetude, but there is no reason to doubt its existence. The piton controversy is of great antiquity. Cf. Samuel Butler's comment in "Hudibras" (Canto 3, vv. 1-2).

"Alas! What perils do environ
The man who meddles with cold iron!"

LE PITON CROUX

E. A. WRANGHAM
(1954)

It lies before me as I write: a rusty thing, serviceable yet perhaps, but looking all its 18 years. It is blunt, straightforward, and I think rather contemp-
tuous of those who criticise it or its friends without having attempted to
savour their qualities. It looks unromantic at first, but the romance is there.
After all it is from Italy, the land of wine, women, and song; though perhaps
the Chianti growers, the belles of Courmayeur, or Signor Gigli would not be
flattered by its company. But romance springs from mystery, and the Piton
Croux has not lacked an atmosphere of mystery. The Guide Vallot, that
opium-den of the alpinist in England, does its best to foster this atmosphere. Pleasant dreams conjured up about the route are punctured by its
rusty, but, elusive, form. All ways seem to lead to or away from the Piton
Croux (and it lies on my desk, so what now ?). It wavers mistily in the mind's
eye in the centre of vertical dièdres, traverses "à la Bavaroise," and hidden
hand traverses. I feel that at any moment I may find myself suspended from
it once more, with the whole vast east face of the Grandes Jorasses beneath
me, watching Antony start across a traverse which Dick is clearly convinced
is impossible.

No doubt the mystery was what attracted initially; for the ridge of the
Grandes Jorasses from Tronchey, perhaps the last great ridge of a major
Alpine Peak to be climbed, had only three ascents recorded. I am still puz-
zled about this state of affairs. For contrast it with the Arête des Hirondelles
which has had countless ascents, or with the Eperon Walker which, despite
its difficulty, has had 16. Yet the Tronchey must be every bit as fine as the
Hirondelles. It confirms what I have long suspected about Alpinists and
Alpine climbs, that they are subject to a capricious fashion which beats
Paris hats or Wall Street to a frazzle. Once a climb has become O.K., has
achieved a certain cachet, it becomes the target of every aspiring Alpinist to
the exclusion of the other, and often finer, climbs just next door. Professor
Graham Brown discovered this when the Sentinelle had had 12 ascents to
the Major's three. Now the boot is on the other foot, with the Sentinelle
scarcely considered and the Major all the rage.

I found, however, that I was not alone in having marked down the
Tronchey. Dick and Antony, whose cordée I had gate-crashed, were looking
that way; and one day in the Café Roma we found that Mike Harris and
Ralph Jones had a similar ambition. So we joined forces.

As we settled down into our gite under the Aiguille de Tronchey, which
we had selected as the starting point for the climb, we reflected on the pioneer character of the expedition so far. Starting from the road in the valley
we had pushed our way on the lower slopes through thick bushes, and on

the upper through flocks of sheep and chamois (the former were even seen glissading a snow slope, under control). The tone of the expedition had also been set by some curious incidents on the way up. Antony had made his first "chute," a trivial affair of a mere hundred feet down snow and a few rocks, hardly worthy of so distinguished a member of the F.F.R.C.*; while Ralph had done a Burgener and broken his ice axe in half. We were comfortable in our gite, warm (sleeping bags), well fed (petrol stoves), and well watered by a stream 10 feet away. Despite all this luxury, the ascent was, in fact, started next day, and after a certain amount of excitement over a loose block in a chimney, the party arrived at the foot of the first of the three towers.

At the same time some cloud also arrived, and we had our first discussion about the weather. These discussions all followed a curiously similar course. First would come an ominous warning from Dick, referring to electric storms and their behaviour on high mountains. Each member of the party in turn would then slowly rotate his right hand backwards and forwards (this being an O.K. gesture meaning that you have no idea what will happen). No decision would be reached, but the party, being by then rested, would in fact proceed.

It did so, but the details seem less interesting now than they did at the time. Ice and rock, interspersed with weather pauses and rain, led to the foot of the third tower. Now this tower, about three or four hundred feet of it, was presided over by the Piton Croux. It had chosen a worthy place. There seemed to be a larger proportion of air to rock than usual, the air being downwards, outwards, and sideways, and the rock upwards. The glacier appeared to be, and was, farther away than usual; one could understand why the intervening space between it and us had been Gervasutti's hardest climb. Now it is a fact that in situations of this kind tension mounts in proportion as the climbers fail to do so. Tension therefore mounted. Eventually two things happened simultaneously. Dick complained that he had not been allowed to move for an hour and a half, and we sighted the Piton Croux. But the climb was, and the story is, by no means over. Earnest members of the Old School, if they have stuck it this far, are strongly advised to read no farther. For in due course the following sight was seen: a member of the Alpine Club dangling over the Frébouze glacier, his rope passing through four pitons, and his hand still trying to clutch a sling in which he had recently been standing. Perhaps the rope should then and there have been cut as an Awful Warning. Instead some unprincipled youth completed the traverse by inserting two more pitons.

At this juncture Antony announced that he was too tired to do any more leading. Not knowing him very well, I believed this, and was preparing to inveigle Dick into doing the next pitch, which looked horribly steep. However, scarcely were the words out of his mouth than Antony disappeared upwards into the gathering clouds and darkness. He had overcome the last difficulties, and we were on the top at 8.15 p.m.

* Fell From Rock Club — Ed.

Bivouac was clearly inevitable, so the descent by the Rochers Whymper was selected, a bivouac being (as one in the party had found three weeks previously) warmer on rock than on snow. The Rochers Whymper are, however, unaccommodating. The ledges are snow filled, sloping, or both; and the less steep side faces the prevailing wind. The wind availed itself of this state of affairs, and blew, fitfully but unremittingly, all night. Life was reduced to the periods of time between bouts of shivering, curious periods, rather like the moment waiting for a sneeze. In the far distance of time, as at the end of a tunnel, one could imagine dawn and a return of warmth. But it is a commonplace how short the memory is for unpleasantness and within an hour of starting down next day we were shedding clothes, and marvelling at the feeling we had had that we would never be warm again.

Descents bore me, and no doubt the reader as well. We reached the road exactly 48 hours after leaving it (30 of those hours had been spent roped). Then came, as usual, sleep and food, food and sleep. But in one of the intervals between food and sleep an awful thing was revealed. We were sorting out pitons, and there in the pile was an unfamiliar rusty one; we turned questioningly to him who had come last, taking the pitons out. His look confirmed our horrified thoughts: he had taken out the Piton Croux! Our minds went back to the Vallot Guide, and how the description of the route revolves round the Piton Croux; and then we were once more up on the face of the third tower, and the cry again was heard: "Swing up more pitons," but faintly, mistily; and again we slept.

THE FACE OF THE BRÉVENT
A STORY

BALDWIN SHAW
(1930)

On New Year's Eve, three men sat in the smoking-room of the Rossett Ghyll Hotel. In that little room the fire, the lamp, the smoke from three pipes combined to produce a fine thick atmosphere. Outside, the full fury of a winter storm hurled great gusts of sleet and hail against the tightly fastened window. But of this the three men took little notice. Two of them, young men from Oxford, played piquet across the table, talking cheerfully and inconsequently of tierces and quints, slabs and arêtes. They had pushed the lamp to one side, where its light fell on the book which the third man was reading. He was deep in the arm-chair before the fire and except that his hair showed grey above the chair-back and that the book was a book of verse, little of him was visible to the others. A couple of sodden rucksacks, kicked anyhow into the corner, and a rope festooned in loops and kinks along the fender bore silent testimony to the beastliness of the weather.

Presently the landord brought in some hot drinks.

"No sign of your young friend yet," he said, as he put down the tray. "I expect as he's gone down to Wasdale most likely. But I've kept some dinner hot for him."

"He'll turn up," said one of the two, cheerfully. "If he said he'll come, he will. I know him. He's as strong as a horse and likes being soaked to the skin. But don't you sit up. We'll see the New Year in and give him a biscuit. He doesn't deserve any dinner as late as this. He'll be all right."

"I hope as he will," said the old man, without much conviction. "But I don't like it. It's after ten o'clock already. Always these chaps as walk about by theirselves as causes all the trouble. They didn't ought to go alone on the fells. No offence meant to you, Sir," he added, with a glance towards the arm-chair, "though I do wish as you had someone with you. Look at that Mr. Middleton and all the trouble he caused. Why, they was out for three days afore they found him and I don't know how many folk there wasn't looking for him." And the good man went out, obviously troubled.

"Master Philip's all right," said one of the players, preparing to deal a new hand. "He'll probably bang in here soon, incredibly hearty and altogether too full of himself."

"I hope so. Not but what a search party would be rather fun."

"Fat lot of good we should be with the whole of the Lakes to search from here to Buttermere. What could two of us do? Or even three —" looking towards the arm-chair.

The older man lowered his book. "Yes," he said, slowly, "you can count me in — tomorrow. But I will not move tonight. It is no good looking for a man in the dark." Then, after a pause, he added, "But a search party is not fun," and went on reading.

The two soon finished their game and were disinclined to start another. A particularly savage gust battered the window.

"Poor old Philip," said one of them. "He may be a strong man, but I bet he has his work cut out on Esk Hause tonight. Who was this Middleton anyway?"

"Dunno. Someone who got lost apparently."

"D'you know, Sir?"

Again the book was slowly lowered. "As a matter of fact I do." Then, after a silence, "It was I who found him."

"What had happened ?"

"It was a queer... a very queer business altogether." For some minutes no one spoke. Then one of the younger men found the courage to ask the necessary question.

"Won't you tell us about it? We're sick of piquet."

"It is a long story. But if you are not going to play any more, it might interest you to hear it. I must get another pipe though: this one refuses to draw properly. You had better pull the chairs up to the fire. I shall not be long." He got up and went out.

"Who and what is he?"

"Don't know. Talked a bit before dinner, while I was waiting for you. Walked over this morning from Seatoller. Says he's only a walker. But those were obviously his tracks at Pavey Ark and there's an ice axe... Here he is."

They looked more closely at the stranger as he came into the lamplight... a tall thin, rather intelligent-looking man, his hair just greying at the temples; neat, methodical and, when he spoke, matter of fact; but in his eyes and about his hands there was something of the artist which was altogether foreign to the level, unemotional voice.

He was clearly in no hurry to tell his story, for he carefully filled his pipe, lighted it, watched it for several minutes and seemed to be wondering how to begin. Then suddenly he said, "It was twenty years ago: exactly twenty years ago today." There was a long pause. "I cannot think why I am telling you this, for you will not believe it. I have told it once, once only, to one man only, and, though he knew me better than most men, he thought that I was pulling his leg. But after all it does not very much matter whether you believe it or not. It is all so long ago now.

"I was spending the New Year at Buttermere. There were plenty of climbers there at the time, but I was by myself, for even then I liked to walk about alone. So did this man Middleton. I had met him more than once on the hills and rather liked him, though he was much older than I was and a morose sort of fellow. He had the devil of a temper. All the Lakeland people hated him. He was always imagining himself insulted and could never make allowances for anybody, least of all for servants. There was a queer streak of revenge in him too and he once pursued some unlucky farmer into the law courts because his dog had attacked him. Most animals disliked him, but they were generally afraid of him; this poor beast tried to be friendly, was repulsed and snapped at him. Middleton went on till he had it shot by the magistrates' order. So you can see that he was hardly likely to be very popular. Men said he would cheerfully sell his soul to get his revenge — but that of course is mediaeval. And yet there was something likeable in the man. For one thing, he was passionately fond of this country. He spent all his holiday here, year after year. He was a great strapping fellow, immensely strong, walked enormous distances and went out in all weathers, which would not, I suppose, commend him to our friend the Landlord.

Then he disappeared. He was staying at Wasdale, which he left in the morning, saying that he would be back for dinner. That night he did not return, nor all the next day; and no one knew in which direction he had gone. During the afternoon they began to look for him. Search parties were out on the Gable and Scafell, but it was clear weather and there seemed to be no reason why he should have come to any harm. Most of the searchers thought that he had gone further than he intended the first day, had slept out that night and was making a second long day of it with another long walk, which would bring him in in the evening. That night he was still away and by the next morning it was obvious that something serious had happened. There was no telephone then and a dalesman brought us the news at Buttermere, for up to that time we had heard nothing about it. We sent word back to the Wasdale people to say that we would be responsible for searching all the Fleetwith area and on into Ennerdale. So a large party of us went off, spread out like a line of beaters, our right somewhere about the Haystacks and our left going up Honister Crag. We were about a hundred yards apart and I was the most left-hand of all.

Half-way up the crag I saw something away to my left and there he was, lying on his back at the foot of a small rock wall. He must have fallen in the dark, coming down; it was the only really steep rock on the slope. He was wearing a bluish tweed coat with patches of grey leather on the shoulders. I said he was a big man. Most dead bodies look unexpectedly small and insignificant. Middleton looked enormous and perhaps it was this which caused me to make an odd remark. The evening before I had been reading a Norwegian Saga, *Grettir the Strong*, and now, as I came towards Middleton's body, I found myself murmuring the words in which the author describes the body of the dead neatherd Glam, 'blue as hell and great as a neat.' As I said this, Middleton's head rolled over towards me, his eyes opened and he gave me a look which I shall never forget. I have never seen such hatred. For a moment I thought he was still alive and I believe I called out to him 'Hallo, Middleton.' But when I touched him, I found that he was cold and stiff, his eyes were shut and his head was fixed immovably. There was a doctor with the party and he now came up with the rest. In his opinion Middleton had been dead for at least twenty-four hours. I told no one what I had seen. It was obvious that the head could not have moved. It must have been some trick of my imagination."

Clough, Streetly, Bray (below) and Walker immediately after the first Whillans Box was erected on the Paine expedition. Photo: Derek Walker.

Bonington and Whillans after the first ascent of the Central Pillar of Frêney in 1961. Photo: Ken Wilson Archive.

Camped at La Bérarde are, left to right, Jane Mortimer, Mike Mortimer, Trevor Jones, Hugh Brown, Ian Roper and Derek Walker, in 1971.
Photo: Bob Allen.

A pre-expedition meet for the 1975 Everest Expedition. Far left, John Hunt, then left to right, Peter Boardman, Dave Clark, Mike Rhodes, Charles Wylie, Nick Estcourt and in the right foreground, Alan Tritton, a director of Barclays Bank. Photo: Chris Bonington.

He paused. Neither of his listeners found anything to say. The whole thing was so strange, coming from one who seemed so essentially practical. Then one of them, a doctor in the making, began to offer some physiological explanation. But he was cut short.

"Yes," said the older man, "I believe it is possible to explain it in that way. I asked a doctor once, putting the case to him hypothetically of course. But that does not really matter. For that is not the end of the business and, if you can believe the rest, you will not need to look for physiological explanations.

Two years later, I was at Chamonix in August. But I ought first to say that, try as I might, I could never quite forget that look that Middleton gave me. It did not worry me very much, but I found myself thinking of it more than I liked. Perhaps it was this that made me imagine once or twice that I saw him, or rather his blue tweed coat. Once it was in the crowd at the Gare du Nord, another time at the Academy and once at Twickenham during the French match. It was always in a crowd and always out of reach. At the Academy, I almost came up to him; but he turned into another room, I was delayed for a moment and, by the time that I reached that room, he had gone. To return to Chamonix. It was a bad August and few of the ordinary climbs were possible. But my companion, for I was not alone that time, was a determined person and, while we waited for the Aiguilles to shed some of their new snow and ice, we decided to climb the face of the Brévent. It had recently been done for the first time, by Ravanel, I believe, and, though the rock was said to be somewhat rotten, there was not likely to be much snow there.

The weather was fairly good when we started, but the day degenerated and, by the time that we were irrevocably committed to our climb, clouds came drifting past us and there were occasional gusts of snow and rain, all rather unpleasant. When we had done about a third of the climb, I realised that there was a party behind us. For a time I could only hear them, but later, looking down while my leader was hunting for a sound belay, of which there are not many, I caught sight of two climbers. There was apparently a guide, dressed in some dark material, and below him a man in light tweeds. I could see little more than the head and shoulders of the second man, but, just as the clouds blotted out the view, a patch of grey leather on his shoulder gave an unpleasant jar to my memory. At that moment my leader summoned me from above and for the next few pitches I forgot all about the others of whom, in any case, I saw and heard nothing. Then we came to that long narrow traverse to the left, not far from the top of the climb. You probably know it. Guides like to stop there, assemble their party and then dramatically hold a stone out at arm's length and tell them to listen for the fall of it. It drops clear for more than a thousand feet. There is nothing very difficult, but the step to the left off the traverse is a little awkward and there is only one small, rather inadequate belay. I had the rope round this — it is almost at the end of the traverse — when I was surprised to hear voices behind me, apparently of the other party, starting on the other end.

They were hidden by the curve of the wall and in any case it was too misty to see much. Now there was clearly no room for two at that belay, so I called out to them to wait until I had gone on up. There was no answer, but a few minutes later there appeared close beside me not, as I expected, the dark guide, but the man in tweeds. There was no mistaking that bluish coat and those enormous shoulders. He was coming, crouching towards, me, his head down against the driving snow, and his face was invisible. But there was no doubt at all in my mind. I think that I said something like 'Go back. There's no room here for two,' and at that moment he stretched out his hand and seized my right arm. I could do nothing. If I pulled my arm away I might send him to the bottom; besides, I am almost certain that I could not have pulled it away. Anyhow, I panicked and shouted up to my leader to be quick, because we were keeping a party waiting. He was round the corner in the chimney and the wind was howling past him, so that there was little chance that he would hear me. But fortunately he was just at the top of the pitch and, almost as I shouted, there came a great bellow for me to come on.

With my left hand I slipped the rope off the belay and then turned with some intention of asking the man to release my arm. As I did so, I felt his grasp slacken and my arm fell to my side, for the moment quite useless. At the same time the man raised his head and looked me full in the face. It was the same face and the same look that I had seen that day at Honister. I do not know what I should have done if I had not at that instant been jerked almost off my balance by the sudden tightening of the rope, as my leader took in the slack. This pulled me together and with my left hand I made a grab at the spike by the *mauvais pas*. I got my left foot on to the step all right and had a good hold for the left hand, but I could do nothing at all with my right. Worse still, as I was raising my right foot, a hand closed round my ankle and dragged me down. I believe that I shouted. I certainly kicked out with all my strength and, according to my leader, came on the rope with a jerk. It is very probable. My foot came in contact with something and my ankle was free, which was all that I cared about. There was no sound from just behind me, but I thought that I heard, above the howling wind, a great shout, almost a shout of triumph, from the other end of the traverse.

At the top I found that my leader had seen and heard nothing, though he was surprised that I had not negotiated the *mauvais pas* more neatly. I told him nothing. We stayed up there some time but no one else appeared. I hardly thought that they would."

The speaker paused and then added, "No, I hardly thought that they would."

"What happened to the other fellow — the guide?"

"Who the devil was the other fellow?"

For a moment the stranger seemed not to have heard either question. Then the even voice began again.

"We came down by the ordinary track. At the point where the path for our face climb diverged from it, there were one or two patches of soft snow. I probably should have noticed nothing myself but my friend called attention to it. He remarked that it was odd that they should leave their cattle up so high in such foul weather and he pointed to the snow, trodden here and there by a cloven hoof. I still said nothing, but the identity of the dark guide..."

There was a hearty shout outside, the door burst open and a dripping figure appeared.

"Hallo you two," it said, cheerfully, "Got anything to eat? I'm ravenous. Lost my way over Esk Hause. Queer goings on up there. Thought at one time that the devil was after me."

THE WEST FACE OF THE DRU

J. BROWN, D. WHILLANS AND A. K. R. (ANTHONY RAWLINSON)
(1955)

"It's the angle that makes it a serious climb," said Joe. "Definitely a terrific climb. Nothing in England like the 90-metre dièdre."

The west face of the Dru was not really in their plans for the summer. But in Chamonix they heard of the second ascent. The successful party they had met earlier on another climb. "We thought, if they can do it, why shouldn't we have a bash?"

They looked up photographs with the route marked. Snell in the sports shop gave them a technical note. They waited for the weather to settle.

"And did it?"

"Well, it was a fine morning when we started," said Joe. "Don and I took the 10.30 train to Montenvers. We walked across the Mer de Glace and over the moraine to the foot of the face. The technical note said there was a pitch of V on leaving the glacier but we didn't find it; perhaps the glacier was higher this year. What we did find was a lot of loose rock. You begin up a 1,000 foot couloir. This was rock at first, mostly easy but steep and very loose. After 600 feet the rock ended. The rest of the couloir was ice. We had to go up and across it. The ice was thin, with bits of icicles sliding down the middle, where falling ice and stones had made a groove. We roped and I led off. I ran out the full 150 feet, hoping to get to a belay before Don had to start, but I couldn't. So we had to move together up the ice, cutting steps and hoping nothing would hit us. It was dicey. Eventually we were up and across, and arrived on the 'terraces inferieurs.'

During the afternoon it had been clouding up. The sun had gone in, and as we got to the terraces, about four o'clock, it started to rain. Then we heard thunder. It was quite a storm. We decided to stop where we were, so as to be able to get back if things didn't improve. We might have gone straight back then, but the idea of going down the icy part of the couloir was so nasty that we thought we'd better stay for a bit to see if we could go on up later. We started to clear a bivouac place. It was raining hard now, with thunder every few seconds, and lightning flashing round the top of the Dru. There was ice over the bivouac ledge. We had one axe-hammer and one piton hammer between us. We started chopping the ice away with them. Then the axe broke. It was no good as a hammer any more, but we kept the head, which might be useful for step cutting. We sat down on the ledge. The storm slackened and about eight o'clock it stopped raining. We cooked a bit and settled down for the night. It wasn't a very good ledge. You couldn't lie down on it. But we could sit with legs out straight and managed to sleep a bit now and then. It didn't rain again during the night, though the clouds chased over. The morning was fine. We had some bacon and boiled eggs and brewed some tea. We moved off about 5.30.

We traversed left about 300 feet, and then began to move up from ledge to ledge. This was the area below the landslide and everywhere was littered with loose shattered rocks. There was a pitch of IV Sup. but not difficult, then a chimney of V with a peg in it. We came to the 'terraces superieurs' and began to feel a long way up the face. The terraces shelved away in steps for 100 feet or so; then there was the big drop of 1,000 feet vertically to the glacier. Immediately above was the giant flake with behind it the long vertical corner. This is the line of the middle and most difficult part of the route, with the long artificial pitches. We knew we were at the start of the big difficulties. We put on the doubled rope and began to lead through.

Two or three pitches led to the Fissure Vignes. We had been told this was the crux. It is really not one, but a series of cracks: you go up each one and then step into the next. The whole pitch is about 75 feet. It was Don's turn to lead. He went up and didn't seem to find it difficult. I followed. It wasn't more than normal V.S. standard. If that's the crux, we thought, we're in for an easy climb. There were three pitons in it, but it wasn't really necessary to use them.

Another pitch and we were under an overhang on the right. Ahead an obvious crack went straight up, but there was a line of pitons to the right underneath the overhang so we thought we'd better follow them. We went across under the overhang on étriers and hand traversed back to the crack above. This brought us to the next big pitch, the 40-metre crack, all overhangs and vertical. I was glad it was Don's turn to lead, but he was crafty. He went up 20 feet, found a stance and stopped; so I had to go on past him. But the crack seemed quite reasonable. It was rather like the first pitch of Curving Crack on Cloggy, but longer and the crack narrower and overhanging. There were wooden wedges in place all the way up, and I climbed on these. This wasn't too easy: most of the slings in the wedges were rotten so I had to use the wedges themselves. At the top I banged in a wedge myself for a belay, the first one we had put in. Don didn't use the wedges at all, but laybacked all the way up.

On the ledge just above the second party had bivouacked. We saw empty milk tubes lying about. The crack went on, with more laybacks and jamming. Then it broadened into a gully, with overhangs all round. The slab below them was running with snow-water. Again it was Don's turn to lead. It looked very hard, but Don found some holds and with a piton got up. This was the half-moon shaped slab, leading into a couloir. The couloir was all ice, but you could bridge across it. Then it steepened to vertical and the ice spread outwards from the back over the walls. We had to cut holds in the ice to get up into the cave underneath the overhang.

It was Don's lead. He got a wooden wedge into a crack under the overhang, and hung an étrier on it. He stepped out on the etrier and swung into space. It was difficult to keep steady to put in the next piton, but after a bit he managed it and got another étrier hung on that. It was more and more awkward, and the étriers seemed to swing always in the wrong direction. Don went up and back to rest, and up and back and rested again. And then at last he forced out over the edge and up. This was the hardest bit of the climb, harder than the Vignes. It was 5 p.m. We were at the top of the great flake and at the foot of the 90-metre dièdre.

It had been clouding up. Now there was mist all round. We sat down for a rest before going up to the dièdre, and brewed some tea. It was cold sitting down and Don put on his duvet.

The dièdre ahead went straight up, smooth and vertical, with a tilt to the right. Don led a free pitch to start, then it was my turn to lead the artificial. There were lots of pegs and wedges in place. Mostly I used these, but I had to put in some more of my own. Half-way up I stopped, standing in étriers, and brought up Don. Then I went on to the top of the dièdre and began to traverse right. Here I had to put in more pitons myself and I wished I had more karabiners. Every few feet I had to go down to bring up the lowest ones to clip into the next pegs. It started to snow. We were sheltered in the corner because of the tilt, but the rock was wet and I began to feel cold. I wished I had put on my duvet when Don had. Now I had to stop to put it on in the middle of the dièdre, one foot on the vertical wall, the other in an étrier. I could only move four or five inches in either way, and it was awkward getting the duvet out of the rucksack. When I moved on, all the rock was running with water and cold and wet and slippery. Hand-jamming up the crack was difficult.

The dièdre ended. It was an impressive place, high above the flake with a vertical drop over the edge to the glacier. We caught glimpses of this now and again through the driving snow. We found the knotted rope left by the first party. On the left was the smooth wall where they made their fantastic traverse in from the north face; we saw their line of expansion bolts. But our way was to the right, down the knotted rope diagonally to a ledge 80 feet below and 40 feet to the right. The knotted rope was tied to a piton at the top, and it hung in a great curve, the other end fixed on the ledge below. It didn't look very safe, so Don belayed my rope through the piton at the top while I went down. The fixed rope creaked and strained and it was slippery with snow, but I got down safely to the bottom of the curve. I climbed up to the ledge, and found two wooden wedges holding the lower end of the rope. We left our own long line running through the top piton so that I could safeguard Don from the ledge while he followed down the fixed rope.

By the time we were both down it was eight o'clock and getting dark. We decided to stop for the night. The ledge was deep in snow, but we cleared it. It was quite a good ledge, about nine feet by three, but there was a big block so you couldn't lie down. We just sat crouched: I had a cagoule and Don a pakamac, and we had the duvets underneath. It was snowing hard, and went on snowing all night. We couldn't sleep.

At last it began to get light. I could hardly see Don: he was covered with snow, with just the ridges of his pakamac showing black. The dawn was grey and misty and it was still snowing, but not so hard. We ate a bit. Soon the snowfall slackened and became patchy, stopping and starting again; occasionally we even caught a glimpse of the valley. We got going about 5.30. We left the ledge by a crack, a pitch of V with two pegs in it. Then down a crack of IV, and up two more cracks, supposed to be V but easy. Then a couloir with four pitons, all running with water. So to the pitch of VI. This was not too bad, but the rocks were pouring with melting snow, and by now we were soaked through, and the duvets were sopping.

All across the upper part of the face is a line of overhangs, but in the middle there is just one weakness. This is the route. First up the edge of a flake, then a crack with a wedge in it. All the way we were knocking down snow and ice off the holds. This brought us above the overhang. We were not sure where to go next. One false cast and then we saw a line of pegs. They led to easier climbing, but on peculiar rock, like stiff mud. And then suddenly we came to a wire ladder. It must have been left by the second party. I pulled: was it secure at the top? It creaked but didn't give way, so Don belayed and I went up. The ladder led to an edge, and over it. It was the edge of the north face. The last pitch. We were up. Only a few hundred feet of the ordinary north face route between us and the top. It must have been about 10.30.

But all the rocks were covered with snow and ice and pouring with water. We lost the route and had some hard pitches. In the end we came out at the brèche between the Petit and the Grand Dru. We climbed up the *passage en Z* to the Grand Dru. It was four o'clock.

Descent was straightforward. We did eight abseils on the 300-foot rope. It was dark when we got to the glacier, but there was a bit of moon. We felt tired. We started across the glacier. Some glacier! It seemed as steep as the Idwal Slabs. Don tried to cross a big crevasse and fell in three times, making impressive pendulum swings on the rope. 'This is fun but monotonous.' We heard avalanches coming down the Dru behind us. There was a terrific one. It seemed to be coming right at us. We dug in the stump of the broken axe and ducked. Snow and ice fragments hissed round us. Then silence.

About 9.30 we decided to stop. We sat down. There was no food left. A long, hungry night. In the morning we found we were only a quarter of an hour from the Charpoua Hut. On down the path and across the glacier. Montenvers. Down the path to Chamonix. Near the bottom was Hamish Nicol to meet us. Excitement and congratulations. On again, down to the camping place. It had been wet here, too. Don was flooded out of his tent."

'MEN OF IRON'

W. M. YOUNGER
(1931)

Next day, after an abortive attempt on the Aletschorn we wandered down the glacier and across to Riederfurka. There we encountered an anxious parent who informed us that her son had had a slight accident on one of the Fusshörner and overwhelmed us with inquiries. I was anxious to appease her, but Neil brushed me aside, and, coldly ignoring her flow of questions, demanded that she should inform us where we could best procure a first-class meal. So, perhaps, we have men of iron at Oxford too.

PETITES JORASSES
(extract)

R. J. WATHEN
(1959)

To have one's mountain dreams dissolve into little puddles of water, and to fail, fall, or be foiled in eighty per cent of one's plans is, it seems, the lot of most Alpinists nowadays. More so for one who is visiting Chamonix for the first time and has not yet learned the golden rule for success there: go up to a hut in the rain, and grab your climb when the weather turns good next day. I reached the Leschaux Hut with Chris Bonington, and there we were for once in step with the weather.

A mile from the "Walker" is a small wall of rock, left of the Col des Hirondelles — small in comparison with the 4,000 feet of its big neighbour — small perhaps, yet very impressive, being a solid rectangle of rock bristling with overhangs, soaring nearly 2,500 feet out of the glacier. And supposed to be hard, too. "The hardest hereabouts: the hardest climb I have ever done," said Bron, the first ascensionist. This was to be our climb, the West Face of the Petites Jorasses.

Frankly, I was rather frightened by the whole thing, and approached the foot of the Wall in some trepidation. I wasn't fit. Chris was. He would lead, of course. But could I keep up with him? I must climb fast, tearing up those cracks and overhangs, carrying my pack to save time. And how would I ride out the bivouacs, and the storm and cold of the two or three nights we might have to spend up there? It is odd how the newcomer to the bigger Alpine routes always imagines these night bivouacs to be a life-and-death affair of sitting on a centimetre of rock counting one's toes and fingers as they plop off one by one and fall to the glacier *"thousands of feet below."* I was a newcomer, and that's what I thought. Perhaps I wasn't exactly frightened. *Tensed*, rather. That's what the guidebook says, for instance, about the "Walker": *tension d'esprit* through the height, the fear of storms, etc. etc.

"Come on, you lazy beggar. We'll be here a week at this rate." It sounded like Chris. (Indeed, who else could it have been?)

I came on, up the first pitch of the climb. The long pitches of the dièdre flew by under our feet. We were moving faster than we had expected. "Well, that's the first 600 feet. Easy enough. Wonder what all the fuss was about?"

I couldn't answer, being somewhat restricted by two rucksacks, one in each ear. Chris had a bad habit of putting the sack-hauling rope through the karabiners on the pegs he was using as running belays, and I had to pay for it by carrying up both the sacks. Another bad habit he has is to drop things — not himself, luckily: he's too good to do that. But small things, like pegs, hammers, karabiners, rucksacks, anoraks, ice-axes, guidebooks, and boots. The occasional peg whistled past my ear. I was glad that the two rucksacks protected me.

Chris led out again. A hard delicate pitch onto the arête out right. I followed. "*Tight rope!*" I was all in. How Chris climbed it so easily, I don't know. With his weight, too. Most of the other top climbers are small men, and go around muttering about weight-to-muscle ratio. Compared with some of these, Chris is positively *fat.*

My turn to lead. Terraces, slabs and ledges up to a wet chimney. Chris went through again, splashing through the water like a dowager mermaid coming up for air.

I followed, with the sacks. We wrung each other out, and traversed back left above the big overhang which we had just by-passed.

Soon after this, the difficulties began. I took a restricted stance in the middle of a chimney and Chris passed out of sight over an overhang. There were a lot of grunts, and the rope went out ever so slowly for about half an hour — so that I had time to take my hands off it and refresh myself with glucose tablets. Chris reached a stance. His sack went up on the rope, got jammed, I climbed up to free it, then followed up the crack wearing my own sack.

It was very thin, and Chris had used a peg and a wedge, which had to be abandoned (*my* wedge, of course). (Whillans, Smith and Brown, coming up the climb next day, took a different line here, traversing left onto a line of pegs planted by the first ascensionists.)

The next pitch was the most interesting. The crux. A mighty overhang, like the Sloth at the Roches, only not so big. The route description said "A3," which indicated high-grade pegging in bad cracks. We got out the étriers, pegs, hammers, and spare karabiners and slings. Chris took some glucose and a deep breath, and advanced to the attack. I prepared for a long wait.

He banged in a peg for protection. And then — suddenly I looked up. He wasn't there. No Chris in sight. Oh, dear. Had he fallen? No, the rope was still there.

"Come on, send up the sack you lazy beggar, or we'll be here a month!" Chris's voice floated sweetly down to me from above the overhang. He was up.

Intrigued, I went up to see what kind of an overhang this could be. In a trice I too was up, sack and all. Large holds above the overhang had solved it neatly. Indeed a kind of Sloth, only much easier: about *V Sup.*

Dear Reader, you gasp at our prowess? — that we should have ambled up so easily where others had struggled and sworn? It's quite simple, really. There weren't any piton cracks worth speaking about, and to have tried to climb it artificially would have taken much more energy than to have climbed it free. Pitons have their drawbacks as well as their advantages.

Chuffed, we flew on upwards. Long traverses up leftwards landed us at the most conspicuous feature of the face, a square ice patch at its northern end. We by-passed this on the rock to its right and then made a curious sort of creeping traverse for 150 feet to the right.

It was getting late. The rock was golden and hot to the touch as the sun sank down over the Aiguilles and Mt. Blanc. We came to the end of the traverse and found ourselves in the chimney where the first party had bivouacked.

"Where's the route go now?"

"No idea. Let's sleep on it."

* * *

I was lowered into the innards of the chimney to hack at ice for supper. Chris made himself at home — trousers off, long pants on, trousers on again. There was no need for me to expose my legs to the night air in this indelicate way. I was already sheathed in my Specials: pyjama trousers, and a pair of Norwegian long string underpants, which I had donned before leaving the hut.

We start supper. I fill the stove. In doing so my trousers get secretly soaked in petrol. A match. *Whoosh!* Flames all over my trousers. I feel like a Christmas pudding. The effort of extinguishing myself nearly throws me off the ledge, so I tie myself on with an ingenious rope system round my feet and under my chin. Unfortunately, this rope under my chin tightens as my feet slide off the ledge, and I am almost strangled.

We eat some of Chris's R.A.F. rations, "for survival in dry climates." They are revolting, but we survive all right.

Supper is over. Night darkens. Glaciers creak. Nose gets cold. Well, let's sing. How about the Bivouac Song? "Far away from the cold night air."

"And how about making me a spot of tea?" mutters Chris, rolling over and knocking me in the ribs. I curse him. "Captain Christian Bonington, how about making it yourself?..."

All I want is a room somewhere,
Far away from the cold night air,
With one e-nor-mous chair,
Luver-ly, luver-ly...

Music, the first and best of the arts. Let's sing. Let us gladden the glaciers with our song. I get dug into that fine example of early folk music, the Ballad of Eskimo Nell. "It may be rare in Berkeley Square, but it's not on the —"

"— How about a spot of tea?" It's Chris again. Apparently, like Dead-Eyed Dick and Mexico Pete, he feels disinclined to take his refreshment in solitude.

"Here's the cooker. And if you drop it —"

He drops it.

Gr-rrr...

Still, can't be helped... No tea. And no soup, be*ooo*tiful soup...

Midnight. Full moon ahead. It is so bright, I am wearing my dark glasses. "Bonattington" rolls again and grunts himself to sleep.

Lots of chocs for me to eat,
Lots of coal making lots of heat.

An hour later. The rope under my chin has tightened and jerked me awake. One o'clock. Ah, an idea: the cigarette...

The cigarette. Only brought up four from Montenvers, one for each day... Smoked the third two hours ago... can I *honestly* smoke another?... Why not? Two hours ago it was Wednesday. Now it's Thursday!

Cigarette over. What now? Four boiled sweets. One every half hour. They'll last till 3 a.m. Wonder why I can't sleep ? It's not, after all, an unpleasant bivouac. Possibly it's the rock sticking in my backside...

* * * *

Slowly the hours pass... "Daylight comes and I wanna go home."

Dawn is touching the peaks. Tone, shine, shape and shadow return to the grey ghosts of the night.

"Top o' da marning to yer." At this hour, Don and the two Joes are reaching the foot of the climb. Unaware of this, we send some rocks smashing down in their direction.

Chris leads off, and we climb two rope-lengths up cracks and open chimneys. They end in walls. These look temptingly easy, but Chris's routefinding genius espies a chance peg out to the right on a most improbable line. Traversing back onto the West Face, we continue upwards. Cracks, walls and easy pitches follow each other in fast succession.

Suddenly we are on the top. We have burst from the cold shadow into the heat of the day. We are on the sharp ridge which delicately severs Italy from France. It is midday. We relax in the sun and look around us. Westward towers the Grandes Jorasses, and we are somewhat humbled to see that our own mountain is only half the height of the mighty Walker Spur — barely up the *Tour Grise,* in fact.

Later we had got ourselves outside a bottle of chianti, which fortified the said hiccough and hastened the said eruption. That night we slept in a local lavatory.

RONNIE'S LAST LONG CLIMB

TERRY GIFFORD
(1992)

" 'Stay off the pop, lad!' Those were Don Whillans's last words to me as we saw him off at the airport: 'Stay off the pop, lad', he said. Of course he'd done nothing of the sort while he'd been here in Majorca. That's the great danger in Deià — for a small village there are an amazing number of bars. Within two months Don was dead."

Ronnie Wathen, CC, poet, and piper, smiled his quizzical smile. Behind his specs there was that characteristic mixture of mystery and mischief. He and I were waiting on a stance whilst Norman searched for the line, little thinking this would be Ronnie's own last climb. He did climb again at Harrison's of course, and in Dalkey Quarry as late as June, before his death from a brain tumour on September 5th 1993. But that was something else.

He'd taken us with typical enthusiasm and poor memory to what must be the best VS in Majorca — 800 feet of varied, sustained climbing spiced by the need for good old-fashioned route finding, if you get up early enough to beat the queue. The soaring ridge of *Sa Gubia* can be seen from Palma air-port. It's the left-hand skyline of a vertical scoop out of the nearest hills. Ronnie told me that *Sa Gubia* means, in Majorquin, (which he had learned fluently) 'the woodworker's gouge'. It is a route of continuing interest whose secrets are not given away by lines of bolts, or by my hinting that descents over the back of the mountain are usually made in the dark and finally involve passing The Three-Headed Dog to reach the road.

It was our third Alpine start for this route, from Ronnie's mountain village of Deià, where he had built a house for his family in 1968. It was Robert Graves who provided the focus for those poets and artists who, like Ronnie himself, have homed in on Deià. Where else would you find that there are two poetry readings in one week? And one of them was Ronnie's reading that night, so we'd better not hang about on *Sa Gubia*. Easier said than done.

We reached the foot of *Sa Gubia* in the cool of a New Year's Eve morning under a cloudless sky. My son, Tom, and Simon from Jersey opted for the bolted right-hand start up a leaning crackline, whilst Norman led off from the red-painted foot of the ridge. It's a scrambly, slightly loose first pitch to a belay in bushes where Ronnie, with his flair for the unpredictable, found behind a bush, a gift of a bottle of water. We accepted it. The second pitch passes two pegs and begins to get into 4b gear. Each belay has double pegs or bolts and is painted with a number. From R2 we should have traversed right beneath a scoop to gain the crest of the ridge, but Norman's instincts led left and back right to a double peg belay on the right of a cave where a large ledge would detain Ronnie and me plus the next team for an increasingly intense impasse.

Norman looked round to the right and returned. Not likely. He looked left and returned. A long way left a line of bolts above and below indicated what he took to be *Super Nova*. Norman tried the cave roof. Ronnie tried teaching me my cue for coming in with a poem of my own in the middle of his reading of his long poem in which he shows Lord Byron around Deià and its inhabitants. It's written in ottava rima, the form perfected by Byron, and it's written by Ron who was quoting:

    " 'the Isles of Greece! The Isles of Greece! are calling

And he hopes that, on a wing and a prayer

He'll leave this Deià which he finds appalling...' "

Cue Gifford:

    " 'In the mountains they have a dance...' " but Ronnie was stopped abruptly by Norman shouting down rather unpoetically: "For Pete's sake shut up! I'm trying to get us out of here and you're reciting poetry!"

He returned to our ledge which was getting crowded. Friendly, but crowded. Another leader had belayed beside us and his second, perhaps motivated by Ron's Byron, looked round to the right and returned. Not likely.

"Well, I've run out of ideas!" Norman declared.

So, having given up hope on this route, the only alternative was any route. Norman crossed the cave to the left again and this time the rope kept moving. A steep bolted wall that Norman was ascending out of our sight proved to be the delightful 4c crux of our version of this route. At the top a delicate traverse right brought a painted belay and a helpful red arrow pointing up right as if by now you might be feeling a little lost. This was Ronnie's fourth ascent and he found it got mysteriously harder each time he did it.

"It's amazing," he said. "You don't need to work at raising your grade. You just do the same route every five years!"

Norman attacked the crack, indicated by the arrow, that slanted up a steep wall. He popped in hexes and Friends, swung out off the crack's edge and disappeared again. Ronnie took off his slippers, which he called his 'Chinese torture socks', and aired his horrible toes. His Majorquin shepherd's shoes were clipped in to his faded Whillans harness. From deep in his sac he offered me olives. I declined. He offered me garlic. I declined. So he popped the clove into his mouth and chewed on it: "Just like Don used to say, 'Don't put any of them olives or garlic in the cooking!' "

He offered me a satsuma.

"Thanks."

"That's alright," he said, "They grow on trees round here."

I tried to peel it whilst belaying. He popped an unpeeled orange into his mouth and chewed on it.

At the top of this pitch Norman hailed Tom, asking him to wait so that we could speed up the route-finding. At R5 Tom's route joined ours. From here the route looked broken by the odd bush above and slightly easier. It's deceptive. Norman raced after Tom.

Ronnie arrived at my stance, then the next two lads, then an English girl who was leading and had to wait at the top holds of her pitch.

"Are you happy?" One of the lads asked.

"I'm ecstatically happy!" she replied, relaxing on her small holds. Fair enough. We all believed her. For the rest of the route Ronnie kept reminding us that people in the queue behind us were "ecstatically happy."

Above the next belay, R6, a steep wall demanded strenuous pull ups, then a stretch left where a manky peg offered a dubious quick clip before jugs tempted sweaty grasps in a groove. To say it's 4b is to convey nothing of the way it reminds you that there's going to be no let up high on this pillar above the plain. The following easier slabs might tease you, but at R7, where there's an *in situ* tape round a natural thread, another wall asks the old question, 'which way?'

Norman took an airy ramp to the left, then came back right, warning about loose blocks. A rightwards-slanting groove led up to a tree in a recess at R8. When Ronnie joined us here, his tale this time was about the amazing etiquette on the stances of this climb. A German had arrived on a stance and asked Ronnie: "Do you mind if I smoke?"

"Here we are, 700 feet up in the air, and he asked my permission to smoke! What did he expect me to say? 'I'm sorry this is a non-smoking stance?'"

"So what did you say, Ronnie?"

"I said, 'It's alright, if you give me one'."

The final pitch of this magnificent climb sustains its interest and quality right up to the unnecessary 'Fin' on the rock at R9. A step right from the alcove reveals sharp fluted rock that tears at the fingertips. Above, pinnacles finally bring into sight the 400ft ridge-walk to gain the summit. The sun may be about to set, but the day is not over yet.

We relaxed as we walked down the long winding roadway off the summit through the olive groves. The sky paled from orange to yellow to green as the moon came up. Talk turned to Cerberus, the three-headed dog that guards the farm before the road. Dave Gregory had warned us about this dog. "It rushes at you suddenly at full pelt, but its chain is just long enough for it to be pulled up with enough room for you to squeeze past with your back to the wall. That's when its neck is jerked back and its back legs swing round to kick you."

Ronnie also vividly remembered this dog and he had plenty of time to give us the gruesome details as the moon rose higher. One by one, as we got closer to the farm, we each picked up an olive branch. It wasn't for peace. We were approaching some outbuildings. A vicious barking started up. Norman shouted back and amazingly the barking stopped. But that was the puppy.

Cerberus was round the corner. And here was the owner, standing by a gate across the track through his farm. Ronnie greeted him in Majorquin and asked if we might pass through. Somehow none of us appeared to be gripping sticks anymore. The owner was charming and kindly told us to keep to the wall. We didn't need telling as the huge black dog came racing out of the darkness snarling at us and doing the business.

Later that night, Ronnie gave an hilarious reading which poked fun at several members of the audience as Lord Byron was introduced to Ronnie's version of the recent history of Deià. To illustrate his poem he continued what he'd begun on the climb, producing props out of a suitcase and flinging them aside. Here he was doing what he loved best, giving his friends fun out of his magical capacity for the unexpected. That it was kindly and intelligent fun, often at his own expense, is what made him so widely loved by all sorts of people, from dons to Don Whillans. It was New Year's Eve. Ronnie took his Irish pipes to the bar and told me that once Mo Antoine had heard him playing in the Royal Vic, and had said to him: "Is it dead yet? I should get it by the throat!"

It seemed impossible that Ronnie would be struck down by the same fatal illness as Mo and that I would never see him again after that precious week in Ronnie's company. I would like to remember him playing his pipes that night when, after the grapes had been eaten on each stroke of midnight, after the firework display over the mountain, the dog's three heads became six in the retelling and Don's advice was toasted again and again: "Stay off the pop, lad."

Ronnie Wathen was a shaman.
Only he knew what it was he blew
From the mountains of his life
Through his poems and his pipe.

Left and Below: Ronnie Wathen in 1957, characteristically showing idiosyncratic style on Brant Direct (HVS), Clogwyn y Grochan. Photos: George Band.

Peter Biven on the first ascent in 1968 of Geronimo (HVS), Seaward Cliff, Bosigran.
Photo: Biven Collection.

Gunn Clarke on Raven Wall (E3 5c), Bosigran 1960. Clarke, who was instrumental in opening up Swanage and made the first British ascent of the Walker Spur on the Grandes Jorasses with Robin Smith, was tragically killed in an avalanche on Buachaille Etive Mor. Photo: John Cleare.

Colin Binks climbing Trevallen Pillar (E4 6a), one of the modern classics of Pembroke climbing.
Photo: Chris Craggs.

AN ASCENT OF POPO

"MR. DOOLEY."
(From the Mexican Herald.)
(Vol.III No.12 June 1901)

"How are yez, Hinnessey, me b'y," said Mr. Dooley as he came up the street walking by the assistance of a cane.

"Foiner 'n silk," replied Hinnessey, "but why the stick; is it lame yez are?"

"Spake in whispers er not at all, an' oi'll be tellin' ye, fer as me ould frind, oi belave ye'll not bethray me. Oive ben away t' th' top iv Popeycapethel..."

"But, Mr. Dooley . . ."

"Hinnessey, be thrue to me. Me woife hez denied me bid an' bard, an' oim a poor outchast in the worruld, charrged with havin' no sinse at all. Oi wint, Hinnessey, in the inthrusts iv Seance, wid me former counthrymon, the Shivvyleer O'Rourke, an' his parthner-in-crime, Bar-ron von Eckenstein. Kape away from him, Hinnessey, er ye'll be inveigle into some deesprate skame be th' which ye'll be robbed iv yure bodily cumfort an' fam'ly thies. Th're a bloomin' pair iv human dayceivers who cahn't till th' diffrence betwane hate and co'ld, upon me soul th' cahn't.

We'll tike yez t' th' top, sid me spurious fellow-cithizen, Misther O'Rourke, er we'll know th' rayson ov it. It's th' topmost pint iv th' sachred mount oim affher tridden, sez oi, worruds oi hev lirnt to raygrit with tears in me oyes."

"Did yez make the trip on becycles er be an autymobile, Mr. Dooley?"

"The S'ints presarve us, Hinnessey! Hez the silver dog lost his lining? or hez the cloud hed its day? or hez the goulden chain ben busthed, or what th' divvle? Thir's no Passy dilly Rayformy laden to th' blarsted crather iv Popey, me b'y. It is a path iv Glury which lades but to th' ghrave, an' fr'm whose borne no traveler ivver hez a sickond birthday. It is a tist iv morrul curridge an' shoe lither. It is not a pliseant dhrive iv a moon-light ave'nin, Mr. Hinnessey. There's no canteenys er fither bids hung up be the way. Th' mounthin was kivvered wid althichude. Iverything use but th' dhust an' wind hed fled fer its loife. Th' wind hed blowed th' atmosphere into a forreign counthry, an' there was nothin' for th' brith iv man but th' althichude. Yez sthop ivery ither sthep to pull in a ghop of condensed air wid yure mouth, an' whin yez close in yer hide to rist yer shoulders on a brist filled wid air, yez'll find it soft an' unsusthainin', an' yer tongue rolls out an' flaps limply in the breezes, upon me honor it do, Hinnessey.

Th' Shivvyleer and th' ither profissor sthrolled along wid hateful haze, an' whrote in books, th' divvle knows what, on th' althichude, the wind, an' so on, an' me wid me pick-axe hackin' off an exthra hunk of hair th' gale hed overlookt. Th' closer hivven we crawled the harder it blew, an' whin it beghan whistlin' the sphots off me vist, ol sid in tones mint to traggick bike dith,

Boys, lit me lodge in some vhast Wilderniss; annyway lit me lodge! It was niver intinded thet oi shud tickle th' fate iv th' angels in hivven. Thir'fure, oi boolt.

It cannot was, sid the gay Shivvyleer. Our agraymint to tike yez t' th' top was saled be th' coorts iv hivven, an' up yez go. A rope was knotted to me lift laig, Hinnessey, an ol wint hippen' along, while th' Shivvyleer an' th' Bar-ron pl'yed chump th' rope achross th' boulders wid mesilf in th' centher iv tha' rope, tied fast. Oi pled as a fellow-counthrymon, thin as a mon wid a woife an' childer an' me juty to thim. Thin, as me last brith hed gone out to th' hivvens, oi fell, swearin' be th' gods oi was a carpse, be the mouth iv th' turrible crather.

Thir she was, Hinnessey, sthamin' and frothin', an' sthinkin' bike a boiled owl, wid wather at th' botthum as grane ez th' damons iv purgathory. It was thot fur down thot she cudden't be sane without lookin' twice. Sez oi, Whar's th' cimmithry fer th' did, an' saylict a sphot, by's, fer oim brathin' me last, an' as oi spoke th' bones iv me body were rhenderin' a snare dhrum solo be the shivvers iv th' wind.

Be iv gude chare, me b'y, sid th' Bar-ron, th' top is not yit r'ached. Th' rist is onsartin in me brain, Hinnessey. I recollict, wid me oyes soked in tears, the how I was jirked fr'm stun t' stun to th' peenackle iv th' crathur, an' hearin' th' Bar-ron announce in treeump thet his bayrommether sid we waresiventane thousan' eight hunert an' ninety fate above the say.

If it's anny wurse siventane thousan' fate unner th' say, thin fade me carkus to th' waves iv the crathur, sez oi. Whither th' did er didn't oi cannot now say. But lit us be movin', or th' polace 'll be on me thracks. Me woife hez tillygraphed me dayscription as bayin' a lunathic."

TONQUANI

ANON
(1951)

With a sigh of relief I escaped from Committee No.3 into the sunlight, picked up a pair of rubbers and a handkerchief and drove out to Pretoria to lunch with H.E. A sleeping bag and a rucksack were borrowed, we were joined by Tobie Louw and drove off 50 miles due West, into the Magaliesberg.

The climate, they tell you, is reliable, and the climber need not provide against wet conditions. We were unprovided. Black clouds laced with lightning piled up on the horizon, then on the nearer hills, then emptied themselves on us. We watched the scanty red African soil washed off the hillsides in streams of tomato soup. We sat in the car under the trees in Visser's farmyard while the ducks enjoyed themselves.

When the storm was spent we marched up to the Nek and down on the far side to the camp site above the Tonquani Gorge. Four or five members of the Mountain Club emerged from a convenient but unsavoury cave. A large fire was already burning. We fetched water, paused to watch white ants drive the males and females from their citadels, got wet in a sharp shower, gathered round the fire to cook and eat and dry our clothes. While the storm rolled farther westwards and a few pioneer stars emerged, I heard of the first ascent of the Devil's Needle in the Drakensberg, of the spread of piton and tension technique, of rival schools of thought on rope and belays. The rocks among which we sat enclosed us as the walls of Helyg kitchen. One by one the party drifted off to their several gites. Tobie took me round with a torch pointing out suitable pieces of ground relatively flat and upholstered with leaves. I chose one and slept.

After breakfast we dropped down into the gorge with intimidating views of the precipitous farther wall. The lower two-thirds appeared vertical while the upper third overhung alarmingly. A pale grey Clogwyn du'r Arddu splashed with red gashes, bone dry but bearing aloes and some tortured trees. I was assured that it was easier than it looked.

Tobie led us up Feng's Folly. Early one morning, Fenger, a Dane, had assaulted this solo and was found by his friends in the evening wedged in the top chimney. His climb starts up an angle in the wall, wanders up reasonably between excellent stances until it lands you at the foot of an overhanging chimney, perhaps 60 feet high. This is the way through the overhangs and the crux of the climb, not difficult if one happens to be the right size for the chimney and provided one keeps far enough out, the last move out of the chimney into a groove at an easy angle being the hardest.

A gully provides a walk-off into the bed of the gorge in which the stream forms a series of rocky pools. A huge rock divides two such pools, the upper being easy of access and the Ladies' Pool, the lower and larger requires a dive or a climb to get into it. Chimneying down between water-worn rocks was reasonable but chimneying up with back, feet and hands wet proved much more formidable and abrasive. H.E. unwisely selected an approach by a descending traverse; this petered out and deposited him in the water rather earlier and with more of a splash than he had intended. Meanwhile two helpful and charming lady members had built a fire and made tea on some flat rocks farther up the gorge. Here we lunched, the party growing as the other two ropes came in with a jangle of pitons and a remarkable collection of hats. South African climbers do not lunch, shivering in a cranny, off a sandwich and a bar of chocolate; they spread themselves in the sun and cook a three-course meal. This is agreeable but takes longer than our less comfortable Welsh practice. It must have been nearly four when my rope set off to climb Reunion, a climb invented by a trio of tigers after long separation. Feng's Folly had been "E," corresponding to our Very Difficult; a bit harder, say, than Avalanche. Reunion was "F" our Severe.

We were now a very international rope; Francisco, an Italian; Eddie, a Swiss; me and Tobie, a South African. Francisco believed in long run-outs. The first pitch goes up a crack on the right of a slab, then traverses delicately downwards across the slab to its left edge, then up the corner with considerable ado, then a long traverse across the top of the slab. One hundred and twenty feet of rope just sufficed owing to the crookedness of the pitch; there was much more than 120 feet of climbing.

I felt I'd been on a journey when I reached the stance. The traverse continued, airily but without difficulty, across the face for 30 feet or so, landing one on top of a flake leaning a little out from the cliff. Below one could see all too much; above was about 20 feet of vertical wall with good holds, but the farther uplook was obstructed by a jutting gable end. Up the wall I went with as stout a heart and as tight a rope as I could decently contrive. The impending roof was avoided with relative ease on the right, but hopes of an easier angle above were disappointed. Holds were solid but distant, enforcing a technique which I dislike, particularly as one's weight had to be held into, as well as hauled up, the cliff. Soon even these inadequate aids appeared to cease. On my left a large block or young tower leaned out; straight up the rock was red, vertical and repellent; on the right a line of feasible holds seemed to offer hope. The rope led resolutely upwards with a slight leftward trend; I was forbidden the right-hand escape. The action required was to place the left foot on an exiguous, steeply-sloping, "hold" on the outward face of the tower, reach round with the left hand till the fingers found a vertical crack. On these holds, which offered but very indirect resistance to gravity, the body was to be forced up till the right hand could clutch the top of the block. My arm was not long enough; I returned with difficulty to my previous holds. Research indicated that the vertical crack broke out again, though more tenuously, higher up. I got my fingers into it and pulled, grasped the top with a desperate right hand and the main difficulty, though not the main exertion, was over. The rock above was magnificent in position and gratifying in the presence of reasonable means of upward progress.

On the summit, while contentedly sucking an orange in the sunset, I complained at the prohibition of the hopeful holds leading to the right from the crux, the hopeful indications being clearly confirmed by a view from above. I was told that this right deviation was, in fact, the recognised climb, but my leader, obviously trained in the *direttissimo* tradition, preferred straight lines. The course followed was, in fact, a private variation of his own and a very fine lead.

We descended a gully into the now gloomy gorge. While doing so I grasped as a brake a substantial-looking tree only to discover painfully that it was a much overgrown nettle about 10 feet high. Mounting to our camping place we collected our scattered possessions and set off to the cars. Just below the Nek we found others brewing tea and coffee which we helped to consume. Singing broke out spontaneously, mostly British and German folk songs; Francisco sang "The Foggy, Foggy Dew" solo to great effect as a finale before we went down the hillside in the dark and sleepily back to Pretoria. There I scandalised the staff of High Commission House by my lack of luggage and by appearing at breakfast in the clothes in which I had climbed, cooked and slept throughout the weekend.

MOUNTAINEERING — AN INDIAN VIEW

G. C. JOSHI
(Bulletin No. 28 3rd Series No.1 October 1964)

The President has received the following communication:

> Wisdom Garden,
> P.O. Kapkote,
> District Almora,
> India.

Adorable Immortal Soul,

Venerably I hail you with most cordial expressions of welcome and am gay with exceeding wondrous merriment in communicating thee in black and white at this special juncture in order to press mine humble material on "Mountaineering" to the Climbers' Club for possible use.

In this connection it is subjoined that this awkward soul is engaged in research on sovereign science for the last 21 years by sojourning in various parts of India and abroad; nowadays, at the above indicated place. The thesis on "The Blissful Rose of Wisdom Garden" is the outcome of my continued and inquisitive quest after wisdom.

Further I pray thee to be abundantly benign in arranging to pass on a copy of "Mountaineering" with a view to broadcasting it over the radio for which humane deed I should feel life-long obligation to you.

If published in any journal be gracious enough to mail me a copy thereof. Please acknowledge receipt. With salutations to the Climbers' Club.

> Thy own soul,
> G. C. Joshi
> (Sovereign Science Scholar).

MOUNTAINEERING

By G. C. Joshi, Sovereign Science Scholar, Wisdom Garden, Glacier View, P.O Kapkote, District Almora, India.

Mountaineering is a divine hobby, a kingly game, a queenly subject, a perilous exercise, an aristocratic pastime, a musical glee, a magical sport, an elevating education and an angelic refreshment. The noble goal of Alpinists towards climbing the loftiest peaks could comfortably be accomplished through the cherubical weapons of constancy; purity of heart; discrimination; freedom from pride, envy, covetousness, gluttony, lust and sloth; fortitude; unhaughtiness; geniality of speech; absence of anger even on provocation; refraining from malicious gossip; absence of the feeling of self-importance; external purity; forgiveness and faith.

Monarchs, saints, scientists, philosophers, artists, poets, travellers and anglers were called upon allured and enamoured by the glamour, sublimity, scenic beauty, grace and elegance of the snow-capped peaks all over the Old World as well as the Western Hemisphere since the dawn of time. The track to snowy peaks is not strewn with roses; on the contrary, it is a path covered with thorns of hazard and peril, nevertheless, at the end of it there is the full-blown rose of mountaineering awaiting the eager-adventurous-cum-heroicly tired Alpinists thus saluting them with most cordial expressions of welcome in a spirit of meekness with a view to enlighten, humanise, refine, and elevate Alpinists' ethical, intellectual, mental and social nature as also instilling in them feelings of fraternity, truth, cosmic love, freedom, justice and equal opportunity whereby they will walk in the light of benevolence, companionableness and the hidden honey of human compassion.

In the fields of all-embracing education, international culture, global fellowship, world understanding and fraternal civilization — the role of gracious Alpinists is paramount in transforming the terrestial globe into a celestial one, thereby sending forth showers of love-embroidered prosperity, everlasting virtue and the holy grail of sublime peace to the benign souls of the Western Hemisphere as well as the Eastern.

The universe is so vast and so ageless that the life of high-spirited Alpinists can only be justified by the measure of their sacrifice, spirit of service and by becoming lovers of hospitality, lovers of goodmen, just, sober, holy, temperate, fearless, and above all, engaged in research on mountaineering craft for human illumination and nurturing congenial feelings of tenderness as well as of marvellous loving kindness towards all created beings.

'A counterblast to the perpendicular'

'Deprivation lay heavy on us in South London that summer'.
Dave Cook
(1979/80)

A COUNTERBLAST TO THE PERPENDICULAR

(extract)

HILTON YOUNG
(1912)

The hopeless irrelevance of mountaineers shows itself in their use of mountains for purposes for which they were not made; and it shows itself, too, in the habit of praising mountains for qualities of beauty which mountaineers can never see, because they can be seen from a distance only. A lover of nature with his nose in the Grépon crack is like an amateur of pictures with his nose in a Turner. The true lover of mountains should never leave the plains. "And the true lover of plains should never leave the mountains," says the mountaineer, sticking to his guns. I have not thought of an answer yet, so it will be best to change the subject, and to turn, without any more odious comparisons, to some of the positive merits of plains.

They are many, both moral and aesthetic; and first of the moral. I will say no more of less important aspects of their merits, such as the hygienic aspect. The exercise of walking is good for the health, no doubt, if it is not overdone. Immoderate indulgence in it ends in nights in which the head and the foot of the bed are confused in space, time and eternity get mixed, and the inn clock is a burden, punctuating relentlessly through evil dreams the passing of ages of fatigue. But it is not for the sake of his digestion that a true walker walks. He leaves that to the constitutionalist, a groundhog whose walks are mere bridges from a full stomach to an empty one. The real walk has higher functions. It is the ritual of a religion, a bridge from emptiness to fulness of the soul. The religion is mystical, and its ritual has the qualities which are common to the rituals of all mystical religions. There is, for instance, a family likeness between the practices of the sect of walkers and those of certain Dervish sects. There are Dervishes, they say, who obtain close communion with the Infinite by means of repetitions which induce trance. They howl, or twirl, or gaze at some near and arresting object, and presently there dawns upon them the uncreated light. A walker sets out, and, by repeating familiar movements of his legs, he leads himself by degrees into a state of great peace and content. The earth and he draw closer together, and, whether by night or day, the further he walks the better friends do they become. They become not friends only, but near relations. At starting, earth is at best his crabbed grandmother; by midday they are cousins; and when they part at the inn door they part as brothers. Could anyone walk long enough and with movements of the legs regular enough, I believe that he would find the relationship grow closer still. The object of his mystical longing would be attained, and earth and he would become one. Perhaps that may explain mysterious disappearances which have puzzled people from time to time. Someone has walked himself out of his personal identity into the ultimate unity.

Now it is in plains that this walker's trance can best be found. Path-finding on a hillside holds the attention and breaks the pace. It is the regular heel and toe of roads and fields that brings soonest the *hypnosis* which the walker wants who walks as a ritual exercise. A long day's walk in mountainous country is an affair altogether too exciting. There is seldom a minute in which there is not something happening, finding the way, or stopping to look at the view, or having whisky and sandwiches in a puddle. The mind, too, is for ever busy answering a string of tiny and tiresome questions about the business of walking, such as which lump to step on next, or which way to go round the next rock. A walk in a plain is free from those disturbances. To tramp all day in level country is to drown the mind in a calm, clear sea of stupidity. A day so spent is a continuous, unbroken thing. Under the sleepy influence of gentle, monotonous movements, consciousness stops hopping from point to point of time, striking sparks at each hop. It glides quietly through the head, the shrill chatter which at other times it makes in passing stilled to a low, musical hum; and the day when it is over lives in memory as one of those rare days which are whole days, not a collection of moments, like a day spent in some exciting occupation, nor a patchwork of morning, afternoon, and evening cemented together by meals, like a working day in town.

Plains are truly solitary places, and it is in their solitude alone that the pleasant quality of perfect silence can be found. A range of mountains is as talkative as an old wives' tea-party; the peaks chatter and shout at each other with the voices of streams and stones and avalanches, and the wind snuffles round them with distressing noises, as of blown noses. But the rustling of moorland grass and the sighing of fenland sedge serves only to remind the listener of the absence of more sociable noises. Besides, mountains never sleep. In the Alps, as in a London drawing-room, the most active social hours do not begin till sunset. Like London hostesses, the mountains are visited all night, as the poet justly says, by troops of wheeling stars. To see nature at rest, you must see the moon shining in the marshes upon the sleeping armies of the reeds. This restfulness and sleepiness of plains is bound up with another and a kindred quality which is theirs alone, the quality of age. Big mountains, and especially big snow mountains, look so painfully new. The Weisshorn, for instance, with its glittering ice and snow, seems to have come straight from the confectioner. It cries aloud for its base of wedding-cake. Compare with its spick and span neatness the look of a landscape in the fens. There, in every square foot of untidy soil, rough and blotchy with old age, you see how the ferments of earth have been at work since time began. Nature is dying of senile decay, and beginning to rot. The active forces of wind and water have stopped hurrying about, scooping out valleys and tearing down crags. They are worn out and resting, pleasanter companions in that state than when you meet them hard at work, like busy young professional persons, clearing away Mont Blanc.

EAST ANGLIAN MOUNTAINEERING

(A report made by Raymond Lister at the Annual Dinner in February)

RAYMOND LISTER
(1962)

Mountaineering is a comparatively new sport in the fenlands of eastern England, yet its progress there has been, to say the least, spectacular, whether it be in the form of simple rodham climbing, or of full-scale attacks on such classic climbs as the tower of Ely Cathedral or the peak of Shippea Hill. The local Sherpas are men of skill, loyalty and courage, and excellent base camps abound.

There are many centres from which operations may be conducted — Prickwillow, Stuntney, Burnt Fen, Bluntisham-cum-Willingham — these are but a few, each one of which has excellent climbs in its vicinity, which range from a comparatively simple ascent like that of the Aldreth Causeway, to a steep and difficult climb like that of the Car Dyke.

Such, indeed, is the variety, that the well-known Denver Sherpa, "Boggy" Black, was able to make the ascent of Brandon Creek and Burnt Fen Pumphouses on the same evening in the summer of 1947, producing from his colleague, "Sluice" Parker, the witty if ribald comment: "What — *twice* a night at *your* age?"

Alas, the great "Boggy" overdid it in the end. In endeavouring, during the latter part of the 1949 climbing season, to add a third climb to his record — that of Stretham pumphouse — he fell into a hole of peat and had to be dug out by the local fire-brigade, who were brought to the spot by his pitiful cries for assistance. However, when at last he was dug out, he had expired, and his body was reverently carried back to March on a litter, later to be buried at an impressive funeral service conducted by the Reverend Mr. Knocker Carter of the Ebenezer and Mount Tabor Primitive Baptist Chapel at Manea.

Today "Boggy" Black's memory is perpetuated by a magnificent cast-iron urinal, erected by public subscription in the market square at March.

It will not be out of place at this point to attempt a description of this remarkable erection, the design of the Six Mile Bottom architect, "Windy" Tighte-Hoppitt. Nothing more well-bred or genteel could be imagined than this convenient arbour of cast-iron gothick lattice, surmounted as it is by busts of their late Royal Highnesses Prince Albert of Saxe-Coburg and Albert Edward, Prince of Wales, each attired in costumes of highland chieftains of the time of the '45.

Within, symbolising purity, a fountain plays, and around the top of the inside of the structure representations of palm and pine are interwoven, while each gothick arch, which encloses an imitation marble vestibule bearing the legend:

"DOULTON LAMBETH", is supported by two caryatids, one formed in the likeness of the late Mr. Rudyard Kipling, the other in that of the late Lord Lugard.

Lest its grandeur should cause us to forget its purpose, the urinal is finished off with a life-size statue of "Boggy" Black himself, attired as was his wont in a panama hat, shirt sleeves, braces, an abdominal belt and plimsolls. Beneath is the inscription, in those beautiful and immortal words of Alfred Austin, Poet Laureate:

"Along the wires the electric message came —
" 'He is not better — he is much the same'."

Nothing better could have been provided to celebrate the memory of the great Sherpa, being placed as it is, in the proximity of the ancient hostelry "The Ship and Shovel", where "Boggy" used to relax of an evening to play skittles or dominoes with his friends — those very friends who may now, by means of this monument, combine relief with reverence.

The special equipment used by fenland climbers is not without interest and may be described. First the dress. It is not so much storm, snow and blizzard with which the fenland climber must contend, as flood and mud. Accordingly, the usual dress is a bathing costume worn beneath a macintosh, with Wellington boots as the standard footwear and a sou'wester for covering the head. These have the essential combination of protection against the elements, combined with ease of discardment, plus a modicum of decency.

All these properties are essential, as witness the occasion when the Westley Waterless climber, "Flushy" Fulcher, in climbing Upware-Saint Uncumber church tower, lost his footing when negotiating the treacherous gargoyle above the east cwm of the roof, and was precipitated into the watery lode beneath. Fortunately he had the presence of mind to discard his macintosh, Wellington boots and sou'wester in the course of his descent, but he had unfortunately forgotten to don his bathing costume before setting out, and was arrested for indecent exposure of his person by the local constable, "Ginger" Gotobed, who was thus provided with his first case for many years.

The *chic* form of bathing wear is, of course, the type fashionable in the early 1920's, and made of loosely-knitted wool with bright horizontal stripes, and reaching to above the knees and beneath the elbows. This makes for absolute decency, so long as it is not shrunk too drastically in the wash.

Crampons and other equipment are rarely seen. Most of the buildings in the climbers' repertory are constructed of clunch, a comparatively soft material, and the natural soil is innocent of hard, rocky substances, and consists, indeed, mainly of black peat, for negotiating which snowshoes are eminently suitable or, failing that, tennis racquets may be affixed to the feet by means of straps.

One item of equipment peculiar to fenland climbing is that ingenious tool known as the spade and becket. Originally used for cutting blocks of peat, it may, however, be used for many other things, from the cutting of footholds in flood-banks to the excavation of a sheltered camping position in the peat itself. In the words of Alexander Pope:

"Let spades be trumps! she said, and beckets they were."

A fishing net also is useful for providing provisions from the natural waterways and man-made canals with which the area abounds. Nobody who has climbed the floodbanks of the Isle of Ely can forget the fragrant and inviting smell of sticklebacks being roasted over a roaring peat fire on a cold night — and this is yet another instance of the use to which the spade and becket may be put, for it makes a splendid roasting-plate. One should be careful in selecting fish for comestibles, and one should see to it that the diet is varied. Sticklebacks *can* pall after a time and with lampreys and pike in such abundance it would be a pity to spoil one's palate by over-indulgence. For those interested in the niceties of technique in stickleback fishing I can do no better than refer them to my own publication, *Tiddlers, or, the Arte of Fishing for Sticklebacks* (London, 1958) in which equipment, dress, and method are all described in great detail.

While on the subject of the fauna in the area it will be convenient to mention the district's particular form of yeti, known locally as the Fen Tiger or abominable fenman (Linnaeus: *Homo Leggbourkeiana).* Traces of the spoor of this creature have been found in great abundance in the peat and mud of the area, and many are the climbers who have laid claim to seeing it. The creature is extremely shy and suspicious, however, and one must be careful to approach it with quiet kindliness. It may be recognised by its ambling, shuffling gait, its half-erect bearing and its expression of extreme vacancy and preoccupation. Its cries are remarkably akin to our own language, but are emitted in a low, guttural growl as if a hot potato has recently been placed in its mouth.

These creatures congregate each evening in communal dens where they seem to amuse themselves by throwing pieces of feathered, pointed metal into discs of cork, marked with radiating stripes. This peculiarity was recently dealt with at length in the *March, Stuntney and Reach Archaeological Society's Journal* by the Reverend Dribble Dampier-Gribble, F.R.G.S. and Bar, in an article entitled "A Curious Survival of Palaeolithic Fertility Rites at Rump Stuntney". Incidentally the article is also of interest in that the learned footnotes occupy three times as much space as the article itself.

Access to the fens may be accomplished in many ways — by motor-car, by railway, on foot, and, more recently, by flying-machine. But the latter is not very useful to the climber, who often will have to take comparatively heavy equipment with him. Best of all, perhaps, is the local train service, which, although not noted for punctuality, does afford one relaxed views of the country with its vast areas of level agricultural land, and every mile or so the sight of a tempting climb, which may be a steep dyke, a pump house, a church or one of the smock mills that still form landmarks in many parts of the area. The trains themselves have a pleasant old-world atmosphere about them which at once transports one back into a more comfortable and spacious age. The cast-iron seats are upholstered in bilious-green plush, and in the first-class compartments spittoons disguised as footstools are provided, although the railway authorities insist upon referring to them as *salivaria*. The carriages, which are illuminated by safety-lamps of a type invented and patented by Sir Humphry Davy, are decorated with crimson and gold lincrusta paper, and are embellished by framed watercolour views of such subjects as Grunty Fen in carnival week, or Burnt Fen in a November mist.

If one is lucky enough to be on a corridor train, a refreshment saloon will almost certainly be provided, where one can purchase, at reasonable terms, the best arrowroot and Garibaldi biscuits, to be washed down with a mug of Messrs. Epps's well-known cocoa. Moustache cups are available for those in need.

Could one imagine a better means of transport into one of England's finest climbing districts? The horseless carriage and the flying machine simply could not do justice to it. May the railway long continue to provide this service.

FROM THE CATALOGUE OF THE C. C. C. LTD. (CRAZY CLIMBERS COMBINE)

H. E. L. PORTER
(1926)

THE GRADUATED BOULDER

You go from office straight to climb, and find
Your flabby muscles and your lack of wind
Make the first day an agony. The fact is
You need a rock at home on which to practise.
"Practice makes perfect" runs the ancient adage;
So why not come and spend an hour at Gladidge,
And see our graduated garden-boulders,
Modelled exclusively by expert moulders,
According to our clients' own designs.
Stock patterns also kept in several lines
E.g., "The Lliwedd," twenty different routes,
Two made for rubbers, all the rest for boots
Or for the Cumbrian expert there's "The Pillar";
None but an active anthropoid gorilla
Could quite exhaust its possibilities.
All these, and others (mark our enterprise)
Supplied in granite, gabbro, Dolomite,
Or ferro-concrete, or Labradorite,
In various qualities, to suit all purses:
No business done with minors or their nurses!

A NEW CLIMB

TO THE EDITOR OF THE *CLIMBERS' CLUB JOURNAL*

(Vol. II No. 7 March 1900)

Sir, It has long been a source of grief to climbers living in the south that there are no climbs within easy distance of London. I should like to call the attention of the members of the Climbers' Club to the fact that a problem of considerable merit has recently been discovered in the city itself, and was climbed for the first time on March 1st, by a gentleman whose name I have been unable to learn, though I was an admiring witness of his ascent, and able to obtain a sketch of the finish. I trust if this gentleman is a member of the Club, he will not allow his modesty to keep us in ignorance of the fact, and that he will excuse my having, somewhat presumptuously, taken upon myself to describe his climb. The new climb is situated in front of the Mansion House, and cannot well be overlooked when approaching either by Cheapside or Queen Victoria Street. It is within five minutes of at least six railway stations, and is sure to be popular.

The problem was attacked on March 1st by a party of two, the second man starting when the leader had reached the summit. No rope was used. The leader swarmed up the lower part of the climb, and, standing on tip-toe on the hold immediately under the overhanging boulder, was just able to grasp the knob on the summit, and skilfully drew himself up over the overhanging portion, till he was able to seat himself on the top — a remarkably neat performance when the unreliable nature of the rock and the scarcity of holds is considered.

He was greeted with enthusiastic cheers from the spectators, the neighbourhood being rather crowded on that occasion. The second man was unable to pass the overhanging boulder, and, having put his head through the climb, and sent down a quantity of loose material, he wisely gave up the attempt.

Future climbers should endeavour to avoid certain rather obtrusive handholds which they will find at the base of the climb.

Yours truly,

F. E. R.

Mike Browell on Suicide Wall Route 1 (E2), Idwal, July 1981. Photo: Browell Collection.

Above: 'Hot' Henry Barber (left) and Al Harris on Gogarth for an ABC TV (US) programme on British sea cliffs in June 1976. Photo: John Cleare.

Below: 'Positively Chris Bonington's last fling in the margarine world'. John Cleare filming a TV commercial for Blue Band Margarine on Lavaredo Wall (VS) in September 1970. Photo: Ken Wilson/Cleare Collection.

Roy Smith of the Rock and Ice, one of the sherpas for the BBC TV live outside broadcast from Red Wall, Gogarth at Easter 1966. Photo: John Cleare.

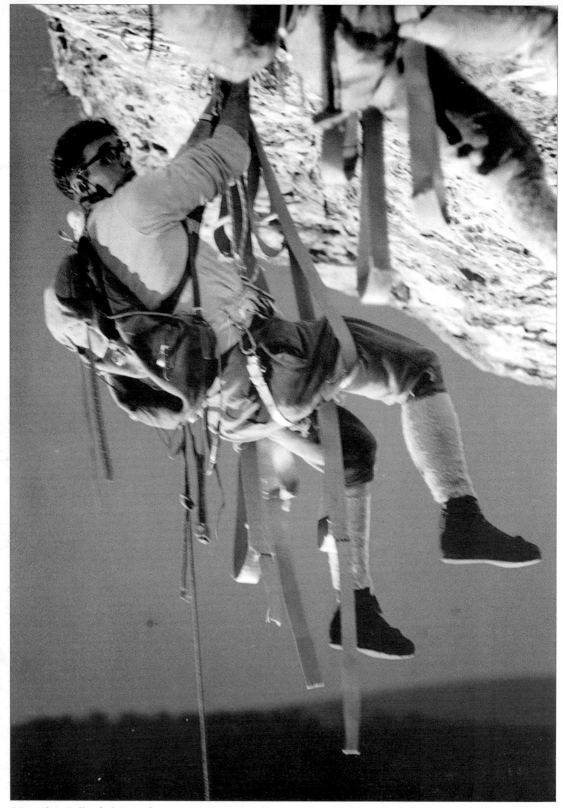

'Mac the Telly fighting for survival in the glare of floodlights after dark during the BBC TV Kilnsey Crag outside broadcast in July 1964'. Photo: John Cleare.

SANDINISTA

DAVE COOK
(1979/80)

Deprivation lay heavy on us in South London that summer.

In hearts made mean in smoky weekend rooms, it was hard to find much charity for Monday morning phone calls that crowed exultant descriptions of days of wine and gritstone. Other people's hit lists fell like salt into the wounds of envy, rubbed in deep by clumsy good intentions. "Christ, Cooky, you should have been there!"

Steve and I weren't. We too had our sports plans, but time was scarcer than a pint of bitter-tasting beer in London. We were stuck close to home.

Stolen hours on canal walls, in sports centres and on sandstone gave brief respite, but they were not as satisfying as some other substitutes I know. Clearly, something had to be done

Pigott, when he inserted a chockstone and used it for an aid on the first ascent of his climb on Cloggy, wrote, "The sole responsibility for the conception and execution of the devilish plan was Linnell's". Anyway, if he didn't, he meant to. I'll do likewise. To climb at Warlingham chalk quarry was Steve's idea.

Steve is in many ways the discovery of the decade. Every ageing climber yearns to find a young apprentice who can be pointed at the nasty ones. 'Off the peg' seconds are common enough, but 'off the peg' leaders are a prize indeed. He drank at the Prince of Wales, and idly enquired if we were going on any trips because he would like to try his hand. Some months later we tied him onto the rope at the foot of his first route, Undercracker (E1) at Baggy Point, and he padded up it with embarrassing ease. To this day, I'm still not sure if Steve's enthusiasm to climb at Warlingham was an index of his inexperience or his vision.

One and a half miles south of Purley, on the east side of the A22, a giant handful of chalk has been scooped from the hillside. A derelict factory blocks the entrance between viaduct pillars. Not an old Pennine relic this, smoothed and legitimised by the passing years, but a brash, tatty-splintered, pre-fabricated box, slightly shocking in its deindustrialised nakedness.

What lies beyond is that classic habitat, inadequately dealt with by science: 'quarry bottoms'. Here abounds that unique mixture — old bits of iron, elderberry bushes, tyres, dumped cars, small boys and men with airguns — among which climbers feel so much at home.

The far right-hand quarry wall is eighty feet high, vertical, giving one magnificent line, a face crack, almost a unique feature on chalk. You can see it from the road: a riven tower, not unlike a Stoney Middleton buttress. But either cracks don't wink down south, or people don't respond to their advances.

Other steep and overhanging rock abounds, but it is frightening to go close, let alone touch it. The crack, which we called Sandinista, is different. In the old days, an L.P. cover would have described its 'come hither' voice.

We abseiled down onto a steep fan of chalk. I was going to call it scree, but it was more like avalanche debris. Lester Cook, my eight year old son, the third member of our party, rolled snowballs down it, while we rigged up gigantic top ropes from tiny trees at the top

"Dad, the police are coming." Lester was overdramatising things, for a single constable, perspiring in the hot sun, his uniform picking up snow flakes each time he stumbled, approached us up the slope. To our surprise he told us he was in the Metropolitan Police Climbing Section and was glad to see some 'experts' here.

Getting talking, we asked his name. "P.C. Everest", was his rather anxious reply. You could hear the backing group change key, and the string section begin their build-up.

Now, with some replies you can see them coming for miles. They hang, looming, waiting to take verbal form. "This is Sherpa Tensing", I said, introducing Steve. P.C. Everest's eyes narrowed, his face taking on that tired, world-weary, East London look that Cockneys do so well. Even Lester got in on the act. "Dad, where's his ice axe?"

I've not seen one set up like that since long ago at school. A small, new pupil was asked his name. "Paine, Sir", was his reply, "Ivor, Sir".

Sandinista inhabited the same bizarre world. Usually on loose rock a crack is sanctuary. Deep jams will hold when the surface crumbles. However, chalk is nothing if not consistent. If it moves on the outside, it moves in deep as well. Clenched fists caused cracks to become chimneys. Steve, who also does karate, was at an advantage, able to fashion holds at will.

Each probing hand triggered a landslide of chalk dust down the crack. My mind flashed back to the Black Cleft on Cloggy fifteen years before. The body formed a water conduit between hand and trouser leg. Now, on this white cleft, chalk dust followed the same route.

Each move was delicate, tense. You had to hold both yourself on, and the rock together, at the same time. I suppose on solid rock the route would have been 4c/5a technically, but the adjectival grading does not yet exist that can describe its overall character. There is no protection, but with a top rope the only risk is having shovelfuls of chalk dust dumped on you. I've seen plenty of climbers looking pale at the top of climbs, but never 'white as a sheet' before.

But, believe it or not, if you sidle your way up this strange cleft, you will probably be back. Adventure in London comes in many forms. This one is worth a try.

CHALK: A MINIATURE ANTHOLOGY

(extract)

E. C. PYATT
(1952)

Considered as rock climbing, chalk will undoubtedly be very dangerous and will require highly developed safeguarding tactics and particularly thoughtful distributions of limbs and of holds. It will no longer be possible to separate danger from difficulty, at present one of the most established traditions of British climbing. It will need to be done, particularly near Beachy Head, not at the best time of day and season of the year, but when there are no crowds at the top to complicate the problems. It will be as finely situated as climbing anywhere.

The above generalities deal with the sea-cliff aspect. The climber who has a quarry close to his home will certainly try it at least once whatever the rock. Much miscellaneous climbing of chalk must have taken place under these circumstances, without any record being left of the doing.

Almost Prehistory, 1858. "The Hampshire chalk-pits gave fine opportunities for breaking one's neck, and the chalk cliffs of Swanage, Scratchells Bay, and Beachy Head provided me with quite sensational risks. There are bits on all these places as dangerous as anything in the Alps. To glissade down a steep, hard, chalk-slope is not easy, and steps cut in the treacherous, crumbly material are not too reliable. I didn't kill myself, but I had some very close escapes." (J. Stogdon — *A.J.* May, 1916.)

Off to the Alps, 1860. "As we steamed out into the Channel, Beachy Head came into view, and recalled a scramble of many years ago. With the impudence of ignorance, my brother and I, schoolboys both, had tried to scale that great chalk cliff. Not the head itself — where sea-birds circle, and where the flints are arranged in orderly parallel lines — but at a place more to the east, where a pinnacle called the Devil's Chimney had fallen down. Since then we have been often in dangers of different kinds, but never have we more nearly broken our necks than upon that occasion." (Edward Whymper — *Scrambles in the Alps.*)

A Sticky Paste. "... the white cliffs of Old England have proved themselves too much for many of her sons. Chalk is a very troublesome material to climb; it is loose, breaks away, and if wet, either with rain or the draining of the land above, forms a sticky paste, which, lodging between the boot nails, renders them of little use. Doubtless many of those who get into difficulties are only shod for a walk on the promenade or pier, but chalk cliffs must not be treated carelessly even by the well equipped." (Charles Pilkington in C. T. Dent — *Mountaineering,* Badminton Library, 1892.)

Traverses. "Though chalk can hardly be regarded as a good rock for climbing, much excellent practice can be obtained on it. As a general rule, it is only sufficiently solid for real climbing for the first 20 feet above high-water mark, though here and there 40 feet of fairly trustworthy rock may be found. These sections of hard chalk are invariably those which at their base are washed by the sea at high tide; all others are soft and crumbly.

Whilst any considerable ascent, other than up the extremely steep slopes of grass, which sometimes clothe the gullies and faces, is out of the question, traverses of great interest and no slight difficulty are frequently possible for considerable distances. A good *objectif* may be found in the endeavour to work out a route to the various small beaches that are cut off from the outer world by the high tide and cliffs. The best instances of this sort of work are to be found along the coast to the eastward of Dover. Between the ledges by which these traverses are effected and the beach below are some of the hardest *mauvais pas* with which I am acquainted." (W. P. Haskett Smith *Climbing in the British Isles — England*, 1894.)

Etheldreda's Pinnacle. "Directly I saw this magnificent pyramid I determined to climb it at once. Two chimneys, side by side, and since named Castor and Pollux, presented the most obvious route to the ridge joining the pinnacle with the mass of the cliff. The north one (Castor) looked easy, though it was almost entirely filled with chalk dust of the consistency of fine flour, caked on the top, and having blocks of various sizes in the middle. All this, at the touch, came down, and the whole weight jammed on my legs, which were well into the chimney. A convulsive series of amoeboid movements enabled me to get out over the debris, when it immediately thundered down, leaving me in a very comfortable gap. I was soon over the jammed stone and on to the ridge. My friend refused to follow, but as he was roped I put on sudden pressure, and he — well — changed his mind. When he reached the ridge I went on for the north face. This has several natural steps, but the first two yards required a few gentle touches with the magic wand, the chalk being very hard. Thence the route lay westwards to the north-west corner and then back again to the shoulder, only one step being at all awkward. The summit consists of a big square block, which rocked and swayed under me as I sat down upon it." (E. A. Crowley — *S.M.C. Journal*, May, 1895.)

Cuillin Crack. "This chimney is nearly 200 feet high, and affords the finest and most difficult piece of climbing that I have yet found in the whole neighbourhood. It is broken at two places, one near the bottom, and the other about 100 feet higher up. The first break presents terrible difficulty, but after incredible exertion it yielded, and then I got a leg and an arm jammed, and managed to wriggle up about 60 feet higher. At this point the rope and my strength were alike exhausted, some four hours, without any sort of rest, having already passed. Foothold and handhold there were none that could be relied upon to support Grant's additional weight, if any pressure were to be put on the rope. There was nothing for it but to let down a rope from above, or to descend with ignominy and much toil. So Grant sped away to invoke the assistance of the coastguard, and meanwhile I sat wedged in a most uncomfortable position, at the bottom of the second break, up to which I had struggled while waiting Grant's return. And so presently a rope was let down from above..." (E. A. Crowley, *ibid.*)

The Devil's Chimney — 11th July, 1894. "After lunch at the Beachy Head Hotel, we followed the usual high-level route to Pisgah, and then proceeded to do the Tooth as before, of course in much less time than on the first ascent. On this Grant 'fixed himself' — a humorous term we sometimes employ — and I went down the ridge into the Gash, 'fixed myself,' and began my steps. The chalk is much firmer than on the Tooth, but the N. face is, if not undercut, at least vertical, the W. overhangs, and the E. is about 70° if not more. On the N. E. corner, therefore, three steps were cut, going as high as possible to save subsequent work. Five times I tried to cross the Gash, but with no decent handhold it is hardly to be expected that one can pull one's self up to a vertical wall. One chance, however remained. I scooped a hole out in the E. face, inserted my chin and hauled. I had not shaved for a day or two, so was practically enjoying the advantages of Mummery spikes." (E. A. Crowley, *ibid.*)

Coastguard Duties. "Beachy Head is a very fine bold chalk cliff, the first ascent of which is made about once in every two years, if we may believe what we see in the papers. The truth is that there is a treacherous incline of some 600 feet, formed of chalk and grass, both very steep and often danger-ously slippery and during the Eastbourne season the coastguards at the top find their principal occupation in supplying mechanical assistance to exhausted clamberers." (W.P. Haskett Smith. *Climbing in the British Isles — England,* 1894.)

Quarries in a Rock-less Land. "... within two miles of Cambridge are chalk pits which give a specialized sort of climbing and a very pleasant Sunday afternoon's sport as well. It is climbing in miniature, but within their modest height the climbs contain a surprising variety of problems, and they give on a small scale practice in many departments of mountaineering. It is not mere freak climbing, bouldering on peculiar rock; indeed, it can teach a good deal in the way of balance technique. Rush and grab methods simply will not work on a rock of extremely variable quality; for even at its best each hold needs testing, and the climber will do well to maintain as many points of attachment as possible." (E. J. C. Kendall — *Cambridge Mountaineering,* 1934.)

THE LIFT

M. W. HARVEY
(1958)

I heaved my rucksack onto the back seat of the car, climbed in beside the driver, who was a witty-looking business-man of about 35, and was whisked away on another "hitch" of my journey to Wales.

After swapping cigarettes, destinations, and small chat, the driver's curiosity overcame him.

"Why *do* you go climbing, then?" he asked.

I took a deep breath, and prepared myself.

"I'm not exactly sure myself. You see, I give people different reasons according to who they are. You can't carry on an intellectual conversation with a truck-driver and it's no use telling a man with a deformity that you enjoy the physical sensation of movement on a climb."

"What category do I come under?" he asked drily, his eyes on the road as it twisted out of Corwen.

"People that I really try and explain to," I said. "To start with, lots of people imagine that 'getting to the top' is the chief aim, which it is, in mountaineering in the classical sense, I suppose."

"Like Everest," he suggested.

"Exactly" — I became enthusiastic — "and the underlying thought of getting to the top carried on long after the classical Alpine peaks were all climbed, and climbers in Wales before the first World War would almost always go to the top of their mountain after climbing a crag on it. Nowadays they return to the bottom and climb up the same crag a different way, or simply go home satisfied."

I paused as the car checked behind a coughing cement lorry before swinging out and past it, and strove to find a way of expressing myself simply.

"I think I climb for the reason I mentioned before," I said, "because I get physical pleasure out of the movements, or — this is more what I mean — because I like making something difficult seem easy."

I sat back, pleased with such an obscure-sounding approach to the subject, and half wished he would drop it.

"But that's obvious," he said. "It's just technique, probably mixed up with a bit of showmanship, too. You don't climb because you like climbing, but because you like practising your technique."

That gave me time to think and while I thought I observed him out of the corner of my eye, and caught him smiling the crafty smile of the well-prepared arguer; of the man who has yet another chockstone in his pocket.

"I suppose you're right," I said, vaguely, playing for time, "because I like skiing and sailing and driving, and they all require a special technique.

But there must be more to it than that, else people would simply swap from one pastime to another, because your *technique* is a common factor."

He clucked quite distinctly, and I looked to see if he had a beard that he was laughing into.

"That's my argument," he said, "and you're arguing back to front. You're supposed to be telling me why you climb. There must be other reasons besides this universal technique, then, such as love of the high hills, or some 'psycho' reason, or what have you."

He swung his car over the Waterloo bridge at Bettws-y-Coed, and as he did so I seemed to see in him a glimpse of someone I had seen before, but the illusion passed, and we were on the open road again, in the dusk.

"I'll tell you what," I said, rather abruptly. "You won't find many absolutely pure rock-gymnasts. Nearly all climbers like hill walking and" — I searched for a phrase — "Greater Mountaineering, of which rock-climbing is only a part, though admittedly a large one. You see what I mean?"

He considered a moment.

"That's so," he said. "Now I like a walk and I like the sea — I was born on the Essex coast — so naturally I like walking by the sea."

This was a new angle.

"Um. What you are saying, then, is that man's choice of pastimes isn't limited by what he's good at, but by what he is attracted to, possibly for reasons formed during his boyhood? But I never even saw a mountain until I was fourteen, and I was crazy about climbing long before that. How do you explain that? And," I added triumphantly, "I sailed on the sea long before that, and liked it, and I still do."

He was piloting the car silently down the long twisting road into Capel Curig, and I knew time was short, and suddenly I saw the answer to my own question.

"But I know myself. I used to haunt the seashore so much when I couldn't scrounge a boat-trip that I got to be pretty expert on the local sandstone cliffs. In fact I did some things there, one or two out of necessity, that I still find hard. And besides that, I've always liked running and hiking, and I suppose hiking plus rock-gymnastics equals mountaineering."

I stopped, short of words, and felt slightly foolish.

"What you're trying to say," he said ruminatively, "is this. You like climbing because you like the sensation of consciously doing it well; you like exercising your technique, in fact. You acquired this technique by climbing on your local cliffs, to which, paradoxically, you were attracted by a love of the sea, and naturally applied it to mountaineering because you also liked rough country and hard going. And when you took up mountaineering you realised you were right in your choice because everything clicked. You liked the people, the scenery (who doesn't, apart from Doctor Johnson?) and you found you were good at it."

I nodded, surprised at his insight.

"That's about it," I said.

"If you'd had the use of a boat when you were roaming the cliffs, you'd probably never have come climbing; or if there were no cliffs."

"Like Essex." I said, as the headlights plunged down over the tumbled blocks below Gorphwysfa and we purred down towards the Cromlech Bridge.

"Yes," he said abstractedly, "there aren't any cliffs at Clacton." He navigated the bridge with the sureness of foreknowledge, and I turned to ask him how often he travelled by that road, but he was still musing.

"I can't think why *I* took it up," he said, and turned into Ynys Ettws.

'Toasting the Club'

"Let us," he concluded, "drink to the health of the Climbers' Club, both for its own sake, and for its infinite possibilities. The triumphs of mountaineering are advancing with rapid strides. Its literature is increasing by leaps and bounds. Let it be ours to uphold what is best and noblest in the traditions of our craft, and to determine that the future of mountaineering shall be worthy, alike of its present and of its past."

Report of the President C. E. Mathews's 'Toast to the Club'

(Vol. I No. 4 June 1899)

'TO THE HEALTH OF THE CLUB...'

C. E. MATTHEWS
(Vol. II No. 8 June 1900)

After the customary loyal toasts, the Chairman, rising to propose "Success and Prosperity to the Climbers' Club," said:

"Gentlemen, and friends and colleagues of the Climbers' Club. It becomes my duty, as it is certainly my pleasure, to propose to you the now time-honoured toast of "Success and prosperity to the Climbers' Club." I do not suppose that I ever before in my life commenced a speech with an apology, but I have recently passed through a rather severe illness — the first I have ever had. I do not object to other people being ill — that seems to be the ordinary, but part of the inscrutable decree of Providence — but I object to being ill myself. (Laughter.) Unfortunately, I am not yet strong, and if I should be deficient to-night in any of those qualities which you have a right to expect from your President, I am sure that I can rely with confidence upon your forbearance and your consideration. (Hear, hear.) Gentlemen, a few weeks ago I found myself in Naples, and, true to the traditions of our craft, my first business was to go up Vesuvius. You may like to know how mountaineering is conducted in that interesting portion of the globe. Well, on the Naples side of the mountain there is a funicular railway, belonging to Messrs. Cook & Son, by which the ascent is ordinarily made. I need not say that it was impossible for your President to attempt to attain any elevation by such improper means. (Laughter.) On the Pompeii side of the mountain a zigzag road is constructed through the soot and lava, which is made available for ponies. (Laughter.) I do not hesitate to say that I ascended on horse-back — (Laughter.); and when I reached a spot about 300 feet from the summit I was stopped by a gendarme, and he informed me that such were the exigencies of Italian finance that, before I could proceed to the crater, I must pay a tax of four francs to the Italian Government. Well, I paid the money — (Laughter.); but I trust it will be long before an English Chancellor of the Exchequer resorts to such unholy devices for raising the wind at the expense of the tourist and the mountaineer."

WELSH NOTES

P. Y. G.
(Vol. II No.5 September 1899)

Will no one go and explore the climb upon Moel Hebog ? As one stands at the door of the Saracen's Head at Beddgelert, the cliffs of the mountain facing you invite discussion, and an hour and a half is sufficient to bring you to the cairn at the top. The climbs, of course, are on the north east face, and while there is plenty of work to be done, there is certainly one descent which, but for about eight feet, can be used, by a perambulator. Someone should make a serious examination of the whole cliff.

FOOTBRIDGE REPAIR

E. RAYMOND TURNER
(Vol.III No. 9 September 1900)

The footbridge over the Glaslyn river (near Llyn Llydaw), which was destroyed in the early part of the present year, is being replaced at the expense of the Climbers' Club. The work is being carried out under the superintendence of Mr. Clee of Pen-y-Pass.

CORRESPONDENCE: GUIDE-BOOKS

J. N. MILLS
(1951)

To the Editor, *Climbers' Club Journal*
Dear Sir,
I read with horror the proposal that all the rocks of Wales should be explored *and described* in the same detail as the climbs round Helyg. Unless climbers are degenerating into gymnasts, plenty must agree with me that the most worthwhile climbing is to lead an unfamiliar route and the less one is told of technique, the more interest in finding out for oneself. The pioneers of new routes must presumably enjoy the process. Why, then, spoil the fun for others by publishing descriptions?

EDITORIAL NOTES

E. RAYMOND TURNER
(Vol. IV No.13 September 1901)

Foiled in their endeavour to disfigure the Pass of Aberglaslyn, the railway makers are now turning their attention to the Vale of Gwynant. The latest scheme is to carry an electric railway from Portmadoc to the foot of Snowdon on its south side, and although the promoters have undertaken to tunnel through the Pass of Aberglaslyn, a fresh storm of criticism has been aroused by the proposal to impound the waters of Llyn Llidau and Llyn Teyrn for the purpose of generating the electricity needed.

When the matter came before the House of Commons, Lord Balcarres, Mr. Bryce, and Mr. John Burns endeavoured to dissuade their fellow members from allowing the Dyli Falls to succumb to the same fate as the Falls of Foyers, but their eloquence was unsuccessful, and as it was believed that the railway would be abandoned if the water were not supplied at the head of the valley, the House sacrificed the mountain stream, and gave its consent to the conversion of Llyn Llidau into a reservoir.

When the Light Railways Bill was under discussion, the House of Commons inserted a provision that natural scenery was not to be injured by the construction of such lines, but we think the formation of an artificial dam across Cwm Dyli, and the interment of the Glaslyn River in pipes, may justly be considered as a wanton injury to one of the grandest pieces of natural scenery in the principality.

The inhabitants of Beddgelert are not unreasonable in their wish to have railway communication with the adjacent towns and villages, but surely this could be effected without allowing them to complete the disfigurement already so far advanced by the works at the copper mines.

COMMITTEE NOTES

A.W. ANDREWS (ED.)
(Vol. II No. 27 1905)

The memorial regarding the proposed light railway from Beddgelert to Betws-y-Coed was read, and carefully considered. It was worded as follows, and signed by 66 members:

"We, the undersigned members of the Club, have observed with regret that up to the present time no action has been taken by the Club in connection with the proposed light railway from Beddgelert to Betws-y-Coed, through Nant Gwynant and Capel Curig.

We are of opinion that the undertaking is one which adversely affects the vital interests of the Club, and that it is not yet too late to oppose it.

We therefore respectfully call upon you to take all such steps as may be necessary to enable the Club to pronounce a collective opinion, and, if so decided, to use every possible means of opposition to the scheme, and to register against it their most emphatic protest."

Letters were also read from two other members in opposition to the undertaking.

The Committee had in fact given full consideration to this matter at their meeting of the 18th March, 1904, and reached the conclusion that opposition to the scheme must be left to individual action. A petition against the railway, sent in last year, bore the signatures of a good number of members of our Club. On the 15th November last, at a meeting of the Board of Trade, the various parties were heard by counsel (including the Alpine Club), but the result was that the railway from Lake Gwynant to Betws-y-Coed was "recommended." The Committee were informed that the scheme would be officially sanctioned as a matter of course.

TELL ME NOT IN MOURNFUL NUMBERS

R. A. MALLET
(1945-46)

Begone, all those who bound from cliff to cliff,
Enmeshed in fifty yards of nylon rope,
Who finding Hard Severes not really stiff
And Avalanche a reasonable slope,
And who, without a semblance of apology
Has wished on us this blasted numerology.
But we, who climb in tennis shoes and hope,
Whose faith sustains us as we clutch and strive,
Whose need is charity and tautened rope,
Whose paradise is merely to survive,
If we should climb a Very Difficult's asperities,
We like to boast of overcoming such severities.
Come ye whose knees are gashed by every crag
Come ye, the short of breath and scant of skill,
Come, let us raise on high rebellion's flag,
Attack the weakest spot The Treasurer's till.
We are the chaps who pay the most subscriptions,
We won't have numbers; we want plain descriptions.

'LYING'

CLAUDE E. BENSON
(1929)

... Meanwhile, nothing can deprive advancing years of the inestimable opportunities they afford for artistic lying. Of course we all lie, often quite
unconsciously. A naked fact in the course of a very short time clothes itself
in frills and thereafter bedizens itself with meretricious ornament. I know a
man who kicked down a big chunk of rock one August and in the following
November assured me that it had shaved his ear. What is strange is that he
believed it, absolutely and honestly. I am not referring to these innocent
mistakes of memory. I have in my mind deliberate, calculated, joyous, artistic lying. I read all the Club *Journals*, but that which I treasure most is the
Journal of the F. R. C. C. The man who invented that noble and most valuable conception, "Climbs New and Old," can have had no idea of the Field of
Exploitation he was opening to Veterans who might be feeling out in the
cold. With a little unscrupulousness you can soon get back into the grateful
warmth. Listen!

Some time ago I was skimming through the Borrowdale List and was
quite surprised to find how many difficult climbs I had taken part in, and a
good deal disgusted to find how many I had missed. But had I missed them?
Never too late to mend. I hunted around and came on a gem, a perfect pig of
a place, at any rate in late October when it is sleeting. I used to go to the
Lakes in October mostly, so as to combine hunting with climbing. There is a
most vile buttress and after a bit you have to get round a corner. The only
way of accomplishing this seemed to be to jam your thigh in a slippery,
sleety groove, reach round, catch hold of a spout of water and pull yourself
up by it. Whether this latter were possible was not ascertained because the
leg refused to do anything but cruise greasily out of the groove. By research
I came on a full account of this climb after it had become an accomplished
fact, and I got to know all about the rest of the course. What then ?

What then? Half a dozen of the younger generation are talking climbing shop and, though they are courteous, you cannot but recognise that
they regard you as a Has-been, which, incidentally, is exactly what you are.
Moreover, you fancy that your presence may make them feel awkward, a
solecism to be amended at all hazards. Wherefore you lead the conversation
round to the desired quarter and at the proper moment break in with:

"I wonder. I wonder. Surely that can't be the place, let me see, twenty-
eight or thirty years ago, was it? Thirty, yes, thirty. That can't be the place.
No, from what you say, far too difficult."

Someone asks the desired question and you reply:

"Oh, the place where, about halfway up, rather less, you stick your leg
in a kind of slot..."

General assent. Then someone says:

"By Jove, sir, you must have been hot stuff."

"Oh, no! Oh, no! Only moderate. Not so bad. Nothing like you fellows though. Climbing's gone up — gone up."

And there you are not only back in the warmth, but in the limelight, and observe that you have never said that you got up. Observe also that no one can ask you to make good your words by doing it over again.

The assembled multitude of members and guests at the celebrations to mark the 60th anniversary of the Club's purchase of Helyg. The first successful attempt at creating a mountain hut in Britain. Photo: Ian Smith.

At the opening of the R. O. Downes Hut below Froggatt, in 1961. Left to right, Veronica (Ronnie) Phillips, Frank Fitzgerald, Mrs Downes (Bob's mum), Geoff Sutton, a dapper A. B. Hargreaves and others. Photo: Harry Pretty.

Chris Jackson (left) and Roy Small huddling round the feeble fire at Ynys Ettws, New Year 1981. Photo: Jackson Collection.

What the well-dressed climber was wearing in the early '80s. Positively Adey Hubbard's last fling in the sun-cream advertising world. Photo: Chris Jackson.

HORATIO'S HORROR

TERRY GIFFORD
(1994)

Yesterday the geese were going north
rippling their V uncertainly, high
above the moors in the sun-scoured sky.

Today the 'Golden Oldies' of the Climbers' Club
emerge under a far buttress of Birchen Edge,
white hair hidden by Joe Brown helmets

or suspiciously new woollen army caps.
Ex-WD to a man, they were killers.
They fought for this day. They offer

each other a rope, biscuits, stories
about the innocent wisdom of recruits
and a 70th birthday night on Cader Idris.

Arriving late, I heave my 'winter fat'
onto rock until halted by the roof
of *Horatio's Horror.* I can't hang left.

'Would you prefer your lunch sent up?'
I descend under tension from rope and hubris.
Later it is led by a man of sixty-two.

Mike Burt, even bolder, strides out right,
exposed to the face of *Nelson's Nemesis.*
Seconding, I can only marvel at how

fingers fit the tilted gritstone grooves
of the final moves and the mind is calmed
by the wide sky, that untracked wild moor.

Such a day a sailor (who's not a climber)
might give his right arm for! Two drops of blood
on the rocking chockstone of *Victory Vice*

are all the price we pay today, plus past
horrors buried under sincere politeness:
as they leave they thank each other.

Mike Banks says, 'Do you think you could write
a pithy poem about today?'
Obviously not. But thank you. Thank you.

PRISONERS OF WAR

F. A. PULLINGER
(1941)

Six members of the Club are prisoners of war in Germany. They are:

Lt. J. S. M. Bingham.
2nd-Lieut. L. S. Deuchar, No.1001, Oflag V B.
Capt. B. G. Evers, No.1561, Stalag XX A.
Lt. R. M. Longstaff, No.945, Stalag XXI D.
Capt. W. W. Price Rees, No.351, Oflag VII D.
Major E. M. Viney, No.877, Oflag VII C/H.

Originally they were thought to be mostly in Oflag VII and the Club has been
sending parcels of mountaineering books to Major Viney in that camp for
distribution.

HOW BIG A CLUB?

A. K. RAWLINSON
(1955)

Domestically, the Club has again been considering the problem of its continually increasing membership. Increasing size must gradually change the character of the Club, for a large club cannot have the intimacy and fellowship of a small one, which the majority of our members probably prefer. But the problem of numbers in the Club is but a symptom of the larger problem of numbers on the hills. In one way one welcomes the popularization of climbing; one likes to see more people enjoying a good thing. And yet each would enjoy it more if other climbers were fewer. But welcome or not, and perhaps it is selfish not to welcome it, popularization is a fact. And it brings a dilemma to our Club. Either the Club continues to multiply, gradually losing its character, or it limits its membership. But this can only be done by such drastic restriction of recruitment as would change the Club's character much more radically and, to most of us, distastefully, than size alone. A waiting list would keep out young climbers in their most active years and sever our traditional links with the University and similar clubs. A formal qualification of climbing achievement would have to be stiff to be an effective sieve, and would keep out many for whom the Club has traditionally found room, who make up in enthusiasm what they may lack in rock climbing technique and who are often among our most loyal and best loved members. The Committee's policy is therefore to continue expansion at a limited rate, maintaining the traditional criteria for membership but keeping our door open to recruits known to fulfil them. Of two discomfortables oedema is preferable to hara-kiri.

RUBBERS

A. W. ANDREWS
(1941)

Who was it raised rebellion first and went
One step beyond the immemorial law,
And freed us from the bonds of precedent
Which fixed the footgear that all climbers wore?
Was it perhaps some atavistic urge
From ancestors who made their cave fool-proof,
So that the way to enter or emerge
Was by an overhang upon the roof,
On which the heavy tread of Alpine boots
Would have been little use for surface worn
And smoothed by constant trial of new routes,
Where even naked feet in time had torn
The lesser knobs away in scrambling through?

And did he feel his skin was not so tough
As he could wish and used a rubber shoe
With a thin sole, to grip on smooth or rough?
And turned our climbing on this downward trend,
Towards the use of artificial aid
By those who had forgotten the true end
Of mountain climbing for which boots were made?

MEMORIES OF LLIWEDD

G. W. Y.
(1955)

To the Editor, *Climbers' Club JournaL*
Dear Editor,
The recollections by A.W.A. in your last *Journal,* describing his pre-historic explorations on Lliwedd, have been most welcome; and may we hope that they are the forerunner of the book so long awaited from the originator of Cornish climbing and a pioneer on Welsh cliffs?

In this hope, may I reassure him beforehand upon a few points of doubt, raised in his article ? Was it not a " Girdle " of the whole buttresses, and not the " Garter" of the east buttress, which he climbed with such rapidity, and with H.O. Jones? H.O. was killed in 1912, and the Garter was first climbed in 1919; nor could the Garter traverse, with our then technique, have been taken "touch and pass."

The Slab, to which his name was attached, was in fact climbed by George Mallory to recover his pipe; and the new Lliwedd guide is in error in calling it a "fable." The feat was entirely in the Mallory vein; but it was not so accidental as it may sound. Many of us were concerned with that large unclimbed facet, and while lunching on the terrace above it during a climbing day, we had been looking down and discussing it. In the evening, George — only an occasional smoker — remembered leaving his pipe on the ledge. Next morning, in the first sunshine, when the rest of the Shack ran up to bathe in the little lake, George ran up the opposite way, on to Lliwedd, and up the Slab, down by an easier way, and back in time for our (traditionally) late breakfast at Pen-y-Pass. On the next day a large party of us repeated the climb.

The "Thank-god" hold on Route II. This name was not "invented" in the first Lliwedd guidebook. The name would have had no point but for its origin, and for the comic value of the repetition of the same exclamation, in turn, by a succession of relieved climbers. The incident is related in Carr and Lister's *Snowdonia,* on p.84 in the new edition. The name was current with my parties by 1907, and had become almost a generic term for this type of surprise hold by the time we issued A. W. A.'s *Lliwedd* guidebook, in 1909. The author's wording in the earliest edition of the guide indicates that he had, then, the incident in mind.

Lliwedd assuredly will never cease to be haunted, and attractively, by the sturdy figure with blond hair, spectacles and rubbers, which used to wander alone among its high recesses, and look down blandly from surprising niches upon our struggles up "unclimbed" cracks.

BOOK REVIEWS

The Fell and Rock Journal Vol. XIV No. 3 1946
J. L. L. (1947)

This number of the *Fell and Rock Journal* after the period of magnificent profusion of photographs and general air of opulence that marked the late G. R. Speaker's period as Editor, and the high level of literary and artistic quality sponsored by Katherine Chorley, has reverted to its local and in places almost defiantly parochial character.

We find the President on the frontispiece — there is no need to ask what part of the country *he* comes from — and pride of place is given to Bentley Beetham's admirable collection of new discoveries in Borrowdale. Later come memories of J. Wilson Robinson, as local a figure as the President, and F. H. F. Simpson evoking the charm of the Lake District through the frames of the Club's collection of lantern slides, and even Howard Somervell at the end of his characteristically modest and perfectly keyed account of his explorations in Kulu comes back very firmly to Bowfell Buttress at the close.

Among all these expressions of local patriotism the special gratitude of members of other clubs will go to Bentley Beetham, who has given us all an object lesson in the new climbing that can be found by going and rubbing your nose into odd corners of a valley in which all the familiar climbs are guarded by waiting queues. Any party that find themselves near Borrowdale on a day clearing from bad weather or with an hour or two to spare before they leave for home will find special cause to bless Beetham for his excellent discoveries.

A tougher reminder that this is not only a Fell and Rock Climbing Club, but *of* the English Lake District — and to hell with foreigners — comes from J. Carswell writing on a "Welsh Week-end." The author carries round his parochialism in his rucksack, and is resolute in attacking the "contention that Welsh climbing is so much superior to Cumbrian." We are glad he intends to visit Wales again, because he may forget his prejudices and realise that Lliwedd has more to offer than Avalanche and Red Wall, and he may feel less certain that Menlove Edwards' classifications overrate the climbs, when he has had time to look at Central Chimney, the Child's and Elliptical Faces, and the direct climbs on Central Gully. He may also learn that our liking for the natural hazards of a range of rock-surfaces, vegetation, and variety of firmness of rock is not mere cussedness, and is besides a training for the much greater range of technique needed on bigger mountains elsewhere. He may even find he wants to do Colin Kirkus's lovely and ingenious climb up Dinas Mot again, when once he has had the chance to set it against the background of the much more continuous effort and strain of the best routes on Du'r Arddu.

Perhaps a similar word about H. Keith Gregory's appreciative notes on climbing in Northumberland will not seem too ungracious. It is very pleasant, on cliffs where nail scratches are infrequent or have mercifully been covered again with a skin of lichen, to feel that we are probably doing new climbs, but it is prudent to verify our references before we claim them as new. Main Wall at Craig Lough is an old favourite, and A. P. Rossiter, among other climbers living in the North-East, worked out a wide range of climbs at Great Wanney some years ago, including the Girdle Traverse. And the assertion that most of the climbs on Simonside "were first done by a man called Emley," is enough to call up the wrathful shade of Raymond Bicknell, if he had not been so modest about his many discoveries in the district. But a really good mark to Mr. Gregory for what he says about the peculiar charm and wildness of the hill-walking between Upper Tyne and Cheviot, where a man may go all day and see nothing but wild duck and wild goats.

And a specially good mark should go to S. B. Beck, who will certainly not be accused of not knowing his Lake District climbing, but who writes to inspire younger members, without previous experience of big mountaineering or much money in their pockets, to turn their eyes to the Alps. His article is full of most valuable tips about post-war conditions there, and of encouragement to those who want to spend a fortnight climbing as hard and as cheaply as possible. He ought to wean himself from Chamonix, which has a fatal fascination for British-trained climbers, or they will never learn that a glacier has more uses than serving as an approach road to the rocks. But he has blazed a good trail, and the toughest of his successors will find it hard to live up to the slogan "peak-peak-change of hut," by which he has replaced the classic and more leisurely "hut-peak-rest day" of our forbears.

Everyone who wants to see "les jeunes britanniques" breaking free from the spell of their own home districts and learning new methods on other mountains will shout "Hear! hear!" to the rousing exhortations with which he ends his very valuable article. S. B. Beck's contribution and F. L. Jenkins' "Raid on Rum" are encouraging signs that some members of the Fell and Rock Club still continue to lift their eyes to other hills.

One last tilt — this time against E. W. Hodge's paper on "Amenity and All That." The author makes you think, as no doubt he intended, and he has good things to say against the tendency of amenity societies to try to preserve what has long ceased to exist. But the general line of his argument is perverse, and, in view of the small size and irreplaceability of the Lake District, at times downright dangerous. He is muddle-headed about afforestation; the Forestry Commission's occasional screens of hardwood, usually only planted after sustained pressure from the amenity societies, are no real compensation for the serried masses of conifers, which they usually screen only from one angle and at one eye-level. And his championship of Thirlmere, including the abrupt variations in the water-level and the dirty bath-water rim that these leave all round, is even more perverse. The Lake District is too precious a possession for us to listen to perversely ingenious arguments in favour of its despoilers — we should be cleaning our guns instead.

Among Club happenings and tributes, there is a particularly good notice on Haskett-Smith from the pen of Geoffrey Winthrop Young, which places "Haskett" delicately and firmly in his appointed place among the great ones.

Scafell No. 2 of the Group Climbing Guides to the English Lake District by A. T. Hargreaves (1936. 2/6.)
J. M. E. (1937)

This guide is an honest piece of work. There are between 80 and 90 climbs in it, with some very exact details about each. The descriptions are concise, neatly tabulated, clean and accurate, pitch by pitch. It is No.2 of the Lakes series — there are going to be five and, they tell me, they are all going to be exactly alike, these guides, as like as pins.

And it is very difficult to think of things to say about it, for the sight of it does not stir me that way, but only to memories. How I hadn't climbed on the cliff at the time; was a beginner, not allowed out on such things; but I read it, read it again, poured myself over it, and photos and diagrams; later on used to get lost on the cliffs, among its buttresses.

There is not much to be said about detail. I have only been to Scafell half a dozen times, but I am sure of that, that everything is as right as makes no matter. And apart from detail there is nothing in the guide; even the historical note is stuffy with detail. So I may as well say straight off that I think it excellent, a very great improvement on the previous edition, and on Kelly's Pillar guide too; that it gives me a headache to have to read it; and that I wish to attack it.

Firstly, on the score of use. It seems to me to be wrong in plan. The description is a tiny, narrow spotlight moving in a single line, "a chimney," "a little slab," then it travels on, "a crack," "20'," "a grass ledge"; and that is all; the rocks might be any rocks, and the conformation of cliff and climb might be any conformation, might be in mid-air, for the spotlight sheds no rays aside, and gives no light on such matters. So, strictly speaking, you do not know where you are. If for instance, you once lost the track, it would be no good looking round at how the rocks stood, you would have to go down and start again. But for the diagrams the method would again and again be useless. The diagrams are luckily fairly adequate and do give quite a good idea of the main areas. I have heard others praise them more highly. There is also an excellent frontispiece drawing much better than the Pillar one, but there are no photographs, no relief. I admired the terse engineering touch that made the best of a bad method: it gives more grip than there is in the Pillar guide. But, even so, the network on these cliffs is not portrayed by it.

Then the headache. Just as there is not a scrap of visual power in the guide, so, among these 80 to 90 individual tracks, there is not one type brought out, and not one character. The history is prep. school history, epics, crowns, best days still to come, just as much as the classificatory scheme is a stupid, prep. school, straight up-and-down scheme, with the old kings treated in charity. You can see nothing, and you can feel nothing. You can read it, the dry print, but only with headache.

I do not know. To write a guide like this takes a great amount of trouble, and to write one as well on the larger scale would take more. It may not be worthwhile for a man to spend so much effort on a climbing guide. But at present we are considering only the point, how good is this one. And for that

I have laboured these as my opinions and can stop there: that progress is a thing of ups and downs, but mostly also of desire; that this guide is best yet of its kind: that there is danger of standardisation at this low level: and that, as for stultification, the method has gone far enough, being sufficient already to cause pain.

A Treasury of Mountaineering Stories Edited by Daniel Talbot (Peter Davies 279 pages 15/- net)
Kevin Fitzgerald (1956)

Mr. Talbot writes in his preface to these 19 stories that he has seen no mountains other than the Alleghenies and that he has never attempted to climb one. I trust that on his first serious ascent, say Moel Siabod from P.y.G., he is more suitably accompanied than most of the characters in this collection. For consider. William and Alfred go for a walk ("The Stream") and Alfred, as well he might, gets on William's nerves. In the result Alfred is pushed over a small cliff by William and breaks his legs. The next day William returns to the spot with a rucksack full of stones and bashes in Alfred's skull as a preparatory move in his own suicide plan. Climb alone would seem to be the moral of this rather dreary little tale.

Mr. Ullman's well-known "Top man" is here, in which, having caused the death of his leader, a young American mountaineer, Osborn, produces a trick ending to the story by a combination of valour and understatement which would have been out of place in the *Boy's Own Paper* of the 'nineties. But Mr. Talbot must not go climbing with that fictional Osborn.

These stories create in the mind of the reader a strong impression that women invariably cause trouble in the hills. They fall in love with guides ("Maiden, Maiden") and tragic consequences ensue, they venture on great mountains with bounders and witness porters left to die for the sake of the peak ("A Splendid Fellow"), and they thrill into full womanhood ("The Ascent") when after a piece of sheer stupidity they feel the "subdued purr of his breath" against their cheeks, and something about "slender artist's fingers" pressing their arms. Mr. Talbot must at all costs seek male company. He doesn't want to find himself looking down in the direction of Capel only to discover that his companion has gone nuts about him and generally nuts as well. That kind of thing complicates any walk.

But Mummery is in this collection (full of Bouvier and *bonhomie)* and so is Miss Knowlton with her delicious "Petite Première in the Mont Blanc Massif." No fictional characters these. C. E. Montague is here but represented by, as I think, his rather poor story, "Action." A most beautiful little tale, "Their Kingdom," by R. Frison Roche, seems to me to possess all the smell and feel of mountains, and there is a strange story by St. John Ervine, "The Mountain," which I liked very much indeed.

Finally there are two comic tales. The classic, "Little Mother up the Mörderberg," by H. G. Wells and, for all that I think death out of place in humorous stories, a magnificent skit on artificial climbing, "The Great Match," by Etienne Bruhl. For anyone who has ever sat in a bar in hill country when the climbers arrive for beer and reminiscence, this story is worth the whole price of admission.

Songs For Climbers Ed. B. H. Humble and W. M. McLellan
A. D. M. Cox (1939)
... And what of *Songs for Climbers?* It was perhaps a pity that one of the Editors of this collection also happened to be a printer and publisher. Climbing songs are all very well. A few in this collection read moderately well, though my own impression is that singing would dull their flavour; on the other hand it is *possible*, I suppose, that singing would redeem some of those which to the eye seem to lack pep.

> *Chorus:*   Yo ho! You climbers!
> Yo ho! You climbers!
> Yo ho! Yo ho! Yo ho!

Or again:

> *Chorus:*   Oh! the climbers. Oh! the climbers,
> Oh! the men who go to climb.
> I'm so happy when I'm climbing,
> For the sport is so sublime.

But it would have to be no mean choir. Anyhow, let us admit that this book fills a need, because otherwise someone may come along and fill it again.

Nanga Parbat Pilgrimage by Hermann Buhl (Hodder & Stoughton)
The Siege of Nanga Parbat 1856-1953 by Paul Bauer (Rupert Hart-Davis)
C. W. Brasher (1957)
One approaches the autobiography of a person such as Hermann Buhl with a great sense of expectation. Here surely will be revealed the great inner force that must have kept him still moving, still alive, during those two incredible days on Nanga Parbat. It is perhaps only this sense of expectation that keeps one reading on through the overwhelming succession of vertical faces and overhanging cracks — each described in minute detail — hoping that sometime Buhl will reveal a little of himself, a little of his philosophy. But it is not to be.

After the first thirty or so pages I lost count of the death roll of Buhl's friends and climbing acquaintances and became submerged in the pitch by pitch description of every climb of note around Innsbruck. The narrative does begin to show signs of life once the story of the great Alpine climbs starts, and the labour of reading is eventually made worthwhile by Buhl's account of the final days on Nanga Parbat; but this we have had in substance already in the *Alpine Journal.*

One is left with a slight shudder. If this is mountaineering, it cannot be for many people. Certainly any non-climber picking up the book must give thanks that he has never ventured into the sport. I cannot believe that it is a true picture of Buhl himself; there must be some softness, some relaxation in his character. His was the greatest solo feat in the history of mountaineering; sheer animal force could not have sustained him throughout. I only wish that someone other than Buhl had written this book. Perhaps they could have revealed more of the man.

Whereas *Nanga Parbat Pilgrimage* is overlong, Paul Bauer's book, *The Siege of Nanga Parbat, 1856-1953*, is overshort. In two hundred and eleven pages of large print the whole story is told from before Mummery to Buhl's final ascent. If you are interested in the mountain itself, then this book gives you a very clear picture of the history of the attempts on the summit by the man best qualified to do so.

As a summary or as an introduction to a closer study of those attempts, it is admirable, although made less useful by the omission of an index; but it is not literature.

THE CHIMNEY CLIMB, EAST BUTTRESS, CLOGWYN DU'R ARDDU

J. M. E.
(1931)

Right of *Pigott's Climb*, between it and the curving chimney, there is an obvious deep crack, narrowing half-way up and then overhanging a little. The route follows the crack throughout.

First ascent, August 3, 1931. C. F. K., J. M. E.

(1)   60 feet. Deep cut chimney of the good old type, awkward where it narrows. Then straightforward bridging. Fine belay.

(2)   80 feet. Crack becomes narrower and harder. Sixty-five feet up ledge on right. Crack becomes ornamental. Small piton (don't let it fall out) and sadly depleted sod enable one to rise to good stance and belay.

(3)   80 feet. Sweaty and rib-caving crack provides another old-fashioned interlude, debouching on to a slab on right half-way up which is thread belay (thread left in).

(4)   80 feet. Overhanging crack above has good large belay on its right-hand base which is reached by the help of number two based on a small belay about half-way from the thread. Crack itself has good holds in addition to the more obvious loose ones. This leads to easy sloping crack with good belay and the Terrace on the left.

Note. — The whole climb is very severe and exposed with one move based on the aforesaid sod of doubtful stability. "Opportunities for lateral deviation" are strictly limited throughout. Gardening operations were carried out incessantly by the leader, who therefore saw very little of number two beneath the sods. Cracks were greasy and leader wore stockings. Stances and belays good throughout, but not extravagantly so towards the top. Rock all excellent except for the obviously rickety innards of the last overhang. There is no "impurity" except the piton and that will be found quite susceptible of removal by even the weakest purist.

NEW CLIMBS

ADDENDA

(1955)

CWM SILYN

The fisherman's hut in the Cwm no longer exists, having been blown away in recent gales.

OPENING OF THE R. W. LLOYD HUT

R. M. V.
(1950)

No special mobilisation had been ordered and no official guests had been invited, but about 50 members attended the ceremonies at the official opening of the R. W. Lloyd Hut, Ynys Ettws, on 20th May, 1950. The day was warm, overcast and without a breath of wind. This allowed the proceedings to be carried out with due dignity, but prevented there being anything so inappropriate to the Welsh tradition as a hot sun. The admirable stone bridge was first dedicated by the Rev. J. E. Grosvenor to the memory of those members of the Club who lost their lives in the late war, and a brief memorial service was held around the stone inscription. The gathering then moved to the hut itself and R. W. Lloyd formally declared it open. After a detailed inspection of the interior of the hut the assembly came out again to be photographed. Those present appeared to be drawn from every generation of the Club's members, and they were dressed in every variety of clothing from business suits to the climbing costume of the 1890s.

The exterior appearance of the hut is in every way suitable to the valley, and the architect, S. McLachlan, received many congratulations. Inside it is heavily mechanized and very spacious. The general opinion of those present seemed to be very favourable, and while this view may have been aided by the champagne which was liberally handed around by the Hon. Custodian, there can be no doubt that the hut is worthy of the Club and of the years of hard work put into its planning and construction. Some conservatives pined for the sunlit lavatory of Helyg, and all viewed the palatial electric drying room with a profound suspicion, which was deepened by the fact that it had short circuited the better part of North Wales on the previous evening, but among the innovations the shelves in the dormitory, the bath of normal shape, and the large kitchen with its fine fireplace were particularly admired. The bunks are comfortable. The hut has nothing that can quite compare with Helyg's view of Tryfan, but the green pasture in front is a charming feature, and there is a promising bathing place in the stream.

In the evening the same members reappeared in ties for the dinner at P. Y. G., where they were entertained by speeches from G. S. Summers, the President and R. W. Lloyd himself who graced the occasion with a felicitous exposition of his own views on climbing and climbers.

YNYS ETTWS LOG BOOK

(extracts)
(1978)

25.2.78   Rained on and off continuously all weekend. Didn't do any thing, just sat in the hut thinking of warm, dry rock and plenty of chalk. Phil and Gaz

4/6.4.78   C. U. M. C. & Hon. C. U. M. C. meet. Steam Team did all the old classics.

21.5.78   Lovely weather. Had a look at Jayway. Didn't like what I saw so Gaz went to do Zangorilla and nearly killed himself on the first pitch. Hold came off. Bad weekend.

21/22.5.78 This is the first time I have stayed in a C.C. hut as a member. Mike Mortimer has left the table in a mess and his cat food out. Hate the colour of the shower curtain.
Geoff Birtles
(Note: the above entry which was fictitious (?)caused a storm of rude comments and further pointed entries. Ed.)

June 78   There seems to be a lot of unmentioned frigging (modern tech-niques?) on several of the recent new routes — abseiling inspec tions — top-roping — nuts for aid — all make routes easier and should be mentioned. It is becoming increasingly apparent that the honesty of several climbers leaves much to be desired. This is a bad thing. Jeremy Frost (Brrrrrrr!)

17.7.78   ... also soloed Suicide Wall Route 1. P. D., T. J.

3.9.78   Terry fell off the Corner after the crux (cos it was too wet to stay on). It seemed the right thing to do at the time.

15/19.9.78 Spent 4 days exploring Clogwyn Mawr Cwm Glas.
Met many nice young men. Stewart Palmer

10.11.78   I'm getting really pissed off with the way members are treating Ynys...
... just to let you know that I'm reaching my limit. D. C.

MORE FROM THE YNYS ETTWS LOG BOOK

(extracts)
(1979/80)

15.2.79	Craig y Rhaeadr — Central Ice Wall exiting left at overhangs. D. Pearce & C. Bonington (Leading through)
17.4.79	Today we had a swim in the high level tarn in Cwm Silyn — just below the snow line. G.M.
28.4.79	Rockfall on Shadow Wall destroyed part of second stance.
May 79	J.A.Y.W.A.Y. Shriek! A modern horror
5.5.79	I spent the same wet afternoon climbing, but then that's what I'm here for. Mike Browell OR Bob Bradley.
13.5.79	2nd ascent of Brut 33 — 'Very Butch'. P. Thomas and Andy Sharp.
1.6.79	TO ALL WHOM IT MAY CONCERN. Arrived at noon on 28/5/79, and was appalled. Hut full of large hairy monsters making a lot of noise. Most left soon thereafter etc. But I fear that a Yobbo is, and always will be, a Yobbo, despite birth or breeding. C. H. S. R. P.
2.6.79	... nobody has the slightest idea who is a member and who is not. Phil Bartlett.
June 79	I volunteer to be obnoxious to non-members who don't pay. Signed, Clive Jones.
19.6.79	I'm afraid all this writing isn't doing any good though. We've all got to get nasty. Smiler.
June 79	It appears to me that the place is phlegmmed up durinq and after large meets by other clubs. C.J.

7.7.79	Did Zukator at Tremadoc. Well-protected though desperate. If it is 6b (which we reckoned it was compared to Cream) then there are 6c routes on Gritstone. Andy Grondowski, Dave Wiggin. Everybody's known that for years. Then it's about time they were graded as such, eh.
August 79	Jeremy Frost failed on Right Wall and on his washing up, but at least he tried Right Wall!
1.9.79	Why don't YOU - both large hairy monsters and geriatric has-beens (apologies to C. H. S. R. P. and Pete Botterill) look after our hut? Ron Prior.
Sept. 79	Personally I like a bit of squalor. J. F.
27.10.79	Bonny Masson U.F.O. (O.K.!)
29.10.79	We recovered!
Feb.80	In my opinion Mongoose has not yet had a second ascent. When people climb routes of this type, i.e. no line, not classic — in fact just boulder problems, and then miss out the crux they have NOT ascended the route. They have climbed some easier alternative. If people climb routes of this type there should be a 'purity of judgement' when considering what exactly is the route. P. L. Gomersall.
June 80	Having completed 140 (half) the Munros between 1925 and 1978 in easy stages, almost by accident, I have in the last 1½ years, at the age of 73, just completed the other half (Not by accident). Ivan Waller. (The above quote was from a letter, not the Ynys log.)

CC MEET REPORT

(1977)

22-24 April 1977. C.C. Meet pathetically organised with little notable success climbing-wise, but a superb night's drinking in conjunction with the B.M.C. A.G.M. The sleeping arrangements were a total disaster and I suggest we do not ask Al Evans to organise any more such meets.

A. J. Evans (Meet Leader)

Derek Walker, Hilary Walker and Ian McNaught-Davis in deep discussion below Goliath's Groove, Stanage, 1988. Photo: Mike Mortimer.

'Hot' Henry Barber surrounded by activists in the St Govan's pub at Easter 1981, one of the legendary Easter Pembroke gatherings with '... routes going up like machine-gun bullets...' Photo and quote: Ken Wilson Archive.

Gloria Wilson
Mark Hutchinson
Sam Whinster
Jim Curran
Ken Wilson
Brian Hall
John Porter
Al Evans
Dave Cook
Ruth Colton
Andrea Evans
Hilary Barnes
Tony Riley
Sue Lawty
Blob Wyvill
Ben Wintringham
Marion Wintringham
Steve Bancroft
Pat Littlejohn
Sue Carrington
Roy Thomas
Nadim Siddiqui
Willie Todd
Henry Barber
Steve Beresford
Rab Carrington
Sue Owen

Climbers' Club meet at Brackenclose, Wasdale 1972. Back row, left to right, Collie Taylor, Ian Campbell, Chris Bonington, Maggie Boysen, Ginger Caine, Dave Potts, Martin Boysen, John Kingston, Di Parkes, Terry Parker, Robin Ford. Front row, left to right, Sylvia Mercer, Mike Thompson, Frank Cannings, Mo Anthoine, Dave Atchison. Photo: Ken Wilson Archive.

John Moss and Will Barker with the ubiquitous Morris van below Carreg Hyll-drem c. 1965. Photo: Ken Wilson.

THE COTTAGE

DAVE GREGORY
(1986/87)

Of Helyg much has been spoken and written, particularly in the last, commemorative year. That each man should have his own favourite location and that the favourite location of many men should be the same is understandable. The friendly roof from which they strode to conquer and under which they now gather to celebrate those blue remembered hills is not that for me, for I have never liked the place. I have, in fact, never entered its doors and would not admit to the indefensible admission had I not recently read in *Menlove* that the writer felt of "Cwm Glas Cottage", the scene of one of Edwards's suicide attempts, that "If houses can be said to have atmospheres this one's is not of the happiest. I have stayed there alone myself and felt unnerved and depressed by the place." Here, I feel, the wish is father to the writer's thought and afterknowledge used as evidence for I too have stayed in what we both call the Cottage and a friendlier place never gave shelter.

My first climbing journey to Wales, those thirty five years ago started in good weather and comfort, but as the Black Vinny wheels rolled on, the sky darkened and the pillion seat hardened. As we approached Ogwen the deluge came in earnest and Tryfan's dragon back was lost in grey wrack and the sheets of rain swept over the bowed, lashed, twisted torment of the trees surrounding the wretched hovel. The depression of the sodden journey deepened the malevolence of that Grimm residence. Home it could have been of any number of wicked witches and hollow-fanged princes of darkness.

Our residence for the week was, in fact, even less salubrious. A hexagonal blockhouse, a machine gun post from Hitler's war standing just above the Ogwen shoreline in the line of seepage from the slopes of Pen yr Oleu Wen. As the week passed, with the drain blocked, the water level rose and the squalor grew, but Helyg stayed its inferior, for here brave spirits throve and there, the unknown evil lurked in its yew-green fastnesses.

The fashion for Ogwen was dying and with the hordes I thronged the Pass and my acquaintance with Cwm Glas began. Triple-staged it has been: illicit, official guest and member.

The sun always shone in the illicit days and from its sunny terrace one could trace the many ways up the more than Three Cliffs, as Menlove may well have done. One evening from the grandstand wall we saw a team rope up under Brant Direct as the yellow sun dipped towards Caernarfon. The leader struggled as the light fell and by dint of spraying gear over the cracks and ribs he reached the V-chimney and struggled rightwards to the tree. His second started as the scarlet cannonball was extinguished in the sea and made a fruitless effort in the growing dark. At least eight pieces of gear they left and by six a.m. we had the lot.

There were and are disadvantages to staying there. One is apt to find, the place alive with Cadet Corps pongos, the table a molecular model of rows and layers of bone domes, the dorms a resonance of far-back falsettos.

I have contributed my share to cramming the Cottage with adolescents. I planned a weekend once — four adults in the hut and sixteen fouth formers in tents around it. The weather was ill. From noon on Friday the heavens wept. The hillside ran with water two inches deep. It came through the kitchen wall, across the lounge and out across the terrace. No water graced the taps however and what we needed we ran for, wellied and shirtless, to the toilet block. The wind flattened every tent we put up and, the floor awash, we slept everywhere else. Two deep in the window bottoms. Top to tail in the bunks. I was cajoled to lash the smallest member of the party to the bookshelf, but Will refused the adventure. A night with Wolf Solent might have been more water than he could have stomached. Mirabile dictu, the Sabbath dawned fine, if windy, and they all made it to the top of Snowdon. On the journey back they all swore they'd enjoyed it and one of the window-sill sleepers went up in my estimation. "What a smashing little cottage", he said. What a smasher indeed.

I was there again that winter. J. P. had decided to emigrate to Tasmania and wanted one last breath of Wales. Just the pair of us there were in The Cottage and the weather was hill perfect. Cold and clear to the sea, Passwords. The tops around so sharp you could reach to grasp them as handholds.

We were the first in the Pen-y-Pass car park and the Miners' Track to Llydaw was deserted. The minor noises associated with putting on crampons and unstrapping the axes seemed as sacrilegious as shouting in church and disgust at the racket made by a squad of the soft and barmy who caught us up drove us early up Central Trinity. There were four inches of powder for the leader to pull down onto the second but hard snow underneath and we were quickly up to the railway ridge and the summit.

There were more people there than watch Sheffield United most Saturdays. The sight would have warmed the cockles of the gear-shop owner's heart (were such an organ capable of so human a response). The slopes were covered in parodies of magazine advertisement models, fibre pile and Gore-Tex teddy bears all sweating in the hot sun. Brand new crampons bought in the flush of enthusiasm in the spring of '79 were seeing snow for the first time, tripping up their owners and punching holes in those lovely gaiters.

Purple Alpinistes were laid by every bulge on the summit cone. Ice axes of every colour, length and droop decorated the hill like a United Nations urinal. A few minutes of this was too much and we crunched off down the slope and round to Crib-y-Ddysgl, over Crib Goch and back to Pen-y-Pass. Two people only we saw and the weather held perfect.

A day to remember.

And the next day dawned as good a day, with one blemish. John's heels were a fair imitation of a pair of steaks and not far above Cwm Glas Mawr he packed up and hobbled over to the foot of Craig Rhaeadr to watch a pair yo-yoing on the ice flutes. I plodded up the path beside Cyrn Las and sat on a boulder in the upper cwm to soak up the view before strapping on the crampons and following some innocuous gully by the side of Cyrn Las to the ridge. Then down the ridge a spell, looking for a gully to break down towards The Cottage. There was no sign of any passage on the higher section. The snow was powdery still and little compacted beneath. Negotiating the rock steps was tricky. Facing inward and scraping down the rock. The gully fingers held sufficient harder snow to face out and stride down relying on the thrust-in axe for support and partway down one of these were the first hare tracks.

For a hundred feet or so as I looked ahead for the easiest way down, the hare had already found it and our tracks coincided. I guessed he knew the mountain better than I did. I gave up trying to find my own way and followed the hare. Faultess it was, the old jack rabbit, and went along a thread of snow and down a gully picking out the easiest line in immaculate fashion. Its trail of prints ran up over the blunt ridge by The Cottage and across its snow-covered terrace. I wished it well, a long pellet and fox-free retirement, and went into another evening in front of The Cottage fire.

At Easter that same year Will and I spent a few days at The Cottage looking to get him started on the easier Pass classics. He had been a member of the water polo party, one of the smaller sardines and was a slightly unwilling companion, expecting the Pass to be a deluge above and below. It was dry and clear, however, and although it took some hard persuading to get him up the Everest of the slope to Flying Buttress, once reached, the rock won four star status. We compounded the bliss by climbing the Spiral Stairs to heaven.

The next day we made our pilgrimage to Crackstone Rib and met there another old man showing a youngster the ropes: The Brown and Alan McHardy. Who was looking after whom? Will was thunderstruck. Two legends on one rope. On our return to the crag foot there was The Master sitting on Will's rucksack. The sandwiches were a bit squashed but who cared? Has Joe Brown sat on your rucksack? I'll bet not. I had made him the sack to fit him just before and since then I've had to lengthen the straps and move their fixings so that he can still wear it. It's half the size of mine and won't really take all his gear, but it has a cachet that outweighs those disadvantages.

A watershed for him, that weekend at The Cottage. He was hooked and for him and for me Cwm Glas Mawr is not just a cottage but a gateway to the hills. I suppose that I can no longer go there now without thinking of poor tortured Menlove, but it still remains my favourite mountain shelter. Helyg? I suppose I shall have to stay there sometime, but do those dismal evergreens still harbour the powers of darkness?

HELYG: A NOTE
TO THE EDITOR OF THE *CENTENARY JOURNAL*

HAROLD DRASDO
(1996)

The 1926 *Journal* quotes George Borrow's famous remarks about Helyg and I suppose you could say they came to us with the house. Borrow gives 'Allt-y-Gog' for 'Gallt-yr-Ogof', equally plausible. (Gog cuckoo; Ogof cave.)
(By the way: did you know that an esteemed Bethesda prostitute of the pre-war years went by the name of Marie Helyg? She'd been brought up there. My authority is Dr David Roberts, died c.20 years ago.)

EDITOR'S NOTE

F. A. PULLINGER
(1945-6)

Users of Helyg are reminded that the log is intended to be a record of their climbs and expeditions and of their observations on the hills. There is no harm in gilding the bare factual record if there is anything interesting to say, and in the past the book has maintained a high standard both as a record of achievement and as good reading. Recently, however, the standard has been declining; there have been too many entries, mainly facetious, which are of interest to none but the writer.

I SPY

ANON
(1983)

Graham Hoey did **not** write the more libellous bits!
First to manage 4,000 points wins a Little Chief (Dennis Gray) I-Spy rock
climber's badge.

	points
Reading a Jim Perrin article	20
Understanding a Jim Periin article	200
Pat Littlejohn using chalk	600
Ken Wilson talking	1
Ken Wilson not talking	600
Martin Berzins handing out compliments	700
Gary Gibson putting up a route	5
Gary Gibson putting up a good new route	250
Trevor Jones resting on a nut	100
(note each I-spy can be used only once!)	
Staying asleep in the same room as Trevor Jones	200
A copy of the '82 *CCJ* which stays in one piece when open	500
Geoff Milburn undergrading a route	500
Chris Jackson overgrading a route	500
Seeing more than 4 people in the Pembroke Hut outside Bank	
Holidays, Christmas and Easter	250
Ron Force It chipping a hold	2000
Pete Live Sea chipping a hold	1000
Receiving payment from Geoff Britles (sic)	400
Mick Fowler climbing on sound rock	600
Nat Allen Climbing (30) Joe Brown climbing (45)	
Don Whillans climbing (75) Pete Crew climbing (600)	
Tom Proctor in a pothole	300
Mike Mortimer's dog	45
Dennis Gray buying a round	450
Graham Hoey placing a 'hand inserted piece of metal'	250
Stevie Haston's latest girl friend	69
Steve Bancroft not in Paris/France	100
Ken Wilson's baggy shorts	65
Bernard Newman on Bamford Edge	850
A contributor to the 1983 *CCJ*	350
Bob Moulton in Wales	400
Al Parker on limestone	800
Doug Scott not wearing crampons	200
Smiler Cuthbertson in a bad mood	600

Mike Browell leading a hard, sustained, poky pitch	500
Mike Browell seconding a hard, sustained, poky pitch	20
Mike Browell in plaster	13
A climber bolting on gritstone	3000
John Redhead bolting on Cloggy	2000
Paul Williams & Welsh lads bolting on Pen Trwyn	70
Gary Gibson bolting on Peak Limestone	15
A fully paid up C.C. Member	150
An ex-Member of the C.C.	50
A leader on The Bells! The Bells!	800
A leader on Master's Wall	900
Gabriel Regan without a drink in hand	400
Al Evans	200
Ron Fawcett not moving when on rock	99
John Laycock's 1913 *Some Gritstone Climbs*	700
A first-class guidebook to Yorkshire crags	900
A climber on the Black Cleft in winter	445
A climber on Cilan Head	007
A friend of Mark Vallance	1
Martin Boysen unable to reach a hold	20
A climber enjoying The Vice	600
Tom Leppert on Carnedd y Filiast	350
An article in *Mountain* or *High* without an obscenity	30
A climber on a route CARRYING the new Stanage guide	500
A climber using ex-W.D. karabiners	350
Chris Bonington with ice-axe on Gogarth	600
A new route on Lliwedd	900
Climbers on Cloggy on New Year's Day	500
A non-paying climber staying at Ynys Ettws	30
A hungry climber at a Pat Green supper	1
The Discipline Sub-Committee in action	800
The Publications Sub-Committee finishing before 2 a.m.	800
A quiet C.C. Committee meeting	1000
The mines Inspector at Great Rocks Dale	300
The summit of Everest	5
An avalanche coming down on top of you	GAME
Smiler on the Eiger North Wall	999

A BRIEF HISTORY OF THE CLIMBERS' CLUB

A PERSONAL VIEW BY PIP HOPKINSON

In August and September during the 1890s a group of about 40 men met regularly at the Pen y Gwryd to climb and explore the Welsh hills and crags. After one Saturday evening's dinner it was proposed that a club be formed. This idea was pursued at a dinner in London on 19th May 1897 at the Cafe Monico and the next dinner was fixed for 6th December 1897 at Pen y Gwryd. This was not well-attended; only 25 of the group turned up. Nevertheless the foundations of the Club were laid at this dinner. The resolution 'That a Climbing Club be formed' was proposed by Mr Roderick Williams and seconded by Mr H. G. Gotch, both of whom were already Alpine Club members. This was approved by the group and a provisional Club committee was elected.

The provisional committee drafted and sent out a circular to all those known as climbers whose names could be obtained from various sources. It read:

The Climbers' Club

Dear Sir,

It has been determined to establish a Club under the above title.

The object of the Club will be to encourage mountaineering, particularly in England, Ireland and Wales, and to serve as a bond of union amongst all lovers of mountain activity.

The qualifications of members will be determined by the Committee, who have the sole power of election.

The officers will be a President, two Vice-Presidents, an Honorary Secretary and an Honorary Treasurer.

The Committee will consist of the officers and nine additional members all to be elected annually at the Annual Meeting.

The first officers will be:

President C. E. Matthews

Vice-Presidents Frederick Morshead

F. H. Bowring

Hon Secretary George B. Bryant

Hon Treasurer T. K. Rose

The Annual Subscription will be half a guinea and there will be an entrance fee of the same amount after the first hundred members are elected.

The Annual Meeting will take place in London at the end of April in each year, and will be followed by a dinner.

The first Annual Dinner will take place about the end of April next, on a day and at a place which will be duly notified.

The Club will be in no sense antagonistic to any existing institution; but will, it is hoped, gather together all those who are interested in mountaineering in England, Ireland and Wales.

Should you be willing to join, will you be good enough to return the enclosed form immediately to Mr C. E. Matthews, The Hurst, Four Oaks, near Birmingham.

At the First Annual Meeting the Formal Laws of the Club will be presented for adoption and the First Annual Dinner will follow.

Yours faithfully,

C. E. Matthews

F. Morshead

F. H. Bowring

G. B. Bryant

T. K. Rose

25th March 1898

The response exceeded expectations. Despite the limited number of the initial circular, by the first AGM exactly 200 applications for membership had been received and all were admitted as founder members.

The first AGM was held in the Alpine Club rooms in Saville Row on 28th April 1898; 62 members attended. Of the membership approximately one third were already members of the Alpine Club. The first committee included W. C. Slingsby (President, Yorkshire Ramblers' Club), R. A. Robertson (President, Scottish Mountaineering Club), Owen Glynne Jones and W. P. Haskett Smith.

The President knew about founding clubs. He was a founder member of the Alpine Club and described himself in his inaugural speech as a 'professional mid-wife at the birth of a new bantling which is destined to be as healthy and prosperous as any previous member of the great family' (of mountaineering clubs, following the formation of the Alpine Club, the Austrians, Swiss, Italians , Germans, and French had formed their Alpine Clubs in that order). The President also reminded members (as many have done since!) 'that the Club is an institution towards which every man must contribute his share'.[1]

The initial members were drawn very much from the professions and senior universities. In those times the common man needed to earn at least a guinea a week to keep a wife and three children (without holidays and if he didn't drink). There was much short-term working and hence little security.[2] It would have been impossible for him to join in the luxury of climbing.

1. The founding of the Club is dealt with in great detail in Volume 1 Number 1 of the *CC Journal.*
2. Seebohm Rowntree, *Poverty: A Study of Town Life* (1901).

Today we would find some of the founder members' views and ideas ill-conceived. There appears in the first President's speech the notion that "climbing is a sport that appeals to the cultivated intellect - 'arry or 'arriet would never climb a hill." As Brecht later said: "What keeps a man alive?... Food is the thing — morals follow on."[3] It would take two major wars to change these attitudes towards class.

The first meets were held in the Lakes at Wasdale and in Wales around Pen y Gwryd. Notices were to be sent to members of these. Winter meets were also proposed for both venues at Christmas and Easter.

The initial rules were circulated and adopted. In general, they are not dissimilar from the rules that we have today. Rule 1's first sentence survives intact from these rules. One may just speculate, if, considering the stated aims of the Club, the founders wanted an all male Club, or whether they would have embraced a mixed membership had that membership been there.

The Club grew slowly. Its more adventurous members started to make their mark as they have continued to do on mountains around the world. Not surprisingly, by 1903, women had started to appear on meets, usually someone's wife or someone's daughter, but not all fell into that category. Oscar Eckenstein did Kern Knotts Crack with a lady, giving her a shoulder at the niche so that she could successfully lead the top section of the crack.[4] This was a climb that in 1903 was a *tour de force* in anyone's book.

These developments did not go unnoticed. But already the CC had mandarins, an old guard of traditional Alpine Club members and their sons who would defend the all-male membership.

Owen Glynne Jones first published his *Rock Climbing in the English Lake District* in 1897. The Second (posthumous) Edition was published in 1901, a book by a founder member which may have given others the idea of a separate club for those interested in Lakeland climbing. Archer Thomson[5] was working on his guides to Lliwedd and to the Ogwen District. Rock climbing was a growing sport.

Gradually the Club started to aquire its second generation of distinguished members: Puttrell, Winthrop Young and the young man described by Sir Francis Younghusband as "slim and supple if not broad and beefy, the delectable George Leigh Mallory." [6] Their arrival was fortuitous. They were going to save the Club.

In 1910 the Club's rules were revised and the rule that very nearly destroyed the Club some 60 years later was introduced: 'Rule 2: All gentlemen interested in the objects of the Club as defined in Rule 1 shall be eligible as members'.[7] The new rule could not have been inserted into the rules without the President's and Secretary's approval: Professor J. B. Farmer MA

---

3. (Erst kommt das Fressen dann kommt die Moral), Brecht 'What Keeps A Man Alive?', *The Threepenny Opera*, 1928.
4. The woman was Miss S. Nicolls.
5. Archer Thomson together with Bretland Farmer could well be considered the first 'weekend' climbers.
6. *Younghusband*, Patrick French.
7. *CCJ*

DSc FRGS and C. Myles Matthews BA LLB.[8] These two were both very much products of their class and their times. They had gone to public schools followed by a senior university education. Relations between the sexes were often strained, especially within the same social class.[9] There was also a new 'breed' of women, increasingly violent, shouting and demonstrating for universal suffrage. I have no doubt that these distinguished gentlemen thought, paternally, that the membership should be protected from them and not embrace them. It was an attitude that stayed with Myles Matthews all of his life.

By 1912 the Club membership had slowly risen to a comfortable 300. It was a gentlemen's climbing club and the Committee's job was to maintain the status quo. Unfortunately, other people in other countries had different ideas and Europe descended into the misery of the First World War. The stable class system and attitudes towards women would never be quite the same again despite the Establishment, despite the Club's Committees.

Like most British clubs and organisations, the Club encouraged its young men to go to war with enthusiasm and patriotism.[10] Only pacifists such as Geoffrey Winthrop Young resisted the 'call' and he lost his leg driving ambulances around the Front in the Friends Medical Corps.

By the end of the war, the Club had lost most of its younger members. Membership was falling and it could no longer rely on its Alpine Club connections to provide it with new members. Other than the *Journal* and its social dinners, it had little to offer anyone.

With A. W. Andrews as President, George Leigh Mallory took over editorship of the *Journal* and Winthrop Young was in charge of publications. The main Committee looked for new members and realised that if there were going to be any, they would be in the universities. The only universities at the time with mountaineering clubs were Oxford and Cambridge, so the Presidents of the OUMC and the CUMC were elected onto the main Committee, a practice that was to continue until 1965. This may have been a necessity at the time, but it echoed into the future.

Slowly the Club started to recover. The main Committee decided that it either needed rooms in London where members could relax and read the morning papers, or that it should find a property in Wales where members might have cheap accommodation. The Committee was divided equally. S. A. Marples had the casting vote and voted in favour of finding a cottage in Wales. Two of the Club's new young members, Raymond Greene and Herbert Carr, searched for a property and were principally responsible for finding Helyg. It was to become, for many, the jewel in the crown of the Club. Helyg was opened on 31st October 1925 by the Vice-President S. A. Marples.

The younger members proposed to the main committee that the rules governing the use of Helyg should allow women guests. Once again, Myles

8. Both were also AC members.
9. A. F. Rodda, historian, to P. H. H.
10. With hindsight, knowing the horrors of this war it is difficult to appreciate how popular it was initially. Football teams, groups from factories joined en masse to fight. The War Office expected 50,000 volunteers in the first three months of war; it got 500,000.

Matthews exerted his authority. (He was now President, having succeeded Mallory who had died on Everest in 1924.) He was not going to have women staying at his Club huts! But it was too late. Before he made his pronouncement a woman had already stayed at Helyg and the rules were not broken — there were no rules![11] From then on nearly every generation would conspire to break that particular rule in their own way, until 1975 when women were finally admitted to the Club. Energy that could have been used for better purposes would be used by the young to defy and confuse their elders.

With the opening of Helyg the Club's future became assured.

In 1927 a small man stomped down the path to a group of members outside the hut and asked what was going on. He was politely told that this was a Climbers' Club hut. He instantly asked to join the Club, thinking that any club that had a hut situated where Helyg was, was a good club to join. To their credit the Committee elected him almost immediately[12] and the Club gained for many what was a characteristic member and one of its great enthusiasts, A. B. Hargreaves.

If the Club only had one Golden Era it was the one which was about to start. H. R. C. Carr's *A Climbers' Club Guide to Snowdon and the Beddgelert District* had just been published by the Club, the last in the first series of guidebooks. It gave a new generation of climbers a lot of routes and it also showed the gaps in the cliffs where no routes existed. The Club once again had competent and good climbers, Ivan Waller and Jack Longland being at that time amongst the best and attracting similar enthusiasts to them.

It is hard to realise today, but at that time everyone worked on Saturday mornings. The weekend started with a mad dash to the hills at Saturday lunchtime, by whatever transport was available. Having transport at all implied a certain social status. For most of the year, in the bigger hills at least, the 'arry's and the 'arriets were still being kept in their place.[13]

Wales was becoming an exciting place to climb. The Rucksack Club had its route on Cloggy, the East Buttress Route (later to be called Pigott's), and the West Buttress Route (Longland's) had been climbed by a joint CC/Rucksack Club party. For the first time men who were trained on gritstone and sandstone (Helsby) were showing what could happen when those techniques were applied to granite. Colin Kirkus often accompanied by A. B. Hargreaves was redefining the art of the possible, backed up by a solid team of people such as Hicks, Linnell, Cooper and Bridge. The Club had a Northern Committee that was the driving force in the Club.[14] Then the next great climber arrived leading the newly formed Liverpool University Rock Climbing Club meet — its President — one J. M. Edwards.

Leading Club members were then arguably the best rock-climbers in Great Britain. The only ones who could gainsay this were the 'arrys and

11. *Helyg*, Geoff Milburn.
12. A. B. H. to P. H. H.
13. When they did get out to bigger hills they were content to do traditional routes — to build up the knowledge that already existed in the major clubs. E. Byne to P. H. H. c1957.
14. A. B. H. to P. H. H.

'arriets breaking out of the northern towns during the long depression to make their mark on the moors and gritstone edges of the central Pennines. But their word was not yet strong and it would take another war before their potential was unleashed on the rather exclusive and genteel world of Welsh and English rock-climbing.[15]

The Club carried on with its business. It expanded Helyg and started to produce, with Edwards and Kirkus, the second set of definitive climbing guides to North Wales. In doing so it defined British guidebook writing.

Sadly towards the end of the decade, Colin Kirkus, understandably slightly taciturn and no longer climbing his best after his traumatic fall on Ben Nevis in 1934, felt uncomfortable in using Helyg and started to stay at the youth hostel in Ogwen where many young climbers benefited from his tuition. But there remains a strongly lingering suspicion that the Club's old guard did not really like an insurance clerk in their hut and made him unwelcome.[16]

Once again thoughts of war started to disturb people's minds.

Despite the loss of good members during the Second World War, these were not entirely unproductive years for the Club. At the beginning of the war the Committee had taken out a 250 year lease on a broken down cottage in the Llanberis Pass that had no access to it. The price was cheap — £10 p.a. for Ynys Ettws. Edwards and Barford (one a conscientious objector and one exempt from military service) produced the first guidebooks to Clogwyn Du'r Arddu and the Three Cliffs. Cox and Kretschmer produced the Craig yr Ysfa guide.

During the war occasional meets were still held at Helyg and it became for many a small haven of peace in those difficult times.

Many Club members worked during the war at training mountain and cliff assault troops. As the troops came home the Club was in good shape. It now had two huts, Helyg and Bosigran, and was refurbishing Ynys Ettws. Its members in the South West had started seriously climbing the cliffs of West Penwith as A. W. Andrews had always predicted that they would. In North Wales CC members were climbing at the current top grades.

The Club asked Peter Harding to rewrite the fastest developing area guide — The Three Cliffs. There is no doubt that this stopped him from doing many other first ascents. For 10 years this book became known as the 'Bumper Fun Book', partly for the area it covered (Llanberis and Clogwyn Du'r Arddu) and partly because of some of the proof reading and 'typos'.[17]

15. Compare the technical standard of Wall End Slab Direct and Count's Buttress on Stanage with Welsh routes of this era.
16. This is hinted at in Steve Dean's *Hands of a Climber*, and in conversations with A. B. H. A. B. H. always advised cutting mandarin's legs off at their knees to remove their pomposity. Paul Orkney Work was more forthright and said to Jim Perrin that Colin had told him that he found some CC members' attitude towards him snobbish and that he preferred the more liberal attitudes at Idwal Cottage. Connie Alexander, the first Idwal Cottage Warden was also a good friend to Colin. She is portrayed as Miss Elliott in Elizabeth Coxhead's *One Green Bottle*.
17. I remember leading my first VS in the Pass. The guide described a 20-foot pitch which today has become 90 feet! I had originally thought, reading the description, that it was a slightly soft touch — the technical grade is 5a!

Ironically the guidebook, as many have been since, was out of date before it was published — for this was the beginning of the days of 'arry and 'arriet.[18]

To the newly emerging post-war clubs of the late '40s the Climbers' Club looked and behaved like the Establishment. This was compounded when they sent details of their new routes to the Club. Nat Allen, the Rock and Ice chronicler, sent the details of Noah's Warning, Cemetery Gates and Cobweb Crack. The reply from one of the Club's officials[19] suggested that interesting as these routes were, they were only 'fillers in' of detail and suggested that the Rock and Ice might be better employed applying its talents to something more serious, like the Nose of the Ogof.[20]

Peter Harding was now sitting on the Northern Committee. One of the functions of this committee was to vet candidates to the Club before the main Committee approved them. His climbing partner, Gordon Dyke, came up for election. One of the Club's officials[21] blackballed him on the basis that Dyke had addressed him by his Christian name when introduced to him and when questioned by the Committee about this replied "Dyke himself is probably okay — but he has some rather objectionable friends." Later in the meeting Peter was asked to support another candidate, G. W. S. Pigott. Peter objected, saying, "Remember G. W. S. P. like myself, is a friend of Gordon Dyke."[22] At another clash with the Club's old guard, Peter and Alf Bridge, the Club Secretary, resigned from the Club.

The Club had two new huts, Cwm Glas[23] — where things were more relaxed and women occasionally stayed — and Ynys Ettws. Ynys was set in an ideal position. It was ruled with a rod of iron by the Custodian, Roy Beard, no doubt following the example set by Stuart Chantrell at Helyg.[24] When the custodian was away things were a little more relaxed. When the Rock and Ice visited on one such day to record some routes, they found a sink full of unwashed crockery and not a clean cup in the hut. They never forgot it. Neither their mothers nor their NCOs (many had done National Service) would have allowed them to get away with that.[25]

If members of the Club could no longer do the hardest routes in Llanberis, they started to make up for that in explorations elsewhere. Tony Moulam was especially active in discovering new areas of rock and producing stunning lines on them. Many others made their mark on the Greater Ranges. Most UK expeditions of the 1950s had CC members on them or organising them. In the Alps members were helping to write a new edition of English Alpine guidebooks.

18. This guide was criticized in a CC after-dinner speech by Stuart Chantrell for having too many hard climbs and too few easy ones. The guide incorporated a Dinas Mot section written earlier by H. A. Carsten.
19. E. C. Pyatt.
20. E. C. Pyatt in a letter to J. R. Allen.
21. Stuart Chantrell.
22. Peter Harding to P. H. H.
23. Cwm Glas Custodian was B. McKenna — he who planted the Helyg trees and those on the island in Llyn Bach.
24. P. R. J. H. and H. Banner to P. H. H.
25. J. R. Allen and D. Whillans to P. H. H.

Membership at this time had very much of an Oxbridge bias, a legacy from the '20s. The Club was still one of gentlemen, despite the high jinks of a well-known athlete[26] walking his muddy Vibram boots over the newly painted Ynys ceiling and the making of a film of a young lady from Pen y Gwryd taking a bath in the men-only hut of Ynys.[27] Hard climbers who might have joined the Club didn't, although thankfully there were a few notable exceptions. The Club was not exactly welcoming to those who might have been from the 'other ranks'.[28]

From its early days, the Club had always had a healthy radical liberal strain in some of its members and in their politics. It could be traced back, I suspect, to people like Eckenstein, but certainly to Winthrop Young, Longland, Waller, Hargreaves, Edwards, Cox and Barford. The old guard had not managed to extinguish it. Geoff Sutton (CC) was climbing fairly regularly with Don Roscoe from the Rock and Ice and new friendships were being made. Geoff proposed his climbing partner for membership. Don didn't think too much about this but was astonished to be told by one of the mandarins[29] on his election that "I don't think you are the sort of chap we want in the Club. I'll be watching you very carefully." To be fair, this particular member apologised three years later for his remark and said he had been wrong.[30]

By 1955 the second series of guidebooks was out of date. The Ogwen guides were not too hard to update, but a mammoth task — one to which Tony Moulam valiantly responded. When Don Roscoe was asked to write the new Llanberis guide, he climbed all but five routes. Noticeably the first acknowledgments in the guidebook are to his Rock and Ice partners.[31] Hugh Banner started to write the Cloggy guide. He was determined to climb all the routes on the cliff before publishing the guide. He had got down to the last two (Woubits Left-Hand and Taurus) when his climbing partner offered to help.[32] Giving Pete Crew a draft up-to-date manuscript to Cloggy fired him and his club, the Alpha, on to great things. They quickly added another 12 new routes before the guidebook was published. Trevor Jones — another star at that time — produced the first major guide to Tremadog.[33]

Peter Crew's guidebook writing helped the Club recruit members of his club, the Alpha. All this started to give the Club momentum. A. B. Hargreaves, still full of fire, suceeded the wonderfully gentle don David Cox as President, and once again young climbers wanted to join the Club. By then, they felt that it was their Club, their heritage, and if some of the rules were not to their liking, that wasn't too serious; rules could be changed.

26. Chris Brasher (J. R. Allen to P. H. H.).
27. You don't expect me to name names here do you? The incident was told to me by J. H. Longland.
28. P. Vaughan and J. R. Allen to P. H. H.
29. Roy Beard, Custodian, Ynys Ettws.
30. Don Roscoe (diaries) to P. H. H.
31. Don Roscoe to P. H. H.
32. H. Banner to P. H. H.
33. This wasn't a great guide. It was quickly superseded by Peter Crew's West Col guide to the area.

This was the generation in rebellion — driving to Wales as fast as you could on a Friday night, living hard and fast through the weekend. Inevitably on Saturday nights they wanted their girlfriends/partners to come into the hut to share the late-night argument and debate. For a while, when custodians were present, cups of tea were passed to the girls outside.[34] But this generation could argue its case well and this strange practice didn't last too much longer. In the midst of this were two major figures, Ken Wilson and Dave Cook, both very articulate, 'politically correct' before those words were fashionable, skilled in analysis and debate, and competent as climbers.

Perhaps the most important difference between this generation and those that had preceded it was that the former generations expected, or accepted, an establishment, conservative leadership whilst the new members were progressives to the core. This is an important distinction and one that had far-reaching implications for the Club. (Members of both the AC and the F&RCC have said to me that their clubs too, at that time, were controlled in the same way.)

In 1964 Peter Crew turned his attention to the newly discovered Gogarth Cliffs, climbing some 50 new routes in five years — a record only beaten at that time by the Club's newest Honorary Member, Joe Brown, who claimed 51 in the same period.

It was at the 1966 AGM that the rule change allowing women to join was first proposed. This was among six motions proposed by K. Wilson at his first AGM. He proposed changing the wording of Rule 2 from 'gentlemen' to 'persons'. The committee thought that this was about letting working-class men join the Club. The motion was treated sympathetically by the President, Sir John Hunt, and the Hon Sec, The Right Hon Roger Chorley. Later, one J. M. Baldock was proposed for membership without a hint of her gender. She would have been elected, but somebody informed the Committee that this was a woman (later to be President). Many said that if a less controversial figure than Ken Wilson had proposed the motion it might have just passed, but the time was not yet right for the old guard to be defeated. This was to be a running sore in the Club for the next eight years. It was obvious to many that it was an anachronism that women could not use the Club's main huts or join the Club. There were very competent women climbers around such as the aforementioned Jancis Baldock, Janet Rogers, Barbara Sparks, Jo Scars, Denise Evans, Sally Westmacott, Jo Fuller, many of whom climbed regularly with Club members. Why was a major Club ignoring them?

As a future President said in one of the debates, "If I can stay with my boyfriend, my lover, my catamite in Ynys Ettws, why can't I also stay with my wife?"[35] The younger members responded in the only way they could — they encouraged no one to join the Club. If, occasionally, on a stormy night some bunks had two sleeping bags on them, then this new generation said nothing.

34. Brian Evans to P. H. H.
35. Harry Sales.

Membership started slowly to fall. Despite this, the Club's guidebook activity continued and to help the emerging BMC, the Club published the new limestone guides to the Peak District.

Eventually, in 1972, a President came into office who was a new convert to the cause of women. Hamish Nicol had a pedigree to suit the Club's old guard: ex-Oxford, a reserve (due to a broken jaw) for the 1953 Everest expedition,[36] a leading Alpinist in his time with a dry acerbic humour. His regular climbing partner was Robin Prager, the Club secretary, who appeared externally to be conventional English Public School. In fact, Robin was Anglo-Indian and radical in his politics.[37] They were both persuaded of the rights of women and Hamish wanted them to be eligible to join the Club during his presidency.

At his final AGM in 1975 the motion was passed that 'All people interested in the objects of the Club shall be eligible as members' and a sufficient majority obtained to allow the rule to be changed. Happily Club members who voted against the rule have since proposed women for the Club.[38]

Gradually the Club took its bearings; it wasn't overwhelmed with women wanting to join. Membership was at a 15-year low and falling. The Club's guidebooks were losing money. The Club's huts, which by now had increased to five, were scruffy. On the positive side there was a will to turn the Club around.

Membership was initially a problem. Many climbers knew what the Climber's Club was and wanted no part of it. The image had to be changed and young climbers recruited to the Club. Alec Sharp was one of the first of these. He rewrote the Cloggy guide and a new guide to the still developing Gogarth cliffs for the Club. The committee made sure that it had a high profile so that they became well-known to active climbers. This policy paid off. Once again the Club had the leading climbers of the day in all spheres as members.

After two disastrous A4 editions, the *Journal* needed reviving. Ken Wilson (by then a very able magazine editor) and Bill O'Connor edited the first one before handing it into the capable hands of Geoff Milburn. Later at the 1979 AGM Ken and David Cox proposed the motion that the *Journal* be published three times every five years, ensuring its continuance.

At the end of the 1970s the committee could look back with satisfaction. It had made the Club accessible to everyone who was qualified to join,

---

36. Also led by a CC member, John Hunt (now Lord Llanfairwaterdine). It is not generally known that John Hunt was the third CC member to be asked to lead this expedition. Charles Evans was asked first. He said he would lead it if he could include the current 'hard men' of the Rock and Ice — the Alpine Club mandarins on the Himalayan Committee refused this, wanting only Oxbridge chaps on the team. Shipton was asked next — but the Committee felt his team selection was too small to give them the success they desired. Finally, John Hunt was asked. All his army training and extremely powerful personal and organisational capabilities were called into play and ensured the deserved success of the chosen team. (Sir Jack Longland to P. H. H.).

37. At a later AGM a blimpish member asked the chair if "having let women into the Club would we be allowing coloured gentlemen in next?" Robin addressed the chair and said, "Excuse me please, but I think the Hon Member should know I am a wog."

38. Frank Fitzgerald for one.

Access to the crags and tops in Scotland and elsewhere remains an unresolved issue from the great *C. C. J.* debate begun in 1901. Unknown climber on Black Mamba (VS), Creagh an Dubh Loch. Photo: Chris Jackson.

Left to right, Roy Small, Chris Jackson, Dave Edwards, Bob Conway, Bill Wintrip and Paul Carling in Pembroke, Easter 1981. Photo: Jackson Collection.

Above: Pete Thexton, Pat Littlejohn and Keith Darbyshire after the first ascent of Spacewalk (E2), Devil's Chimney area of Lundy, 18th April 1974. Photo: Ken Wilson.

Below: The 'paint tray' (Boat Squadron) *en route* to Lundy in 1971. Martin Chambers, Pat Littlejohn, Ken Wilson, Bob Moulton, Frank Cannings and Ed Grindley can be spotted. Photo: Ken Wilson Archive.

Landing operations on Lundy beach on a military-aided early trip to the island, 28th August 1970. Photo: Martin Chambers.

regardless of class, creed, colour or gender. It would never revert to the stilted gentlemanly days of the 1950s.

During his presidency Hamish Nicol also started to re-organise the Club's guidebooks. Up until that time the Club had regarded guideboks as charitable work and did not aim to make a profit from them. Then it recognised that if it did not aim to make a profit it would make a loss. The Committee were not prepared to subsidise every climber in North Wales. Initially Hamish became the first publications business manager and recruited Bob Moulton to be the guidebook editor. A quick glance at the Club's 5th, 6th, and 7th series shows what a powerful force this Sub-Committe became. At first the guidebook finances were handled through the main Committee, but this became unwieldy. Also, there was the suspicion that guidebook sales were subsidising other Club activities. It wasn't until the early 1980s, after acrimonious debate,[39] that the guidebook finances were split from the main Committee finances. Again, this reform has worked well to the benefit of the Club.

Not unnaturally, the Club, reconciled within itself, started to prosper. South Pembroke was the newly developing climbing area, and in that area, under the presidency of Trevor Jones, the Club purchased its sixth hut. The huts gradually, under Henry Adler, started to improve in condition and standard, though Tim Lewis's axiom of 'Cleanliness is next to Godliness — make friends in high places — clean the hut before your next route', should be upheld by a Club of active climbers.

Having missed Helyg's 50th anniversary as a hut (it was still a men-only hut) the Club celebrated its 60th anniversary with style and produced a definitive history of the hut, its life and times. Further modifications to the accommodation at the hut brought back its atmosphere and once again it is a pleasant place to stay, even if, like this *Journal's* editor, you have to nod to the occasional ghost.

Almost as a matter of course, some 15 years after allowing women to become members of the Club, the Club elected its first woman President, Jancis Allison. Appropriately, she was someone who on cold stormy nights in the '60s had slept in the outside toilet at Ynys Ettws, not being allowed then into the hut. At this point the Club moved quietly into the 1990s.

It is obvious that throughout all of its history the Club had the potential to lead, inform, and form opinion. It needs to keep its established place at the centre of debate. There is a tremendous survival instinct within the Club. Consider the Club's life to date: in the 1900s it mixed English provincial intelligensia with the Welsh members; in the 1920s and 30s the Oxbridge members with the hard men from Liverpool; in the 1950s it accommodated, albeit slowly, the new, often working-class, provincial clubs; in the 1960s it reinvented itself and almost adopted the Alpha; in the 1970s it elected women and the Yorkshire activists. All this is reflected in our membership. We should

---

39. Principally between the Treasurer, J. H. Longland, the guidebook business manager, A. H. Jones and K. Wilson.

be very proud of this.

In writing this version (I have no doubt that there are others) of the Club's history I have almost lost count of the times that I realised that a crisis was emerging. Yet we are better than this. The last 20 years have shown that. The ferocity of debate surrounding the Club shows not only how diverse we are, but how highly members treasure the Club. This needs to be remembered by all generations. The Club needs to focus on the main climbing issues of the day and not be complacent about them. They need to be debated and managed, and we can all play a very full part in this. We need to encourage adventure climbing in all its aspects, and most of all we should ratify a sin of omission from the 1930s and start to fight very hard for the freedom of access legislation for all the high uncultivated ground and open country in our land. In doing this not only will it benefit our own and future generations, but it will help to realise the most important dream that our founding members believed in.

Postscript

In writing this article I am aware that there are many omissions; the article could easily have been many times its length. Any writers of history have problems of what to put in and leave out. I have tried to follow the trends and patterns of the Club's history as I have perceived them. Many members have helped me. It may not have been historically important to record A.B.'s arrival to the Club, for example, but I have no doubts that many would want this celebrated in a history of the Club.

I have made no pretence about my political stance. I could not have written any kind of history without it. I regret not being able to delve more deeply into the 1940s and 1950s, especially in the establishing of the R. O. Downes hut, but again length prohibited that.

I can hear a certain Salford/Rossendale plumber saying, "He was alright, was Bob..." but I had better stop. Talking with ghosts has its own reward.

'Access to mountains'

'In my opinion mountains should not belong to private individuals. Great natural objects belong, or should belong, to the nation'.
A. L. Bagley
(Vol. IV No.13 September 1901)

DEER AND DEER FORESTS

A. L. BAGLEY
(Vol. IV No. 13 September 1901)

Two articles have appeared in the May number of the *Scottish Mountaineering Club Journal* on the above subject; one of them by Duncan Darroch of Torridon, the other by A. E. Maylard. The subject, to climbers and mountaineers, is obviously of supremest importance. I, a humble member of the mountaineering brotherhood, had awaited these articles with eagerness, and opened my new number of the *S. M. C. J.* the other day in anxious expectation. I am bitterly disappointed. I hardly expected to find much comfort in Mr. Duncan Darroch's paper, but 1 am equally disappointed in Mr. Maylard's.

Mr. Darroch's paper opens very nicely. "To the majority of the owners and occupiers of deer forests in Scotland it is a great pleasure to be able to allow the climbing and scientific public to share as far as possible in the delights of climbing the hills and enjoying the scenery." Well, we must be thankful for small mercies, especially when no others seem likely to be forthcoming. The value of Mr. Darroch's benevolent proclamation is perhaps somewhat impaired by the qualifying words "as far as possible," since there is likely to be much difference of opinion between the Highland laird and the Sassenach tourist as to the limits of possibility; also it is a little discouraging to the tourist, who without any claim to be considered a climber, yet loves the moors and hills, to find even the meagre privileges which Mr. Darroch is willing to accord, restricted to "the climbing and scientific public"; still Mr. Darroch might conceivably have written, "The majority of the owners and occupiers of deer forests in Scotland are absolutely determined to prevent the public, whether climbing, scientific or otherwise, from sharing in the delights of climbing the hills and enjoying the scenery." Probably a good many owners and occupiers of deer forests would very much like to issue such a proclamation, and I will do Mr. Darroch the bare justice to admit that he is a little more liberal-minded than many of his class.

After some remarks on the habits of the deer, Mr. Darroch goes on to define *his* views of the limits imposed by those fateful words "as far as possible," and sums up by remarking that during the months of February, March, April, May, no real harm can be done to the sporting interests by those who wish to visit the hills for mountaineering or scientific purposes. I am glad to see, be it remarked *en passant*, that this time he uses the wider word "mountaineering" instead of "climbing." There are many mountaineers who are not, in any sense of the word, climbers. I myself love the mountains, and have set my foot on many of Scotland's loftiest summits, but a stalwart of the Scottish Mountaineering Club would laugh to scorn my claims to be considered a climber, because I have never held on to invisible ledges by my eyelids, or climbed rock faces by means of a living ladder of my fellow-men, or performed any others of the marvellous feats whereof one occasionally reads in their annals. However, enough of quibbling.

Unfortunately, Mr. Darroch goes on to say that notice should be given to the keepers beforehand. It is difficult to understand why this should be necessary, if, in his own words, "no real harm can be done." It may be said that this is a little thing to ask, but I think otherwise. In the first place, one has first to find the keeper, and this is not always easy in many parts of Scotland, where one's hotel, or head-quarters, is often at a great distance from the mountain which one means to ascend. Moreover, we all know the uncertainty of the weather, especially in the Western Highlands. To give notice to the keeper beforehand means deciding on your expedition a few days beforehand; when the day arrives, it is possibly pouring in torrents; if you have given notice to the keeper, he is probably awaiting you somewhere; you feel that he will be deeply disappointed if you do not keep your appointment; you either go, and get miserably soaked, or you decide, with unusual strength of mind, to stay indoors; in the latter case the keeper will probably feel, and possibly express, intense contempt of your prudence, you will have to make all your arrangements over again, and the keeper will probably expect a double douceur. "Giving notice beforehand" opens up a vista of innumerable difficulties and drawbacks, and I for one will have none of it, if I can possibly help it.

Mr. Darroch goes on to say that we others — tourists, mountaineers, &c. — have no conception of the damage that may be done unintentionally. I will admit at once that this is probably the case. I am earnestly desirous, and I hope Mr Darroch believes that we all are, of avoiding the committal of any damage, and I am open to instruction. I would like to ask whether it is literally true that a tourist, walking quietly across a moor or up a mountain, will banish a stag to a neighbouring forest? If it *is* true, then it seems to me that even if some of Mr. Darroch's stags fly to another man's forest, and do not return, some other stags will be in a similar manner frightened off the other man's ground, and fly for refuge to Mr. Darroch's forest.

I may as well say here, that I do not expect to be allowed to go anywhere and everywhere at my own sweet will. I do not expect, or desire, to interfere with sport by strolling over moors while stalking is going on, nor at all during the shooting season. I always endeavour to get my trips to Scotland as early in the year as I possibly can, and I never attempt to walk over deer forests or to ascend mountains, which are included in deer forests, after the beginning of July, unless of course there are public paths up them, as there is up Cairn Gorm for instance. In fact if Mr. Darroch could only extend the period, during which "no real harm could be done," to include the month of June, and would withdraw the suggestion as to giving notice, this article would never have been written. But in the last paragraph Mr. Darroch goes on to make special mention of the month of June, inasmuch as he states his willingness to allow tourists to go over his ground during that

month, "if accompanied by a keeper." I can only say, speaking for myself;
that I would far rather not go at all, fond as I am of Scotland, and of Scottish
hills. To me, and I imagine to most mountaineers, the pleasure of the day
would be entirely spoiled, if I had to be personally conducted up a mountain; the greater part of the pleasure lies in making out one's own way, in the
indulgence of the exploring instinct, which we all possess in a greater or less
degree. Besides, I fancy Scottish gamekeepers might prove rather an expensive luxury, and personally I do not feel that I can afford such an addition to
my holiday expenses.

I always try, as I just remarked, to arrange my Scotch trips as early in
the summer as possible, but I have never yet found it possible to get to the
Highlands before the end of May or the beginning of June. I expect many
others are in the same position, and it seems rather hard that, because the
nature of our respective avocations prevents us from taking our holidays
before the beginning of June, therefore we are to be debarred from ascending the innumerable Scottish mountains which lie in deer forests, or are
only to be personally conducted to the summit under the stern and expensive guidance of a gamekeeper.

It seems to amply prove the arrogance of Scottish landowners, as a
class, when one of the most liberal of them thinks it worth while to enunci-
ate with unction, that permission to go on the hills will always be given, at a
time when "no real harm can be done," and when the majority of *nous autres*
are unable to go; but when, in addition, a prominent member of our own
camp accepts that enunciation with tears of gratitude and joy, and kow-
tows, as it were, at the feet of the benevolent enunciator, showering down
blessings upon the latter's head, it is really time for somebody to take up
their parable, if only to protest that Mr. Maylard does not speak for all mountaineers. I cannot help doubting whether the glow of pleasure with which he
seems to have been so profusely pervaded by the perusal of Mr. Darroch's
paper, will be quite so universal among the members of the Scottish Mountaineering Club, as he thinks, and feel convinced that very little of that pleasure will cross the Border and be transmitted to the various English climbing
clubs.

There is a certain "stately home of England" built on a cliff, overhanging a river. I have been told that this river is really navigable, and that there
still exists in the town archives a charter, centuries old, declaring the river
navigable up to, and including, the town, which, be it noted, is situated
above the castle. An ancestor of the present noble proprietor took a fancy to
the site, wherein truly I find it difficult to blame him, built his castle, and
then said, "Now, you base-born churls, clear out, you're not to pollute my
river, or the neighbourhood of my castle with your presence"; forgetting, or
ignoring the fact, that the river was there before either he or his castle, and
that the base-born churls had more right to it than he. Similarly, a Scottish
landowner takes a few square miles of moorland, on which incidentally are
several mountains, converts it into a deer forest, and then says in effect:
"Now, you base-born Sassenach tourists, clear out, this is a deer forest,"

&c., &c. I will admit that the parallel is not quite complete, inasmuch as the Sassenach tourist was not on the spot before the laird, but the spirit is the same, and everybody who knows anything of the Highlands, knows of innumerable cases where the most bare-faced attempts have been made to close up public paths.

There is a certain shooting-lodge in the Highlands built on a public road; the front door opens on the road, the lawns and gardens on each side of the road are not separated from it by any fence or anything of the kind, and at the boundary of the private grounds a gate is thrown across the road, which is thereby converted, to all semblance, into a private drive; passing the house one comes to another similar gate, then the road winds between various stables and outbuildings, out to the open moor. Now, this is obviously not right; no proprietor, whoever he may be, has the right to enclose a portion of the public highway within his private grounds. The average tourist, arriving at the first gate, would naturally conclude that he had reached the entrance of a private domain, and would probably retrace his steps; which very likely was the precise object which the noble proprietor had in view when the gates were placed there. I myself was driven along this road some few years ago, and, on arriving at the gate, my driver concluded, not unnaturally, that we had no right to go on, and thought he had taken a wrong turning (he had never been on this road before); fortunately, I knew something of the road, and insisted upon his going on.

Not very long ago I was myself stopped on the public road by one of Mr. Darroch's keepers; at least I conclude he was Mr. Darroch's keeper, since it happened near Torridon, who insisted upon knowing whether I had been on the hills. Have Mr. Darroch, or his myrmidons, the right to stop peaceful pedestrians on the King's highway, and demand whether they had dared to set a sacrilegious foot upon his — Mr. Darroch's — hills? I may further remark that this took place very early in June. As a matter of fact, I *had* been on the hills, but I might easily have been a simple pedestrian from Torridon, and the keeper had no reason to suppose that I was otherwise. I will, however, do Mr. Darroch the justice to believe that the keeper in this case exceeded his instructions.

In my opinion mountains should not belong to private individuals. Great natural objects belong, or should belong, to the nation. A great waterfall, like Niagara or the Skjaeggedalsfos, is open to the whole world. What would be thought of the proprietor of the ground round the Skjaeggedalsfos, if he were to put up a fence round it, and announce that in future tourists would only be allowed access at a period of the year when most of them could not go and would not care to, say the middle of winter? Everybody has a right to ascend Ben Nevis; everybody ought to have a right to ascend Liathach, which is indeed, in my opinion, a far more interesting mountain than Ben Nevis. It is unfortunate that the country around Liathach, including, I suppose, that interesting mountain, belongs to Mr. Darroch, but the proprietor is, after all, only a sort of trustee; the public have certain indefinable rights, and when they see a noble mountain like Liathach rising up almost immediately from the high road, and a magnificent corrie with most singular terraces, the like of which I never remember to have seen elsewhere, it is not reasonable to expect them to sit down on the road and look at it, and be satisfied therewith. If Liathach, or a similar mountain, were situated in my back garden, and I wish to Heaven it were, I should not consider myself justified in putting a brick wall round my garden, and rigidly excluding the public therefrom, nor in issuing a proclamation to the effect that certain sections of the public would be allowed, during a certain part of the year, to go round the property under the guidance of my gardener. I should not, certainly, throw open my garden gates, and invite every Tom, Dick and Harry to walk in, to go where he listed, to pluck my fruit, to pull my flowers, to play football with my cabbages. But I would allow everybody showing a genuine interest in mountains free access whensoever they might wish; possibly now and then this indulgence might be abused, but I fancy very rarely.

The British public, as a rule, are law-abiding, and respect the rights of property, and the mountaineering section of the public are almost invariably gentlemen, although Mr. Darroch seems rather unpleasantly to hint the contrary. At all events, after relating how a "distinguished scientist" had asked permission to "go along the watershed of my principal hill," and giving the gist of his own reply, Mr. Darroch goes on to observe, "Our friend... was a gentleman, and wrote at once to say that he would put off his trip for another year." Certainly he could hardly have done otherwise, in view of the snub he had received, and the moral of this instructive anecdote seems to be: "Don't ask permission to go over a certain hill, lest you should be snubbed." I should have thought it hardly necessary to state that a distinguished scientist was a gentleman, and believe they usually are, but the inference certainly seems that Mr. Darroch in general considers men who desire to explore his hills are not likely to be gentlemen.

There was a little bill brought into the House of Commons last year, I believe by Mr. Bryce, entitled "the Access to Mountains Bill," and I regret deeply that it was negatived. I do not know any details of it, but the general principle, viz., that the public should be allowed access to all mountains, should certainly, in my opinion, be affirmed by Parliament, and recorded in the laws of the nation.

One more personal experience, and I have done. There is a certain noble group of mountains in the Highlands, which I have long wished to explore more thoroughly than is usually possible, owing to their remoteness from the habitations of men. I have been on all the principal summits, but they lie so far from the nearest inn or lodgings that I have never been able to do more than the summits, while a vast amount of interesting detail lies among them almost entirely unexplored. There is, especially, a vast corrie with glorious encircling precipices, which I have gazed at longingly, both from above and from below, but have never been able to explore. Close to this corrie, within a few hundred yards of its gloomy portals, is a small wooden hut, or bothy, used I suppose in the stalking season. I wrote to the mighty potentate, to whom the whole countryside, for miles around, belongs, and asked whether he would allow a friend and myself to occupy the hut for a few nights, in order that we might explore the surrounding mountains, and particularly the corrie. I believe it was the end of May when I proposed to go, and in any case I could, on that occasion, have arranged the time to suit him and would of course have done so. There is an undoubtedly public path within a few hundred yards of the bothy, so that there could not be much fear of frightening the deer; moreover I asked him to place any restrictions upon us, in the way of leaving special sanctuaries for the deer, and such restrictions would of course have been religiously observed. The potentate refused absolutely, not on account of the deer, which would indeed have been more consistent, and perhaps more pardonable, or at least comprehensible, but the sole reason given for the rejection was, "that were he to accede to my request, he would be inundated with many similar requests, which it would be difficult for him to consistently refuse." Ye gods! Is it likely that the British public will ever flock in their thousands, or desire to do so, to a spot about 15 miles, over some of the roughest ground in Britain, from a shop, post-office, inn, railway station, or any other of the adjuncts of civilisation, which to ninety-nine British tourists out of every hundred, are absolute necessities of their existence? Remember too, that all baggage, all provisions, everything, in fact, has to be in some way transported over these 15 miles, and that the ground for a great part of the distance is, I should imagine, far too rough for any beast of burden; it is obvious that the whole affair would be a most arduous undertaking, and that not many, even among keen mountaineers, would care to take it on.

Moreover, the bothy would be required, I suppose, for the game watchers during the month of July, and after that by the sportsmen themselves; nobody would want to camp (and it would practically be camping) in those latitudes and at that elevation, earlier than the end of May, so that there would be only a very few weeks in each year during which it could possibly be occupied by mountaineering parties. It might conceivably lead to a little extra correspondence, a few extra letters per annum for the potentate's secretary to write, but it is absurd to suppose that anything else could result.

This is the more surprising because the same potentate allowed a well-attended gathering of a Scottish climbing club to take place in one of his houses; if I am not mistaken, the house was placed entirely at their disposal; at all events they stayed there two or three nights, slept and feasted there, and were sent on their way rejoicing. I remember reading an account of the proceedings at the time with some envy, and thinking that after all these great Scottish seigneurs had been maligned; and it was in a great measure in consequence of this that I ventured to ask for the use of the bothy. Truly, it does not follow because it pleases a noble seigneur to entertain a company of his compatriots, that he must therefore extend his hospitality to all and sundry who may present themselves. The noble seigneur, however, is a great stickler for consistency; he cannot allow me the use of his bothy, because in that case he could not consistently refuse it to anybody else. He allows the Scottish climbers to use his shooting-lodge; are we to understand that the same principles of logic are extended to it which apply to the bothy? If so, should I have been allowed to occupy the shooting-lodge had I possessed the "cheek" to ask that favour? If not, why should it be possible to consistently refuse me the shooting-lodge, but impossible to refuse other people the bothy? It would have been a graceful act, and I should have esteemed it a great favour, had he allowed me to occupy the bothy. I think if he allowed a company of Scottish climbers to occupy his private house he might have found it possible to have allowed two Sassenach wanderers to occupy his hut.

EDITORIAL NOTES

E. RAYMOND TURNER
(Vol. IV No. 14 December 1901

It has come to the knowledge of the Editor that a paper in the September number of the *Journal*, on the subject of right of access to Scottish deer forests, has caused annoyance to many of our members, whose attitude towards this much debated question differs widely from that of the writer of the paper. While taking the general view that the *Journal* should be open to all sides of questions directly affecting the interests of mountaineers, the Editor sincerely regrets the introduction of remarks which have naturally aroused a strong feeling of objection.

COMMITTEE NOTES

(SECRETARY: GEORGE E. BRYANT)
(Vol. IV No. 15 March 1902)

Several members having enquired what the attitude of the Club is towards the Deer Forest Question, and whether it is correctly represented by an article on the subject which recently appeared in the *Journal*, the Committee wish to state that the article mentioned, precisely like any other article, represents no more and no less than the private opinions of the writer who signs it.

Secondly, that the attitude which they consider that our members should take up towards the owner of a deer forest is precisely the same as they would naturally adopt towards the owner of a library, a picture gallery, a garden, or any other property, the occasional use of which adds to their enjoyment of life. They feel certain that no member of this Club, whatever abstract theories he may choose to discuss, would in practice do anything knowingly to injure property or to interfere with sport, and, in shewing this consideration, each member incidentally procures better treatment for himself and his clubmates on other occasions.

There must, however, be cases where his experience is at fault, and then he can hardly do better than be guided by that of the Scottish Mountaineering Club, which has of necessity given long and close attention to the matter.

KYNDWR CLUB NOTES

(extract)

UNATTRIBUTED
(Vol. IX No. 34 December 1906)

To save a circuit we kept away from the bridge over Ashop, and, striking the river higher up, had to struggle across, from stone to stone. The spot was marked by a boundary, and we used the three wires to support us over the longest strides, fearing all the while that the frail threads would drop us into the eddying scours. Evening was upon us as we walked up the last mile to the Snake. The sky was rosy; there was a whole firmament of light overhead but the vast sombre masses of the Kinder buttresses were like the pillars of a realm of night. The deep brown face of the moor seemed to radiate darkness, itself growing darker and darker, until the whole vast fell, with its rocks and black heather tracts and its profound ravines, was nothing but many gradations in a vortex of gloom.

Our party, in the course of the next hour or two, was augmented by fresh arrivals, until we attained the happy number of a round dozen. We dined and drank each other's health, and finished up by drinking success to the Access to Mountains Bill, which we hoped would one day free the mountains of Derbyshire, as well as those of Scotland, from the iron rule of the gamekeeper, so far at least as concerns the rambler and the climber.

It was after midnight when we went to bed, and by then a perfect moon was shining in a sky of absolute purity. No longer dark and gloomy, the sides of Kinder were transfigured and spiritualised, shining with a pearly lustre, slope beyond slope growing more and more ethereal up to the ghostly skyline of the Edges. The Ashop and the Fairbrook were twisting the moonbeams into chains of silver; the deep and rugged cloughs brimful of moonlit haze; whilst overhead the great orb, no longer a flat disc, as it appears to us in town, shining with reflected beams like a phantom sun, swung in the blue infinity as a globe of light; and the star that watched its progress really seemed, as it really is, a far more distant point of light in the unfathomable depths beyond.

'Just good friends'

'The most enduring friendships he had ever formed would have been impossible but for his love of climbing'.
Report of the President C. E. Mathews's 'Toast to the Club'
(Vol. I No. 4 June 1899)

JUST GOOD FRIENDS

KYM MARTINDALE
(1993)

Intense as lovers our climbing made us
And as precarious,
We dovetailed our dreams
And our gear
Which we bought as carefully as couples in Habitat.

We blazed with triumphs
Savoured like suns in our own universe;
Sharp and hungry,
We crept without breathing up slabs,
Battled on cracked faces,
Swung over and round ledges and edges.

We grew round the climbing too,
Attuned to each other
As we leant burnt and tired from a route across a beer-ringed table,
Or crouched on sky ledges where gulls scavenged.
Loved each other we said at last,
Bleary with whisky the first time,
The second time stonily sober
On a grey washed-up day at the foot of cliffs
Beyond us in every way.

For just as we grew easy
With the warmth we had,
Something cold and sickly crept from us
And between us and the rock.
We began to lose.
And each loss was harder to reason
Or console away.

Our moves became bloodless.
Blunted and stale with futile longing
We stood hostages to our terrors
At the foot of a tide-slapped slab,
Or a wet jug-handled wall;
Months before we would have danced them with quick care,
Fear the spice which gingered the pleasure,
Not the drowning whole.

Raw with loss
We were useless to each other.
Pain mirrored hurts twice.
Chained to the foothills
By our anguished ambition
We toiled only to tangle.
Cutting loose was a confused hacking
And when the ties fell
We blundered uncertainly, you for the plains,
I circling with a dim remembrance of the joy
Until with small steps and a sense of my fate as my own
I returned
And arrived.

But celebrations for myself
Are less for the absence of you,
Sadder for knowing that I could not arrive with you,
As you could no longer with me.

This summer you gave me your gear
And your leaving was no longer words.
Our ground has shifted,
We have found new footing
And I still have in you
All that made me love you.

But the biggest loss
Is clipping your gear to my harness
And when I climb
It is with a resonance of you.

J. M. EDWARDS

WILFRID NOYCE
(1959)

A boy of 17, I was staying at Helyg over an Easter meet. On the Friday evening, while the others descended to Capel, I stayed in. The only other person in the hut was a man in tattered coat and seaman's jersey, a man with powerful looking shoulders and a strange face, handsome in its way. The hair was auburn, almost woolly; the jaw firm and jutting, so as to force a hollow below the full lips; the face smooth, rather childlike but for the eyes, which were those of a man who has seen a good deal.

"Let's have tea," the stranger, whom I knew to be one of my 'heroes,' said. And we got talking.

So it started. Next day Menlove suggested climbing, and we went to the Three Cliffs. "Going to dig in your back garden?" somebody grinned. At that time the Three Cliffs were considered dangerously loose and full of vertical vegetation. We got a lift round to Pen y Pass. "I really go there because I like to walk downhill to my cliff," Menlove said. He never spoke with any pleasure of walking uphill for its own sake, or of the hills themselves with affection, though "Good old Tryfan" might slip out, almost apologetically, at times. It was obvious, that first day, that something else was in the air. Each of the three routes that we did was a struggle, each demanded the power to wrestle in an uncomfortable position. Several times Menlove seemed defeated, whether by rock or grass, but hung on, clinkers scrabbling, while he hitched the rope over a minute projection. Several times those enormously powerful arms got him up. I learned a lot that day.

There is no space to do justice to Menlove's major contribution to rock-climbing, nor even to give much of a picture of him as a climber. He was an originator in the way in which he developed new cliffs ("because other people don't go there," he said), often on variable rock, and in his use of safety de~ices which have now become commonplace. Long before karabiners were used he fell off Eliminate on Helsby, where others had been killed. But he had managed to protect himself with a sling, and this art he found most useful on his hunting grounds round the Devil's Kitchen, on Craig Rhaiadr and the Three Cliffs.

To climb with, Menlove gave the impression of strength rather than of lightness (Colin Kirkus's quality). The whole thing was a wrestling match, and specially so in the clinkers he usually insisted on wearing. In 1935 he struggled for nearly an hour, in clinkers, to repeat his feat of climbing Flake Crack on C.B. unaided. When that failed, he waited placidly for my nailed boot on his head. It was this leaning towards effort which made him the first (and only?) man to row solo across the Minch to the Outer Hebrides and back. Or he would take a canoe to the Isle of Man over a Whit weekend. And

Left to right, Bruce Andrew, Jack Street, Carol Street and Geoff Birtles at Black Rocks, Cromford c. 1968. Photo: Bob Keates/Wilson Archive.

Above: Morty Smith (left) and Joe Brown after their second ascent of Biven and Peck's Bastion Wall (then A3) whilst Biven and Peck were making the first ascent of Fortress Wall (then A3) at High Tor, Matlock, in 1957. Bastion Wall is now free as Robert Brown (E3), Parts of Fortress Wall are now Hot Gossip (E5) and Lyme Cryme (E3). Photo: Biven Collection.
Below: Joe Brown (left) and Don Whillans c.1968. Photo: Ken Wilson Archive.

In 1985 at the BMC's Buxton Conference there was a charity 'beauty contest' won by Donna Whillans. Photos: Ian Smith.

Above: Ruth Allen and Don Whillans at the 1984 C. C. Welsh Dinner. Photo: Chris Jackson.
Below: Left to right, Keith Sharples, Graham Hoey, Ian Smith and Marjorie Allen (with Hugo) below Great Wanney in Northumberland in June 1984. Photo: Mike Mortimer.

yet Western Slabs on Dinas Mot and Bow-Shaped on Clogwyn Du'r Arddu showed that he could be delicate too, when he wished. It was a question of mood, and, as he said himself, on some days he would fail to get up Hope. As a second he gave a feeling of confidence and strength that was not illusory. Under his eye I was made to lead climbs I had not dreamed of, but to profit even more from the experience of his mature and affectionate loyalty than from that of leading.

With people, with writing, it was the same story. "My over great intensity with people is not v. good for them either," he wrote once, "except that it's necessary with patients to be absolutely following every least mental shift" — and that made him a brilliant psychologist. In writing there was the same sense of convulsion, the same conquest of obstacles as much in himself as in the material. Nothing came easily, but what came was worth waiting for. The Climbers' Club owes him three full guides (since my own part was entirely subordinate) and the Clogwyn Du'r Arddu interim offprint. These set a new standard. They took the climber to the rock face, not just to the line up it which somebody had traced, and described that face in remarkable prose. One may quarrel with the underestimations but not with the descriptions, and his talent for this type of writing comes out still more vividly in the few short stories. These, with fragments of tortured and yet wonderful verse, are all that he has left. Being a psychologist, and Menlove, he was one of the few who could come near to putting on paper the states of mind of the climber.

The years after 1939 have been years of tragic waste. Menlove received absolute exemption as a conscientious objector, but he never recovered from the shock of war and the suspicion that his fellows were engaged in a madness which in a real sense threatened him personally. If the war had not come, he would have fulfilled himself in the psychological work he set out to write. As it was, nearly 20 years of frustration are now succeeded by a death which should never have been. We mourn one of the great personalities of climbing, and a man who might have been many things besides.

WILFRID NOYCE

G. J. SUTTON
(1963)

There are two kinds of climbers, those who are happy in motion and those who are happy when still. The first and much smaller category comprises the naturals. You can tell them by a kind of supple, relaxed, flowing movement on rock, which seems to demand little thought. They take easily to skis or crampons. In my experience they reach their top standard early, and they complete a long route much faster than the other sort. The second and larger group is made up of those who have consciously had to overcome a lack of aptitude. Their motions are deliberate, not rhythmic, and they take little rests between hard moves to calm themselves and work things out. Their one real advantage is precisely that their underlying discomfort forces them to think. You get great climbers of both kinds. I have been lucky enough to observe some of the best climbers of several countries in action, and I have no hesitation in saying that Wilfrid Noyce was as good an example of the first category as I have seen.

One's main impression in climbing with Wilf was of ease and lack of tension. His carelessness of danger was sometimes breath-taking, and sprang from his exceptional sureness of foot — or was it the other way round? I could never work it out. It seems indisputable that he was the greatest British mountaineer of his generation, yet he consciously limited his achievement to exclude the great modern Alpine rock routes he could so easily have mastered. I think this was partly because of a lingering distaste for the large-scale use of pitons, born of his pre-war association with Menlove Edwards and his cousin Colin Kirkus, and partly because the slow toilsomeness of artificial climbing removed the wings from his heels.

All this dynamism released itself smoothly and quietly, without any fireworks. He was painstaking of detail in all work and tenacious in pushing things through, always ready to do more than his fair share and let others take the credit. Though I think he basically preferred to keep his own counsel (he never in any sense *confided*) he was conscientious in keeping others in touch with all that concerned them. In daily life he was quiet, modest, amusing, but by no means shy or stumbling when called upon to speak publicly. When we were collaborating on *Snowdon Biography*, Geoffrey Young and I disagreed over the question of whether climbing progress is smooth and imperceptible or goes by jumps, and Wilfrid revealed himself a peacemaker. Indeed he seemed to carry a pot of peace inside him which he could spread on others when required, and loyalty was not so much a principle of his mind as of his inmost nature. When you were with him you could talk or be silent with equal companionableness.

Whether or not Wilfrid was accident-prone, I do not think he consciously took more risks than are unavoidable in mountaineering. A certain insouciance of gesture is at once the strength and the Achilles' heel of the superb natural climber. At the time when he returned to Himalayan mountaineering, because of Everest, he must have made certain conscious decisions about the meaning of life, common perhaps to many who continue in dangerous sports after the age of thirty, which preclude conventional sentiment after his death. "Man is great in that he is a bridge and not a goal", said Nietzsche, and perhaps the emotion of dread resolved in ennoblement which comes from tragedy is more appropriate. The whole thing is much discussed in his novel, *The Gods Are Angry,* with which I once disagreed in print. I no longer do so. Under the layers of the public schoolmaster, the man of culture, the thinker, the poet, one divined a knight at arms, simple in himself and unwilling to dissemble, not born out of his time because his time is the whole struggle of humanity to define its essence.

'THIS GENTLEMAN MUST BE KEPT OUT...'

KYNDWR CLUB NOTES (UNATTRIBUTED)
(Vol. III No. 9 September 1900)

WHARNCLIFFE CRAGS. By the invitation of Mr. J. W. Puttrell, a party went on June 16th to Sheffield, where they were met by Mr. Puttrell and Mr. Watson, and taken to Wharncliffe Crags. These crags are one of the gritstone escarpments, which are usually called "edges," and rise on the crest of a hill overlooking a richly wooded valley, almost within sight of Sheffield. Although the climbs vary in height between the narrow limits of 20 and 40 feet, they comprise almost every conceivable form of mountain gymnastics, and every grade of difficulty. There may be longer climbs in Derbyshire, but certainly no place in Peakland affords anything like the variety and number of these Wharncliffe scrambles. At one spot a little cove, surrounded by towers of gritstone, gives immediate access to seven or eight distinct climbs, mostly difficult; chimneys for back and knee work, chockstones that have to be embraced with fearsome contortions, awkward corners, and, most sensational of all, a rocktower, which the climber has to ascend from another slightly lower by stretching his arms straight overhead and falling horizontally at full length across the intervening rift, 5 feet wide and 40 feet deep. Dropping on the palms of his hands, and toeing the smooth side of the rocktower, he lifts himself by the arms over the edge into safety. The Monkey Jump is a still stranger affair. Leaping a chasm 5 or 6 feet wide, one has to alight on a shelf that is closely overhung by a mass of rock, compelling one to twist slightly in mid-air so as to finish in a stooping position. Altogether a most intimidating nerve-test, though on a small scale. Hard by is another innocent-looking problem — a corner with sloping top that has to be scaled by means of a peculiar "pick-up" on the wrists, with a tumble into a rocky gully for the forfeit.

Our Sheffield friends are in the habit, from strictly scientific motives, of course, of eliminating the more convenient holds from any given climb, much in the way a crafty examiner leaves out the handiest logarithms; and so they can set the newcomer some exceedingly severe problems. A certain face climb, for example, was stiffened by the imaginary removal of a large boulder; and it was gratifying to the Sheffielders to see how regularly the Kinderites dropped off on the rope as, one by one, they reached the level of this desirable stone. A good deal of diversion was created by a non-climbing visitor. Bond and Baker had struggled with much ado up a difficult cleft, when this gentleman, after watching them compassionately, called out, "But why don't you chaps do it this way?" and straightway ran up the cliff after the fashion of a cat storming a wall, quite heedless of the fact that he ought

to have nails in his boots. This gentleman must be kept out of the Climbers'
Club at all hazards, for climbing will soon cease to be an art if our pet scrambles are to be massacred in this summary way.

The day was concluded by an informal concert, the songs and canti-
cles wherewith the peaks of Wales and Cumberland are now so well acquainted, being re-sung with the usual gusto; and the hospitable Sheffielders
departed a little before midnight.

BREAKING THE RULES

JANCIS ALLISON
(1991. President: J. M. Allison**)**

The scene is set in the early '60s, when the Climbers' Club was an all-male club. It should perhaps also be explained that at that time, Ynys Ettws had a bathroom (now the 'members only' bedroom).

There was a time in days of yore
When women were not allowed through the door
Of Ynys, Helyg, nor the Downes Hut neither,
Though not through want of trying either,
To join that great illustrious Club
Of hardy climbers — (ah, there's the rub).
For its numbers were worried they could be outdone
In feats of endurance, so I'm told by some.
Though I'm sure this certainly cannot be true —
More likely they wished to preserve their loo!
For women could use a little cell
Gainst Ynys back wall (I know it full well).
Their women this little room could use
As long as the hut they didn't abuse.

Now I have an awful tale to tell
Of sheer timidity — oh bloody hell.
How weak I was that terrible night;
I should have put up a far better fight.
For I had hitched up from Oxford City
(All on my own 'twas more the pity).
I had, I thought, a faithful friend
Who'd erect a tent for me to attend.

HOWEVER —
The night was rough and wild and wet
When down the road I was duly set;
Then forced to walk from far Nant Peris
To Ynys Ettws in the Pass, Llanberis.
The rain lashed down, the wind did howl
As I trudged on through the night so foul.
No moon shone down to light the road,
Not even the line in the centre showed.
I clung to the wall, until at last
The sign at the entrance to Ynys I passed.

I then plodded up the puddled track,
But a Vango tent the field did lack.
I searched and searched and searched in vain
For all I could see was the driving rain.
For I am very sad to say
My very good friend in Ynys lay,
In total warm and faithless bliss —
Me, he certainly did not miss.
Now, I dared not enter through Ynys door
For that would be breaking Climbers' Club law.
I decided the only place to be
Was the outside loo, for the likes of me.
So in I crept and settled my seat
On the wooden loo, which was quite a feat.
For the room was certainly very small
And not really meant for such a call.
However, I somehow managed to fill the place
With my 'sack and pit, while the water did race
Down the hillside and under the door,
And created a puddle which became more and more
Like the Padarn Lake as the time went by;
And as daylight came how I did sigh
For the days when women could be in the Club —
I would certainly always pay my sub.

However, a stroke of luck at last
For Roy Beard, the custodian, came hurrying fast.
Now Roy was known to be terribly fierce
And no woman I was sure his heart could pierce:
But this hard heart softened and he saw the light
When he realised my truly terrible plight.
For he knocked on my makeshift bedroom door
And an ass he did make of the CC law.
For he asked me in to the forbidden den
Of CC members and then, oh then...
He even offered to run the bath
This I must say caused me to laugh (not half!)
For never in all my life it seems
Nor in my very wildest dreams
Did I ever think I'd get such a chance;
This made me want to shout and dance —
For this was the beginning of the end
Of male domination — 'tis true my friend!
For wickedly through me a thought did run
Of far off days that were yet to come.
When women could walk freely through the door

Of Ynys, Helyg, the Downes — and more.
Well, now it seems, those days have arrived
And very great pleasure I have derived
From sitting proud on the new Ynys loo.
Well, wouldn't you?

CITIZEN KEN*

(1966)

The following is an extract from *C.C. Journal* for 1984:

MINISTRY OF LOVE: CASE FILE — RE-HABILITATION.

SUBJECT. K. J. W.———N.

Subject was originally employed by the Ministry of Truth in the re-writing of climbing guide-books as and when Government policy required it, in November 19—. A number of errors in his work were at first attributed to zeal, but later the true cause was found. Upon investigation by an observer from this Ministry the subject was found to be suffering from the delusion that he was the leader of 'a team' operating from 'the hub'. His capacity for 'newspeech' was shown in the coining of the word 'cream' to describe those he thought to be the climbing meritocracy. The weak sympathies of this group enabled agents to be infiltrated with ease, and upon their evidence his complicity in the ....† . (The rehabilitation of Citizen M—cN ———t-D——s was, in point of fact, coupled to this plot by this Ministry.)

On the 25th December 1979 — in accordance with the slow-moving nature of Min. Truth Climb. Dept. Citizen W——n was removed from his house in Finchley for treatment. (He was subsequently written out of climbing history.) In the early stages of interrogation he proved obdurate — largely through talking too much for our interrogators to interrogate him, but many of his melogamaniac tendencies were revealed, e.g., jealousy on professional grounds of the 'Earl of Snowdon' (sic), whose title he adjudged his own, and the pre-revolutionary notion that the proles are fit to govern themselves. (This last is indicative of his general rashness and basically obsolescent ideology.) The secondary stage of re-conversion consisted of a meeting in Room 204 with the Climbers' Club committee during which the subject was gagged. Breakdown resulted in 2 mins. (For more details see earlier case-history: C. T. J——s.)

Re-habilitation for citizenship consisted of indoctrination with classical music, hill-walking, brightly-coloured Sunday newspapers, miming, deaf and dumb speech (the subject had to be muted), and Yoga/Buddhist relaxation. The subject now runs a children's sweet-shop in Camberley.

ADDENDUM. 1st SEPT.1984.
Subject has again been under surveillance because his weight increased from 12 to 20 stones indicating that most of his stock is not being sold to children.

---

* These puzzling fragments have come to light among a bundle of correspondence and other papers. They were passed on to me as being of possible interest. I publish them in the hope that they may mean something to some members — Ed. (T. I. M. Lewis)
† This section illegible. — Ed.

TIME TO CRY 'ICHABOD'?

MARJORIE ALLEN
(1977)

A very familiar craggy face appeared over the top of a boulder. An even more familiar voice crackled through the mist shattering the air with jackdaw-like intensity,

"Hello, Hello, Hello! Which route are you two going for?"

We were all planning on Ichabod, but Scafell East Buttress was not inviting just then with an atmospheric humidity more appropriate to a London fog in November. Only the first twenty feet or so of the routes were visible. But the fever of competition soon got hold of us. Here was Ken Wilson "elbowing" us from the route with his verbal barrage and as it was important to save a reasonable amount of time and energy for the climb, we conceded to this editorial giant (after all, if we climbed on the route alongside him, who knows what dramatic photographs he may come up with in the next Bumper Fun Book).

Why not sieze this opportunity to enlist his support for my application for the Climbers' Club? Wasn't he the fellow who caused such a fuss and did such a public spirited thing as resign because women weren't acceptable — surely he'd write a supporting letter...

In the relatively commodious sentry-box stance at the foot of Ichabod and Phoenix I felt the atmosphere was a little less humid, a little less hostile. In fact, in the intimate proximity of Ken's aromatic presence, I naively made my request. Wilson never concedes that easily, I've now realised on better (or worse) acquaintance. He'd never miss such an opportunity for an inquisition and detailed analysis which would put any psychoanalyst to shame.

"Applying to the C.C. — Well, now — my philosophy is — support you with pleasure, providing you can prove to me that you really can GO IT ALONE — GET YOURSELF OUT OF A REAL EPIC FIX — Not lean on any man — Stand on your own two feet."

Christ, I thought — here we go — Chauvinist Pig approach within the first two sentences. Poor fool, hasn't he heard that "every woman is a potential Napoleon with a possible empire in each man she meets." NO man to "lean on" — no empire!

My mind whipped through cameo-like scenes of past alpine seasons. Surely, there was enough material here to give him a convincing picture of my competence. My imagination took off into orbit as I moved from crisis to crisis, tasting the mountain "high" of the one who intuitively led the team through a maze of crevasses in whiteout conditions. At dawn I was dodging avalanches with split-second timing in that death-trap of a couloir, when my companions had sworn it was only raked by Piano-sized blocks at 11 a.m. Who was the only one with fingers thin enough to jam that overhanging crack on the crux pitch? Light enough to risk hanging from that bootlace tied off from a bolt? Agile enough to leap the void of a crevasse. Next morning, the only one with energy to arrange that diagonal abseil across a complex face — the rest debilitated with altitude sickness? The team finally staggering back into the hut (with the exception of C. T. Jones who'd been ignominiously dragged across the glacier by his ankles after passing out from the agony of parting with a kidney stone — from-we-all-know-where).

Unfortunately, the cameo scenes were those of pure fantasy. My alpine seasons had been remarkably uneventful — indelibly printed in my mind as traumatic experiences but, no doubt, rather tame by Wilson's standards. He was unlikely to be impressed with the pathetic near-misses I could recall.

— that avalanche on an ice-route in the Bregalia. As I froze in my tracks within inches of the avalanche groove — Bob (safely belayed) called "don't move I want a photograph of this" I felt I was certainly about to "go it alone" — and with some velocity.

— that descent down a rotten rock face in the Pyrenees, all of 3,000 ft. of indescribable rot. As I leapt to one side the gendarme I'd been hugging only seconds before dropped below like a gigantic candle. No chance of leaning on any man there — we'd have dislodged the entire mountain. A situation which called for movements of feline stealth — one graphically described to us by a French climber: "You move with extreme care as eef you 'ave placed an olive between zee cheeks". The locals claimed we were the first to come off the face alive.

— those unexpected bivouacs from some combination of sheer fatigue, incompetence and lack of acclimatisation. My man, at risk of dying of exposure, needed me to lie on top of him to avoid a disastrous drop in temperature. And after all, I might just need his expertise the following morning to get me up that 5 Sup. pitch we had ahead of us before the summit. Score: one all, not much standing-on-my-own-two-feet material here. No use at all, when what I'd be needing was a bionic grip of those blue handholds over that impossible looking overhang — and a snug rope.

— admittedly, I know that once in my life I'd had the opportunity to really savour the exhilaration of being in command — if that's what you could call it, on the vast vertical desert of the Olan when we'd avidly followed the guide book instructions (the one where you need to be smart at knowing the game of chess moves — when to move to the left and not the right: to realise that what is described as a couloir is really a crack and that the "highest" snowfield in 1975 is in fact non-existent in 1976). Those dubious instructions had led us into a stonefall couloir festooned with shreds of scalp sprouting black curly hair and other "petit morsels" of that aspirant guide who'd attempted to solo the route the previous week. There may have been just five seconds between the bombardment of "bricks" that were tipped from the natural quarry above. I think I kept calm — or was it numb, or resigned to a similar fate to the guide when I spotted human spoor prints on a natural terrace cutting across the entire face. Such an escape route was a gift from the Gods for any mountaineer. This qualified, to me, as a real epic fix alright, with Mike's right hand out of commission from one of those stray bricks ricocheting from rock face to helmet to index finger. He felt faint from the steady flow of blood and deliriously insisted that we just sat down and waited for a helicopter. We'd have been suitable fodder for vultures by the time a helicopter had strayed to that remote region of the Alps.

I offered a synopsis of these incidents, but evidently lacking the conviction to really cash in on the situation to reach the Women's Lib. currency that Ken aimed at wringing from me with Shylock tenacity. Each was demolished — not enough evidence, lacking autonomy, no real quality of leadership or the character-forming stuff that men are made of.

"Intuition — you can't compete here", I said, (once arrogantly defined as "what is intuition in a woman, is but transparency in a man"). How often I had instinctively pointed out the correct descent ridge when my male companions were blundering about in fast-fading light, checking and re-checking compass bearings, never admitting to the futility of this when they were in a total whiteout devoid of any reference point. The peal of raucous laughter that followed this caused Wilson's leader to finally protest in a strong Aberdonian accent that he was not confident in making this crux move across the traverse with such little support below. He didn't reckon that parabolic loop of rope to the deck was adequate protection.

Meanwhile, I too, was called to order from above. My leader had reached the top of the first pitch and for once I was confronted with the attractive alternative of stepping on to rock to leave this situation which had turned out to be far more stressful than I'd bargained for. If this fellow had resigned, protesting in favour of women, what formidable force he must have left in the front ranks. After all, I had only asked for a letter of support — not a gold medal in the art of survival.

Ken broke his brief silence after a curious survey of the steep crack I was about to launch myself at. "That looks desperate", he said. I looked around to see who had joined us using such a dulcet tone of voice, full of concern, almost paternal care. But no, there were only the two of us and did I recognise a hint of identification of anxiety on his part that this could be his next climb? "You'll never reach that jug up on the left, tell you what, how about combined tactics — here's my shoulder".

He never did write that letter.

WHAT DOES "X" DO NOW?

A MOUNTAINEERING PROBLEM

BY "X"

(1929)

I am a shy bachelor. This personal introduction, for which I apologise, is necessary to explain my pseudonymity. Incidentally, had I not been shy, my own solution of the problem might have been different: had I not been a bachelor, the problem might never have presented itself. But there it is. I am a shy bachelor and all my efforts to change my state have ended in ignominious failure. But that is another story, several other stories. To return to the problem.

Last summer I was invited to join two very energetic friends, who proposed to climb the mountains of Dauphiny. I accepted their invitation, but, owing to a slight indisposition, decided to go to Grenoble a few days before them, in order, if possible, to fit myself for their company by taking a few walks ("training walks," I believe they are called) amongst the surrounding mountains. I understood that these mountains were not unduly high, nor covered with formidable glaciers: that they were, in fact, mountains where a man might walk in safety by himself. Little did I dream of the terrors that lurk for the lonely traveller.

Having bought a map and consulted the Syndicat d'Initiative, I decided that the Croix de Chamrousse would not be beyond my strength. The Chalet Restaurant de l'—— seemed to offer a suitable starting point and for this I accordingly set forth, one Friday afternoon. My journey was uneventful. Arriving at dusk, I found the most friendly and hospitable of *gerants*, who gave me an admirable dinner, outside the Chalet, where, from my wooden bench, I could admire the lights of Grenoble, some four thousand feet below. My only fellow lodgers were a Frenchman and his wife, spending their honeymoon tramping from hut to hut. The *gerant* had allotted to them one of his two bedrooms and to this they presently retired. I, too, was soon ready for bed and asked the *gerant* to show me the way. He led me to a magnificent room on the first floor, containing four beds, each well supplied with the cleanest of sheets. There was, he explained, a *dortoir* somewhere downstairs. But as it was already eleven o'clock it was impossible that any other parties should arrive and I might therefore have the best bedroom to myself. I chose the bed nearest the window (and furthest from the door), disposed of most of my clothing about the room and, clad only in my shirt, a rather *chic* blue one, climbed into bed. I was soon asleep.

I cannot say how long I had been asleep before I became aware of a great deal of noise. Clearly a party, a large party, had arrived at the Chalet. Drowsily hoping that my privacy would not be disturbed, I soon fell asleep again.

But it was not for long. Once again I was awakened. Footsteps approached my door. There was a flicker of candlelight; the door opened and the *gerant's* voice broke the silence.

"Voilà, mesdemoiselles, il y a trois lits... faut choisir." He ushered in four women.

The situation clearly demanded great tact and great presence of mind. I possess both. I had just made up my mind to leap from my bed, make a polite bow and offer to depart at once for the *dortoir,* when the intruders, catching sight no doubt of my beard, which was lying on the turn-over of the sheet, uttered shrill cries. This, of course, altered the situation completely. If the sight of my masculine visage caused them, as the French would say, to *pousser* such *cris,* I shuddered to think what would happen at the sight of my masculine knees, which could clearly not be concealed by my very *chic,* but rather short, blue shirt. Besides, at this moment, my shyness overcame me. George Birmingham says somewhere, or if he does not say this he says something very like it, that an Englishman reduced to his trousers will gladly face any number of opponents, but that an Englishman reduced to his shirt is a very helpless individual. Of the truth of this statement there can be no possible shadow of doubt.

Still, George Birmingham or no George Birmingham, something had to be done. I hastily summoned the *gerant,* begged him to hand me my *pantalons,* which were across a chair-back at the foot of my bed, prayed him to request the demoiselles to retire for a few instants and firmly declared my intention of descending at once to the dortoir. I had expected to find a friend in this worthy man. I was soon undeceived. On no account must monsieur derange himself. On no account could any more clean sheets be found for this bed and it was forbidden absolutely to give a bed to travellers except with sheets perfectly clean. No. Monsieur must stay where he is. The *dortoir* was already full with the men of the new party and there was no more room in it. "Taisez-vous," he turned on the demoiselles, still *poussing* their plaintive *cris* in the corner furthest from me. "Taisez-vous," he repeated and added the terrible threat to take away the candle if they would not be quiet. Then with the magnificently reassuring sentiment, "Tout le monde est bon dans les montagnes," he quietly left the room and shut the door behind him.

What does "X", 'do now?

* * * * * *

My own solution of this problem can be of no interest to anyone. Suffice it to say that I made one more effort in my best French to induce these ladies to retire long enough to allow me to recover from my dishabillity, but they clearly did not understand me. This is hardly surprising, since, as I subsequently discovered, one was Roumanian, one Czecho-Slovak, and the other two Scotch. While I was still speaking, circumstances compelled me to pull the bedclothes over my head. And there I passed a sleepless night, looking hourly at my luminous watch, until the first pale streaks of dawn and the even breathing around me warned me that it was both safe and expedient to depart.

* * * * *

When women talk, as they sometimes do, of the equality of the sexes, I like to recall that Chalet at the moment when the *gerant* left the room and four figures rushed for the bed nearest the door (and furthest from the window), while four frightened voices exclaimed, in three different languages, what sounded very like "Bags I this one." What it is to be a mere man!

NEVER AGAIN

'SPIKE'
(1965)

It seems rather curious that I won't see P. again. It wasn't that I saw him very often, but when I did it was always a stimulating experience in every way. He arrived just after the War. A curiously sun-burnt nose, gained East of Suez as he would point out, and two half-pippins stuck east and west of his nose; that nose, which had been flung on from fifteen yards without a very accurate sense of aim, a tonsure which could be irreverently ascribed to a monk, and a rather short, stout but vitally athletic body. That was P. His eyes, I should have mentioned, were very bright china-blue and glistened, particularly when he was excited, like a couple of murky marbles soaked in brandy.

I was fourteen at the time, and had to have a go at rock-climbing, for some unknown reason. P. had some reputation of pre-war ascents to his credit, and I took good care to infiltrate. He arranged to go to Wales. "Do you think your Ma will object, boy?" he said. "No, I don't," I said, knowing damned well she'd be pleased to get me out of her hair for two weeks. "What about Mrs. P.?" He gave me a curious look. "Another on the way, boy, due in the Summer" (it now being Easter); "she can't travel." Mrs. P. had got two then and finished up with eleven, a tribute to Hennessy and P.'s devotion to climbing.

We set off in P.'s old Bentley, late 1920's, and seven hours later arrived at Helyg. "Get sorted, boy," P. said, "I must go down to the village and get some lung-syrup." I should point out that P.'s lungs were a constant source of worry, not only to P. but to everyone else. P. had an almost pathological fear that his lungs would be eroded by some air-borne virus, and that one morning he'd wake up, breath out a cloud of lung-dust and croak. Two hours later P. returned. You could hear the Bentley coming up the road, throatily growling along in two gears too high and bumping off the road-side; first one side, then the other. I'd gone to bed in the large room.

P. said he'd sleep in the loft. He had to make a few attempts to mount the ladder. The noise was fantastic. A chuckle, a grunt of effort, "Christ, I'm off again" and a terrible crash as he hit the floor. He made it eventually and the bed never recovered from the impact P. gave it when he fell full length and fast asleep.

Next morning P. was up first and very early. He cooked the porridge, made bacon and eggs and coffee, and gave me a shout. Considering his tumbling-act the night before, he looked fresh and beaming as ever. Just before we left the cottage P. said "I'll first fill up the flask with lung-syrup". Keeping his hand over the label of the bottle, he topped up a half-pint flask and screwed it up well, popped it into his sack and we were off.

Marjorie Allen on Dream of White Horses in 1975. Photo: Mike Mortimer.

Marjorie Allen climbing in the Kaisergebirge in 1980. Photo: Mike Mortimer.

Youngest ever female member, Eve Prickett, elected, aged 17, in 1995, bouldering on the house wall of the *Centenary Journal Editor*. Photo: Terry Gifford.

Stella Adams climbing Meshach (VS), Craig Bwlch y Moch, Tremadog in 1984.
Photo: Ian Smith.

P. had decided views on the teaching of climbing. "Let's get up a proper route", he'd say, "none of these bloody boulders for us." So off to Tryfan and Pinnacle Rib. As you know, the Rib is 600 feet high and not very hard, but it seemed fantastic to me. (It's a curious fact, and one that I'll have to take up with our geologist friend Dave Thomas, that the main structure of the Rib has altered considerably in recent years. I remember when it was vertical. Then for a few brief years it flattened out a bit to about 45°. Now it is getting steeper and steeper again).

The air was really alive that morning. There had been a light frost the night before and now, with a few billowy clouds and the sun doing its best, it was marvellous. We trudged up to the foot of the crag and P. seemed to breathe a bit. "My chest", he said, "seems rather clogged. Must get the pipes sorted out." He took out the lung syrup and gave his chest a good belt; his eyes watered slightly, he coughed, belched, and stowed the flask, and the work began. I will say now that I was impressed with the surprising speed and grace with which P. went aloft, talking the whole time. Instructions and advice gushed out, getting progressively fainter the higher he went. Time went by, then: "Come on up, boy; you'll love it." And it was my turn. We met up, I changed places with P. and with the minimum of delay he was at it again. After two hours it was time for lunch, and, an hour or two later again, tea. Each time P. safeguarded his ailing breathing system. As the sun grew a bit tired of this particular day, I followed P. up the last pitch. I met with him, after struggling up the chimney and arriving at the top of the mountain. P. was looking unusually florid and was positively boisterous. I received a tremendous blow between the shoulder blades. "What do you think of that, boy?" he said. When my eyes had returned to their sockets I managed to reply that I had enjoyed it, but that now and then I had felt frightened. At that, I got another one on the back which sent me reeling across the summit. "You'll soon get used to that, boy," he shouted, and we both staggered down towards home.

The weather remained fine but cold, and we visited most of the less fierce crags. Each evening P. set off to renew his depleted stock of lung syrup and, each evening, renewed his act which would have gained him a fortune in films.

The weather did break one day, at the end of the holiday. P. was undeterred. "We'll do a gully climb and get really wet," he announced. I noticed that, to ensure his continued well-being against particularly virulent attacks by the weather, he brought out an even larger flask and decanted most of a bottle of lung syrup into it. He was right about the gully; I'd never been so wet in my life before and not often since. It was pretty obvious that P.'s pulmonary system was getting a fair attack by the conditions, as he needed plenty of medicine to continue at all. From time to time the gully rang with joyful song and declamations of snatches of poetry. P's face glowed like a torch in the gloom of the chasm, and advice tinted with anecdotes continued to pour out. When we got to the top it was getting dark, and the clouds beginning to scurry off towards England had left the sky a beautiful shade of watered pink. "You look cold, boy," P. said. "You can say that again," I re-plied. Here P. thought for a moment. "You'd better have a drop of this," he said kindly. Expecting something like Auntie Flora's cough mixture, I took the top off the flask and took a fairly hefty slug. For one moment I thought that the volcanic era had returned to North Wales. I felt that the air had left my lungs and some great explosion had occurred near the top of my head. Tears poured down my cheeks and I fought for breath. Suddenly my guts caught fire and continued to glow with almost delectable combustion for the rest of the evening. P. looked concerned. "All right, boy?" he anxiously en-quired. "Yes, now," I replied as soon as I could. "That's the spirit," he shouted, cuffing me over the head; and we staggered down. I must say that cough syrup certainly improved the performance. For some strange reason, though, I twice lost the ground and shot downwards in enormous somersaults, being unhurt both times and hearing great shouts of laughter behind and above me in the night.

Mrs. P. continued her vocation in producing a population explosion single-handed and this gave us plenty of opportunity to get away to the mountains. We were joined by P.'s oldest son in a couple of years; and a most remarkable boy he was. The exact opposite of P., pale, gangling and thought-ful, and with almost no co-ordination in his body at all. (He was deadly on the rugger field; if you placed the ball in his arms, he'd be off flailing down friend and foe alike, his limbs whirling in all directions — and no knowing where he would end up.) He was alike in one respect to P. and that was in his ability on rock. His arms and legs flashed out in all ways at once, and in incredible contortions he would fight up the rock. One time, watching him lead up a difficult crack, P. and I were so full of lung syrup and amazement that we forgot to let out the rope, and down he crashed, uttering the weird-est oaths I've ever heard used.

The Alps came next and the three of us went to Arolla. Looking back on it, it's a wonder that we got up any peak and even more astounding that we returned in one piece. Then, in the years that followed, Zermatt and Chamo-nix, and, finally, finish. I was called up for service and during my medical I heard the doctor say, "It's incredible, I've never detected symptoms like this in anyone his age". But I got through and was sent to Norfolk. After this I found friends of my own age and continued without P.'s guidance, meeting him now and again, still looking much the same. but each time perhaps a little more rotund and amiable.

It was announced recently that P. had died through heart failure, but Mrs. P. and I knew better. Now, when I'm having a drop of P.'s favourite brand of lung syrup, I remember him, not with regret but rather with the hope that I will have the sort of middle age P. had, and it looks as though I might at that.

'It refused to be a mountain'

'Y cynefino a'i gwnaethai'n fynydd...
　　Ond un hwyr o haf fe wrthododd fod yn fynydd

(It was habit which made it a mountain...
　　But one summer evening it refused to be a mountain.)

Euros Bowen 'On Arennig Fawr'

MOUNTAINS IN DREAMS

MRS. O'MALLEY
(1914)

Dreams about mountains are, as far as I know, uncommon. To dream about them twice in a month is a rare thing, even in a man who climbs much and dreams often. They are not less incoherent, fanciful, and exaggerated than other dreams. Mountain dreams are especially suggested by places half-seen: a strange valley at twilight; hill slopes going up into the darkness of clouds; or the white look in the mist up a side valley which betrays the hidden glacier. Our conscious mind is arrested and particularly gratified by such pictures as these, which arouse and haunt the imagination; it may be, perhaps, that some part of our waking consciousness more than the rest is receptive of, and pleased by, the things which furnish the material for our dreams.

Mountain dreams can be fitted roughly into four classes, as follows: the Nightmare ; the Superman, or Impossibly Easy dream; the Scenery dream; the Supernatural dream.

The first two classes are simply two of the most familiar kinds of ordinary dream in a mountaineering setting. In both of them the sense of impossible difficulty or of impossible ease is of more importance, as a rule, than the mountain background. In mountaineering nightmares one climbs up rocks at an increasingly terrifying angle; they become glazed with ice; they thrust the horrified climber further and further into the air, till he loses his hold, falls, and wakes with a bump in his bed. This, in every case known to the writer, is just the same as the falling dream familiar to everybody. (It would he interesting to know whether any climber who *has* fallen dreams of falling, and whether his dream sensations correspond with his waking ones.) Other features of the common nightmare appear in the mountain variety. Half-way up a climb you find that you have forgotten, for some reason, to bring your boots; or it is impossible to start, though the party is dwindling into the distance, because a necessary lemon has been unaccountably mislaid. These are just mountain variants of the well-known nightmares of missing a train or going to Court without clothes. In the same way the mountain dreams of falling stones and impossible icefalls are no more and no less interesting than the favourite nightmare of a friend of mine — not a climber — who habitually drives in a pony-cart down an English lane, which presently crumbles from under the vehicle leaving him clinging like a fly to the underside of an overhanging wall on which housebreakers have been at work. There is one really original and amusing mountaineering nightmare on record, but it is the property of a notorious anti-perpendicularist, and, having been celebrated both in verse and song, it is too well known to need quotation here.

In the Impossibly Easy dream the climber is endowed with superhuman skill, strength, and activity, and climbs up the steepest and coldest rocks in a whirlwind of triumphant case, into warmth and a blaze of sunshine. This dream, too, has its parallel among everyday dreams. As a child I dreamed constantly that I was swarming up tall and slender trees — a thing I could not then, or ever, do; or that I climbed hand over hand up a rope out of a dark and slimy well into light and sunshine. The relation between these dreams is evident; but it is curious that, whereas my dreams as a child had no parallel in facts, I have, when climbing, occasionally felt as every climber must have done — some of the sense of unconquerable power which I experience in my dreams.

The same indifference to danger was shown in another very vivid dream of mine, when several of us were lying in bright sunshine on a slope of intensely green alpenrosen, overhung by grey cliffs, covered with a thick blanket of névé, after the manner of the Tschingelgrat. I can remember now the blue of the ice-cliffs above the rocks over our heads. Presently these cliffs began to fall, in great white and greenish blocks. They flew for the most part clean over our heads and over the precipice below us, where we saw them dropping through the air like birds, and fluttering like butterflies down the stony slopes, on which they smashed. Sometimes, however, a bit of cliff came away clumsily, and then it thundered down the green slopes towards us in such a river as sugar makes. We were not in the least frightened, and lay in the sun for a whole afternoon watching the entertainment. I do not know where this delightful place was, but it was reached by walking out of the window of the top-floor bathroom in the Central Hotel at Glasgow.

The one mountain-dream of a supernatural occurrence which has come to my knowledge is recorded by the dreamer as follows:

"I dreamed that I was stopping with my brother in Zermatt, at the Monte Rosa, and while there, we climbed the Weisshorn. Two climbers, members of the Alpine Club, but not personally known to either of us, had been killed on the mountain six weeks before. Our guides, with a not unusual taste for horror, insisted on our changing the route on our descent in order to visit the scene of the accident. We walked to it over a rounded snowfield, which was much more like the Petersgrat than anything near the Weisshorn, and presently came upon tracks of another party in the snow, quite clear, leading downhill. We knew — I can't tell how — that they belonged to the men who had been lost, and we refused to go any further in that direction.

A day or so afterwards, in Zermatt, I received a card bearing a fresh date and postmark, and the picture of a place near Lake Orta, signed by one of the dead men (whose grave I had seen). He said that he and — I have forgotten the name of the other corpse — were coming over to Zermatt, and hoped to meet us there. For the next few days I received a card every day, always from an address nearer to Zermatt, always hoping to find me there. At last one was brought down by two parties returning early in the day from the Regina Margherita hut, with the words, 'Zermatt this evening — G.'

By this time I was thoroughly disturbed, and took the whole affair to a well-known alpinist, a member of the Club and a friend of mine, who by good luck happened to be at the Monte Rosa. The big man considered all the facts, and then gave his opinion. The two men, he said, obviously wanted to go on climbing, and as they had no longer any bodies to climb with, they were coming to try and get possession of mine and my brother's. He refused to let us stay in Zermatt to meet them, but hurried us off to the Schönbühl Hut, where he put us to bed in the upper room, covered with blankets, and told the Swiss in the hut that we had got bad phthisis. He then gave us an anaesthetic, telling us that while we were under it, he would keep our souls in his pocket-book, and as anaesthetised bodies could not be misappropriated, we should be quite safe. In the meantime, he promised to deal with the intruding spirits. Much comforted, we 'went off.' I did not come out of the anaesthetic till I had come out of my dream, so how the adventure ended I cannot say."

There are some odd omissions in mountain dreams — omissions of things so usual and so important to climbers that it would seem as if they could not fail to find their way into dreams of mountains. In my experience, it is almost unheard of to dream of food, or of other parties, or of heat, cold, or fatigue, or even of jokes in mountain dreams. The dream quoted above is the only instance that I know of, in which a hut occurs. Yet all these things have a large place in mountaineering; and food, heat, cold, and fatigue have their usual place in ordinary dreams. These facts might lead one to imagine that mountain dreams are purely visual, yet this is not the case; action, though slight, does occur, and the sense of fear and danger is strong in the nightmares of mountains, and do occasionally enter into other mountain-dreams. The explanation may be that those elements in mountaineering which make the strongest appeal to the imagination form the material of mountain-dreams as a rule, and that the less important elements only slip in rarely and casually.

If it is true that the study of dreams is of some importance to psychology, it may well be that the collection and study of mountaineering dreams might throw some light on the psychology of mountaineering. This, however, is not offered as an excuse for these observations. Only pressure on the part of the Editor furnishes that.

HOW I BEGAN TO CLIMB

CLAUDE WILSON
(1928)

It was only on receiving an invitation to contribute an item to this series of articles that I began seriously to consider how it had happened, and to realise that my mountaineering really began at the age of six, or seven, among the sandhills at Southport. But on looking back I find that I there learned much of the technique of mountain exploration. Knowledge of the "condition" of sand would, if the heights were equivalent, be as important as is knowledge of the "condition" of snow. Before I was ten I was leading parties among the heights and hollows of this miniature, but intricate, range, in all weathers. In soft, dry sand one sank above the boot-tops, and though one instinctively picked the easiest gradients, the expedition was always a laborious one. On "good" sand — wet, but not too wet — one could walk with comfort as on good snow and could kick steps up very steep places. On "crusted" sand, wet on the surface, but powdery at a depth of two or three inches, danger lurked for all but the experienced; for, though apparently easy and safe, steep slopes were prone to avalanche. Only under very good conditions could vertical walls be scaled, and the climbing was sometimes like serac work and sometimes like rock-climbing. We used no ropes; perhaps it was as well, since the belays were by no means reliable.

I used to know those sandhills pretty well and I ascended the highest, Mount Ararat (now built over), by at least fifteen different routes. Knowledge so gained in early youth is not to be despised.

RAW DEAL FOR A PRECIPICE

A. D. M. COX
(1940)

Modern rock-climbing has been criticised on many grounds and by weighty critics. It has exhibited fascist tendencies. It has failed to bear in mind the distinction between a mountain and a gymnasium. It has used rubbers on cliffs that tradition had made sacred to boots, and boots on holds that posterity required should only be touched by rubbers. The force of these charges may possibly still be open to dispute; but among the evils undoubtedly ascribable to modern rock-climbing is one about which much less is heard — the decay of that noble conception, the precipice. More accurately, it is the precipice itself which is in decay, for the conception of it is exactly as it was a hundred years ago: a crag of fearful size and steepness. But during these hundred years the qualifications necessary for a cliff aspiring to such rank have become steadily stiffer, and the precipice has been pushed steeply up through a great number of degrees. Many were the pleasant, rounded hills which easily passed the test in the days when men grew giddy on the top of Y Wyddfa; later, as Hugh Pope said, "only quite steep slopes were called precipices"; and now an increasing familiarity with steep places has forced the poor precipice back, right to the vertical or beyond it, so that as a mountaineering term it is in danger of complete extinction because too much is expected of it.

FROM *SELECTED POEMS ON WEST PENWITH*

A. W. ANDREWS
(1957)

CAMOUFLAGE
I was pleased
They made me Minister of Camouflage
To see that all direction posts
Showing the way to Babylon
And distances in miles should be removed
At once or otherwise made useless
And a vexation to all invaders.
And I had a free hand and took away all names
On farmyard gates and buildings
Anything on the One Inch Ordnance,
For I knew that any raider
Would carry a map with him
Or there would be one copy in each party.
And I went one better
And had all names deleted
That were printed on the Six Inch
And even on the Twenty-five.
I don't mean I called in the maps;
It wasn't possible,
But I obliterated all the symbols
Carved on stone or painted
And pronounced variously
By natives and residents of recent occupation,
Say thirty years and casual strangers
Who could never get the intonation right.

* * *

And then I thought about the Coast
And I remembered
That I had published in the *C. C. Journal* '38
A climbing guide with photographs,
But luckily the pages had been numbered wrong
And no one could find the places mentioned.
Anyhow no one has ever got anywhere except in a closed gully
Impossible to escape from,
By reading the directions given,
And in addition
The number was out of print.

Also my own unpublished poems
In one of which I said
That you could see Scilly
From Zennor Hill
And as I mentioned Lyonesse
As one of the natural objects
Visible from that spot
I thought if they did get a copy
They would waste so much time
In trying to find it
That the Defence would round them up quite easily.

IS A CRUX CRUCIAL?

D. D. YEOMAN
(1952)

For some time I had been perturbed about the use of the word "Crux" by some climbers. Nowadays no description of a first ascent is complete unless the co-ordinates of "the crux" are recorded to several decimal places. Since most new climbs are much too hard for there to be any possibility of my attempting them, this hasn't worried me unduly, although it is another step towards destroying in climbing the adventure of not quite knowing what is coming next. What did worry me was people finding more than one crux on a route. Waterpipe Gully, for instance, now has at least "... four recognised cruxes..." according to the appendix to the 1948 edition of the *Skye Guide*.

This, I said to myself, is surely nonsense. A "crux" is (is it not?) a crucial point. The *Oxford English Dictionary* defines "Crucial" thus: "2. That finally decides between two rival hypotheses, proving the one and disproving the other; more loosely relating to or adapted to lead to such decision; decisive, critical. (This sense is taken from Bacon's phrase *instantia crucis* explained by him as a metaphor from a *crux* or finger post at a *bivium* or bifurcation of a road. Boyle and Newton use the phrase *experimentum crucis*...)"

If we accept all this, it seems quite reasonable to refer to the crucial point or crux of a climb, i.e. the point at which you find out whether or not you can get up. If this difficulty is overcome all else can be surmounted; if it is not, you must go down. Thus the crux is the point which tests which of the two alternative hypotheses — "I can do this climb" and "I cannot do this climb" — is correct. It is in this sense that it is commonly used in the writings of climbers, e.g. *Glyder Fach Guide*, page 47: "(5) 50 feet. From the left-hand end of the rock ledge rises Gibson's Chimney, the crux of the climb" and on page 49 concerning the same climb: "(10) 30 feet. This constitutes the crux of the climb for Rectangular Excursionists" (who have avoided Gibson's Chimney).

Therefore, I thought, to speak of more than one "crux" on any route is clearly nonsense, and people who do so are havering.

How wrong I was.

In search of ammunition for the barrage I was intending to fire at such people I delved further into the *Oxford English Dictionary*. To my astonishment it declares that a "crux" is simply — I quote — "3. A difficulty which it torments or troubles one greatly to interpret or explain, a thing that puzzles the ingenuity." Obviously this is a word which may very properly be popular with climbers. Equally obviously, there may be any number of cruxes on one climb. Indeed a climb such as Ivy Sepulchre might well be described as a continuous succession of cruxes from bottom to top. (I judge this solely from its appearance and description in the 1948 *Journal*. I am unable to speak with — and quite incapable of acquiring — first-hand experience.)

However, I thought, on this particular word my *Oxford English Dictionary* may be out of date. It was published in 1888 and relies on quotations ranging from Sheridan and Swift in 1718 to Dowden in 1888 ("The consideration of a textual crux in itself sharpens the wits"). The 1933 supplement does not mention it. I therefore consulted in turn *The Century Dictionary* (1899), *Webster's New International Dictionary* (1932), *The Universal Dictionary of the English Language* (1936), *Chamber's 20th Century Dictionary* (1947), and the *Concise Oxford Dictionary* (1950). Opinion is unanimous. Crux, it appears, means no more than an extremely ticklish problem. (I looked in Fowler's *Modern English Usage*, but could find no mention of the word.)

Now it pains me to have to do so, but I must at this point cross swords with that worthy warrior in the war of words, Sir Alan Herbert. I have long been a humble and unknown private in Sir Alan's army for the defence of the proper use of English words, but I have never been able to accept his dictum that — again I quote — "A little knowledge of Latin and Greek, Bobby, would be useful to every citizen... I affirm boldly that the elements of these ancient tongues should be taught more widely not less, than they are to-day;..."*

I submit that these words "crucial" and "crux" show what nonsense it is. Both are derived from the Latin word CRUX: a cross — indeed one of them *IS* the Latin word. Not only do neither of them have more than the haziest connection with the idea of a cross, but they do not even have meanings which are in any way allied to one another. In both cases knowledge of the Latin derivation, far from being a guide towards the accepted meanings, is grossly misleading. I'm sorry, Generalissimo Herbert, but on this point I must "include myself out" of your army.

Well, there we are. Apparently we may have as many cruxes as we like on a climb provided we only have one "crucial crux." Let me, however, utter one word of warning to guidebook writers and tigers who record accounts of first ascents in log books: make sure a crux is truly a crux before you label it as such. Last year I met a man at Lagangarbh who said of Agag's Groove: "The only real difficulty is at the top [or was it the bottom ? — I forget] of the second pitch. If you can manage that you'll romp up the crux." Gosh! What a word!

* *What a Word*: A. P. Herbert, page 163.

MEET ME ON THE MINERS' TRACK

KEVIN FITZGERALD
(1965)

There is a school of thought (my doctor belongs to it) which holds that in the last permitted decade of life, and after serious operations, all mountains should be eschewed. This is demonstrable rubbish. On any fine Sunday between January and December the lame, the blind, and the halt may be seen groping or staggering their way up Snowdon and it is strictly their business if Glaslyn rather than the summit is their objective. They are being, as Alan Hargreaves used to say, "active." It is not only Men of Harlech who can rush about the Welsh Hills; quite a lot of Men of Eighty are capable of reasonable performances. But having said that, there are some reservations to be made.

It has been my unfortunate lot to count among my friends some of the most formidable climbers and walkers of this or, I suspect, any other generation. And what is a man to do, if, caught sitting with his boots on, he is asked to go "out"? The late Mr. Keats held that the word "forlorn" was like a knell. The present Mr. FitzGerald not only hears the tolling of bells, but the rustle of shrouds and the slow clip-clop of plumed horses every time the words "Are you coming out with us?" are addressed to him. There have been times, as he glanced nervously about him, when the very breakfast at Pen-y-Gwryd has taken on the taste and smell of funeral baked meats.

For consider. In my time, unfit, untrained, full of cigarette smoke, Worthington E and brandy, wearing a pair of ill-shaped ill-disposed boots and a corset, grotesque in a leaking anorak, I have been dragged about the countryside over ways designed to tax the stamina of a Whillans or the skill and ingenuity of a Brown. And not just for a few minutes, but for hours and hours and hours. Sometimes I have fallen sobbing to my knees in order to bless the man who invented cameras and thus made possible the phrase "I'm sorry to be such a nuisance but would you mind waiting here just a moment to give the thing scale." I was looking at some of the pictures to which I have given "scale" the other day and I am still wondering how I got to the places. In most of them it is clear that I had stopped breathing some minutes earlier.

There is another type of invitation. That one goes: "Let's all have an easy day." One such, that I recall with hideous clarity, began smoothly at eleven o'clock, that in itself lulling me into a beautiful feeling of complete security. When dusk had become night and I had lost one of my big toe nails someone said: "There's only one difficult place now, and we're only six miles from Llanberis." At that time I had not been off a difficult place since the 20-

minute sandwich break at 3 p.m. We got back just before nine o'clock to the inevitable "Have a good day?" and the invariable lying reply: "Wonderful, thank you." As I got into bed on that particular night I was seized with cramp in both legs and an arm, ALL AT ONCE. At home in those circumstances one would lie screaming for assistance. In Wales one dives under the bedclothes, snapping at the cover of the *Alpine Journal* for 1872. 1 like to think that one day that particular volume, with my teeth marks still visible, will be displayed in one of those illuminated cases of relics now such a feature of the better climbing hotels. I wouldn't like to be an example to the young, only a horrible warning.

It is a dozen years since I allowed myself to be talked into something called "Strolling about looking for a new climb." That involved 23 miles, of which almost the whole of the last four were covered along the side of a mountain on my ankle bones. All that was the easy part. It was raining of course and very cold and there was endless hanging about while experts conferred and differed, tried pitches, sought natural lines, gambolled about on problem boulders or stood around in Anglo-Saxon attitudes. It goes without saying that nothing worthy of being called a climb was found by my companions. I've never had the good fortune to know anyone who liked to spend an hour or two on a common or garden "Difficult"; except Moulam, who once glanced down at me with the never-to-be-forgotten phrase: "You are witnessing a spectacle not often seen: Moulam stuck on a Moderate."

Then there is the "casual walk." Heavens above, where those can lead. I've been on a casual walk which intended to go to the power house on the Lower Road (I was in my slippers) and finished in the refreshment room on Snowdon Summit. I still can't remember what we did or how we did it. I was in a kind of trance most of the time and in my socks for quite a bit of it. And no one would lend me the money to come down on the last train. That is why, in whatever state I may be when you meet me on hill or mountain today, I will always be in a position to lend you at least two pounds, and usually more. Nothing conceivable could get me out on a "casual" walk without a bit of reasonable taxi-hire in my pocket. I've been on too many of them.

"It would be as well to borrow an ice axe," a friend said to me one crisp winter's morning years ago. That is merely one of the foolish things I've done in my time. If you've got an ice axe in your hand there just isn't an excuse for not going on. You are in the business and you look as if you are. Only you know, at first, what a danger you are, and are going to continue to be, to yourself and your companions. It is only after you have speared someone or tripped yourself up, or let go of the thing on the top of Craig-yr-Ysfa, that your real status becomes apparent. And by that time you have given up caring. I've been on top of all the Welsh three-thousanders except Elidir Fawr and on some of them many times. But, except for three of them, my first time up has always been in conditions which would have drawn complaint from men on their way to long terms of penal servitude. I seem to recall that Carnedd Llywelyn was the ice-axe one (I know it snowed all day that time) but it may have been somewhere else. The end product was the same. "Had a good day?" "Wonderful, thank you" and then off upstairs to plug the hole in the leg, get out of the corset and lie flat on the floor for an hour or so.

But the most dangerous of the lot is of a more recent vintage. Certain tigers have found certain utterly impossible, artificial, "attempting places," adjacent to easy ground, in one or two spots within reasonable distance of Llanberis Pass. The invitation to get mixed up in the fringe activities of all that goes like this: "If you felt like going out this evening you could help me a bit." "Yes," you say, cautiously. "Well, Blank and I thought of looking at a thing. He's out with Dash at the moment but I said I'd meet him at Ogwen at five. If you ran me down there and he hasn't turned up I could go for a decent walk and you could stroll up later on and meet me on the Miners' Track."

I have already fallen for that one twice and it might as well be said at once that no one is ever met anywhere. But I can tell you the sort of thing that happens to the man who goes up the Miners' Track. He is, by definition, a member of the Climbers' Club in late middle age; what might be called in the hastening autumn of his days.

And being all that and knowing a thing or two he will avail himself of the excellent new bridge below P-y-G by which to cross the Gwryd and, babbling happily to himself of green fields, will strike up for the corner of the wall. About half way a madness will overcome him. "When I was unfit, years ago," he will say to himself, "I should have been glad enough to get to the corner of the wall. But why don't I forget about the Miners' Track and go straight up to the waterfall from here?"

Now that's steep, however fast you say it, or however slowly you take it, and the waterfall is reached by the ageing C.C. member rather in the way that Paradise is reached by the earnest aspirant. There is of course no sign of Blank, Dash or anybody else. It was five o'clock at Ogwen when all this nonsense started. It is seven o'clock now, or maybe eight. Perhaps it would be a good thing to walk on a bit, across the plateau anyhow, in case they've gone up Tryfan? In a mile or so one could get a view around and about.

There is no one and nothing to be seen from the end of the plateau, but the sun has gone down. It begins to get dark and the member of the Climbers' Club recalls that he has often fallen into the Gwryd after dark. He is too old for all that now. All the same it wouldn't do for these walkers to come charging over something, all muscle and easy breathing, and find him not about. They might think he couldn't get up as far as that. Perhaps one had better get down, around, and up to Bristly Ridge? That would show them. Surely they haven't gone over Glyder Fach? Anyhow it's pitch dark and one cannot very well start shrieking for help. Pity about missing dinner, but just as well to have got off the ridge while it was still possible to see.

That was the first time. The second was like that with variations and there will be no third time. The second time was quite reasonable, really, I was only hanging about at the top of the Track for three or four hours. Weeks later I discovered that the party I had gone up to meet had decided not to go that way after all. I remember getting into P-y-G and sinking down in the smoke room opposite a cynical smile on the face of Emlyn Jones. "You look tired, Kevin," he said, "been doing much?" "No," I said, "nothing very much; just strolling about composing an article for the *Journal*. I'm going to call it: 'Meet me on the Miners' Track'. "

Elaine Owen on Brant Direct (HVS), Clogwyn y Grochan, Llanberis Pass, 1986.
Photo: Mike Mortimer.

Geraldine Taylor climbing El Scoupier (F6c), La Cascade, Flaine, France. Photo: Taylor Collection

Sally Westmacott climbing Bell Vue Bastion (VS) on Tryfan in 1978. Photo: Mike Westmacott.

Sally Westmacott on Kirkus's Route (VS) Craig yr Ogof, Cwm Silyn in 1970.
Photo: Mike Westmacott.

REAL CLIMBERS DON'T
(WITH APOLOGIES TO ALL REAL MEN)

DAVE HOPE
(1983)

Real Climbers are a special breed of men. It takes a combination of the humour of Patey, the integrity of Mummery, the endurance of Buhl and the courage of Croucher to be a Real Climber.

To give you an idea, Joe Brown, Warren Harding, Jan Morris and Don Whillans are Real Climbers. Dennis Gray, Chris Bonington, Reinhold Messner and James Morris are not. Nobody's too sure about Gwen Moffat, Clint Eastwood or McNaught-Davis. Actually McNaught-Davis isn't too sure either. Everyone knows that he isn't. And everyone else knows that he is. The only thing that is certain is that we know that he knows that we know that he knows that no-one knows!

Real Climbers are intelligent. They always defer to mile-wide avalanches, five-day blizzards, eighty-foot seas, and lunatics wielding bolt compressors, Moskvich vans and chalk bags. Real Climbers sometimes say shit to all of these just before they die.

Real Climbers do have rules but climbing ethics are about as clear as the BMC constitution. The Real Climbers' Credo is:

'Never settle anything with words unless they are, "... and then I 'it 'im!" unless, of course, it's an argument with Whillans.'

Then Real Climbers just don't.

Real Climbers are Strong, Quiet Men. Real Climbers think. They never open their mouths or wallets without good reason such as eating or drinking. Real Climbers will always give you a straight answer of yes or no and never beat about the bush.

"Well, according to the latest reports from the upcoming Hunt Commission, at this present moment in time, the position as we see it, because of recently forthcoming evidence, leaves us with an interesting situation to be aware of and gives us reason to believe that negotiations are approaching a point of delicate balance (the crux, you might say), that may or may not be of importance to the successful outcome of the problem." A Real Climber calls this Bullshit.

Real Climbers are never ill. They just have recurrences of old war wounds, previous Himalayan bowel disorders, or hangovers. Hygiene is not so much misunderstood as ignored. Real Climbers think that Herpes is another name for a ladies toilet. Likewise Real Climbers can sleep anywhere. Any bivouac finds him snoring soundly. He generally sleeps his soundest slumped over the pan after throwing up over the floor at an Annual Dinner. Real Climbers only go to Annual Dinners if they've been invited to speak. Afterwards they're expected to throw up over the floor so that anyone who invited them feels no obligation to ask him to sleep back at their place.

Real Climbers don't use chalk, Friends or descenders. What's wrong with a hefty pull from your leader, or a mild steel peg wellied in up to the hilt? Better still, a good solid coach-bolt has few equals. When anyone chops a bolt a Real Climber's trigger-finger itches until it's been replaced by another and backed up with five more. Real Climbers don't wear Calvin Klein Y-fronts. Real Climbers don't wear brown Y-fronts. They don't need to. They just call for their second to send up a man with guts! Failing that, Real Seconds rattle a bag of acid drops, offer a shoulder, or send up a sackful of chockstones.

Climbers who are all chalk and no traction are not Real Climbers. And a final word on the technical side — Real Climbers only use oxygen when cave diving for a little relaxation.

Real Climbers drive small beaten-up vans or old British motor-bikes. They crash them frequently. Occasionally they stop and have running battles with the kneecaps of huge motorcycling giants.

Real Climbers prefer tents to huts. Real Climbers don't cook food. They eat cold beans or cold macaroni cheese straight from the tin with an old mild steel jam-spreader peg. Real Climbers don't allow the weather to upset them. They shrug off blizzards, hurricanes and heat-waves with supreme indifference. They're all one to him because he's in the pub. Real Climbers don't sing in pubs. They just talk quietly between arrows and consume vast amounts of ale to prove that they can keep cold macaroni cheese down. When Real Climbers get up at 3 a.m. for a pee they squelch unflinchingly through several square yards of regurgitated macaroni cheese lying outside the tent flap. Real Climbers don't throw up in pubs. They do it outside, preferably over the local panda car.

Real Climbers don't belong to organisations such as the BMC, the AC, the CC, or the Friends of the Earth. They do have fantasies about belonging to the original Creag Dhu!

Desmaison is a Real Climber but Rebuffat is a Ballerina.

Some Real Climbers have bits missing but it's not obligatory. Winthrop-Young was a Real Climber and so was Herzog. Norman Croucher is a Very Real Climber. Messner has spent so long over 8,000 metres that bits of his brain are missing. Unfortunately his writing is too sensitive and meaningful and thus disqualifies him from Real Climber status. Real Climbers are characterised by their horror of such terms as meaningful, sensitive, relate to, elemental consciousness, etc. Michael Tobias writes Bullshit.

Real Climbers hate midges, farmers' dogs, seagull chicks and wasps (or WASPs). They do have a soft spot for Fulmar Petrels as long as they don't have to share a ledge with them. Real Climbers are not music lovers but will listen to Glenn Miller if they're in Cornwall. Real Climbers can't agree on the kind of music they like but do agree that there's nothing like the sound of crashing waves, the moaning of a nymphet wind(?), and for Real Atmosphere, the Bonzo Dog Doo-Dah Band playing the Sound of Music.

Ron Fawcett look-alikes are not Real Climbers. Pete Livesey is a Real

Climber. Pete Livesey look-alikes are REAL MEN. They have to be!

Real Climbers don't spend all year in the Himalayas, Alps, Patagonia, etc., in order to avoid paying income tax. If they're away that often they don't earn anything but our envy and Real Climbers are not enviable. They are reputed to be able to get to the Alps and back on £20 having spent £19. 19s. 6d on a pair of boots.

Real Climbers don't read much but they do like to look at the pictures. That's why many of them mistakenly bought *Portrait of a Mountaineer*. And even if they get as far as this line they're likely to check for the perforations so that recycling in the time-honoured fashion can take place. Besides, who needs to read when all you need to do is follow the dotted lines.

THE ASCENT OF BUNK THREE

GEOFF MILBURN
(1981)

Only very recently, when the true facts became known, the climbing world was staggered by an unprecedented event which took place in North Wales. Unbelievably Ynys Ettws was the scene of a potentially serious fall during an enforced night ascent of the multi-topped Bunk Peak. On reflection it is extremely lucky that no C.C. member or guest has so far sustained multiple, fatal, or even worse injuries on this harrowing and unprotected 'killer peak'.

Under the prevalent and lethal conditions at the time, which are so typical of the summer monsoon period in North Wales' huts — hot, humid, windless, disgustingly smelly — and in total darkness, such a foolhardy attempt was totally unjustifiable.

This solo, non-sight ascent which was to leave the leading climbers of the day gasping (they say that Ron Fawcett was utterly speechless for minutes on end) was for the record done barefoot, in underpants and without even a hint of chalk. The only actual aid employed on the route was from one of the upright corner posts and the accident certainly occurred only because the left hand upright was not 'in situ' when I unfortunately made a wild and uncontrolled grab for it. Some might consider that a previous daylight inspection of the pitch, although not exactly ethical, might have been advisable.

Having fallen down the East Face Route for some distance accompanied by loud crashings and bangings I eventually landed on a large ledge at ground level. As I fell, time stood still and Joe Brown's whole life passed before my eyes. Having reached the present day I had just started on the life of Whillans when the cold concrete floor brought me back to my senses. Writhing in agony I could only marvel that I was still alive and had incurred no legal responsibilities by injuring any other parties during my headlong flight.

It was impossible to move until the string of curses from the indifferent occupants of the room had subsided into more uniform snoring. Cocooned in their expensive down bags the bodies were oblivious to my plight and the only way out was to fend for myself for a change. It did occur to me that a night out even at that altitude might well prove fatal and in desperation I considered feeling around for a female form on one of the bottom bunks so that I could slide in beside her. (It is a well known fact that the female body can withstand extremely cold conditions during storms.)

Even a cursory glance at the signing-in book of that period will reveal who was present on that fateful night and furthermore why such an action on my part could not be contemplated. Imagine the shock and horror of coming to grips with Chris Gibb to say nothing of... No I just can't bear to think of it, the pain is just too much. After a further exploratory feel of myself — to make certain that I was still functioning properly — I renewed the attack.

On the second assault I was prepared and while gaining height rapidly fate took a turn for the better, in the shape of a foot protruding from the middle bunk (Note: this foothold has since disappeared!), which provided the means to allow progress to the finishing mantelshelf. As the substrate of the summit pyramid was somewhat loose only a further desperate lunge across to the edge of a deep crevasse avoided another headlong fall. Collapsing in a nervous and semi-alcoholic heap on the summit plateau I managed to regain the safety of my own sleeping bag.

For the rest of the night I slept fitfully and it was only when the first cold rays of the dawn struck the buckle of Sheard's rucksack far, far below that I was able to make a more controlled descent to terra firma.

Now it must be plain that such a major catastrophe, which nearly robbed the climbing world of one of its most outstandingly insignificant figures, must not be allowed to happen again. Consequently until the M.L.T.B. has had adequate time to consider the far-reaching ramifications of this episode, which has multinational significance and could even lead to a seasonal ban on this much sought after peak (to say nothing of the time needed to argue the toss with the B.M.C.) the Committee has reluctantly implemented a temporary and logical system. Please note that this has copyright and must not be infringed by the F. R. C.C., West Col or any selected climbing guides.

TOP BUNKS — for the technically proficient may be used by: super stars; old timers who need a training routine (provided that they can second Bancroft 5b); non-drinkers who retire early; anxious virgins of either sex; E1 to E7 leaders and all soloing activists; libbers who don't like to have a man on top of them; smokers who like to get high; Ken Wilson and all magazine editors who aspire to get closer to God; rampant snorers and eccentrics such as Jim Moran who possess noisy alarm clocks; gate-crashers and dossers; last but not least Chris Bonington and all other high altitude snow plodders.

MIDDLE BUNKS — for the élite include: Committee Members, Guide Writers, Hut Custodians and all Honorary Members; experienced climbers not yet in the senile class; Severe to Hard VS leaders (Very Severe (hard) if FRCC); married hard men with wives and countless children to support; honoured guests and Lord Hunt.

BOTTOM BUNKS — our lowest but safest order includes; all senior citizens, pensioners, Dennis Gray and other BMC officials; has beens; leaders up to V. Diff. and seconds who NEVER lead; sleepwalkers; errant potholers who suffer from vertigo; habitual drinkers who 'needs must' walk in the night; nubile and willing females; peggers and chalk users; streakers and flashers; and lastly all M. L. C. holders who, as such, are neither fit nor sufficiently qualified to ascend any higher.

Al Evans and the Lancashire contingent have advised that permanent belay points should be provided for all top bunk climbers (Rowland Edwards's suggestion of bolts was unceremoniously thrown out), that an abseil rope should be left in position for emergency night descents and that there must be a fixed rope ladder in place for those who are ethically weak. It must be made quite clear that the much talked about recommendation of Doug Scott, our intrepid Himalayan ace, that a set of oxygen equipment should be made easily accessible for top bunkers should now be considered as somewhat out-of-date.

As this new innovation is likely to spread it is anticipated that the Livesey column in *C. and R.* will become BUNKSCENE. The sleeping problems of climbers will be discussed, the routes in other huts will be reviewed and ethical problems given an airing. We understand that Pete will not be caught napping while on the job this time. Details of nocturnal first ascents and protectionless night climbs may be sent to Pete's new address which we understand is now somewhere in Bedfordshire.

A SHORT SIESTA ON THE UPPER SLOPES

ANON
(1967)

> 'What do we do now?'
> called Ulf the Unwashed.
> Njal's Saga.

A report on the Keele 1965 Peruvian Andean Expedition in the previous issue of the *Journal** included reference to 'a new route on Chichiccapac made by B. Chase, A. Tomlinson and G. Bonney,' adding 'the latter took a short siesta on the upper slopes while the other two pressed on to the summit.' Such reports are liable to give false impressions, and I feel it my duty to record the facts in fairness to Bonney, who is, alas, still with us.

It is no longer possible to discover with certainty who first suggested that he should join the expedition. Attempts to recall the days when we were selecting personnel produce instant violence and recriminations:

'So you thought he could carry the kit?'

'He could if he didn't eat so much.'

'I always said a woman would have been more use'.

Each insists that he was the first to devise the schemes to get rid of Bonney (known by the code-name GROB). It is not that he is unusually revolting, but when it comes to organising an expedition he is the very antithesis of Major Pingle. I shall say no more.

It is most probable that GROB was initiated by Bonny himself. When we were still unpacking deliveries, he announced that he would not go unless we took an adequate supply of Dr. Gritte's *Muesli*. Almost simultaneously Webster and Gallagher leapt out of their crates to suggest that he should go to Germany to negotiate directly with the *Deutsche Muesli Gesellschaft*. He left the following afternoon and we found to our surprise that although he hadn't actually done anything while he was present everything was much easier in his absence.

So we progressed rapidly during the winter of 1964, and the months passed without news from Germany. Then, without warning, a letter arrived in which he not only claimed to be gainfully employed, but proposed that one of us should join him for a skiing holiday in Austria. This was a disappointment, but we decided to send Tomlinson to see what could be done, with instructions to survive the Alpine Tragedy himself. He did a good job. He met Bonney at Landeck and helped him to hire a pair of ski-boots. They

---

* *C. C. J.* 1966, page 106.

then drove into the Otztaler. After a few days Tomlinson arranged a hard day's skiing which took them, towards nightfall, to the top of the shortest, steepest and most twisted descent in the district. When Tomlinson was about half-way down he heard a howl of agony above him, and was overtaken by a pair of skis carrying only the soles of the pair of boots. He then returned to England.

Our programme for the expedition work in Peru was comprehensive. Not content merely to climb our mountains, we were to make a map to find them with, and then to transport lumps of them complete with adhering vegetation, back to England. When finally assembled, the equipment weighed about three tons and it became clear that the five of us could no longer rely upon wearing it all at the airport baggage check. To this problem was added the return of Bonney, which made poor Webster quite ill for some time. The solution, however, was simple. Baggage and Bonney were taken to Liverpool and put on the next cargo boat to Lima. We told the First Mate that if he could induce Bonney to leap overboard in the course of a game of deck quoits, he would not go unrewarded. As a fail-safe we included among his personal luggage an ex-army bazooka which we told him was a range finder. We were confident that this would ensure his prompt arrest and execution on arrival in Lima.

The rest of us flew out in June, and immediately set about finding the equipment. We found, instead, Bonney, living on a roof in the suburbs, still clutching the bazooka. Our difficulties of living in and leaving Lima are recorded elsewhere,* but we eventually became incorporated in the load of a lorry bound for Arequipa.

At Arequipa we caught a train which hauled us slowly up onto the *altiplano,* and we became intrigued by the spectacle of odd Indians dismounting at unlikely spots, and walking slowly off towards the distant horizon. The idea made an immediate appeal, and at the next stop, we told Bonney that we had arranged for him to meet here a man called Gonzales Gonzales who was to accompany us to our base camp. Without question (not even "Where is the base camp?") he climbed down and standing like an uncomfortable cactus, watched the train grind slowly out of sight.

We were sitting in the back room of an inconspicuous café in Juliaca eating *Guisco de pansa* (stewed paunch) when his dishevelled figure appeared in the doorway surrounded by small children. We retreated to the station waiting room to spend the night, though poor Webster, distraught at Bonney's ubiquity, spent it being sick on the platform, to the utter delight of the small children.

At Tirapata we dropped him again, but despite being savaged by a *plano-wolf,* he caught us up at Ayaviri and stuck with us all the way to Base Camp. It was clear that we should have to stage an Andean Tragedy.

We actually staged two. Neither was successful, but it might be worth

---

* *Procedimiento de Ministerio de Justicia Peruana,* 1965: *Alcholismo,* Vol. XXV p. 11,653. *Extradiccion de Expediciones Extranjeras,* Vol. XII p. 581.

relating them for the benefit of others (other expeditions to the Carabaya have taken one llama too many).

The first was planned with great care and executed without a hitch. We climbed Huayaccapac (5,500 metres),* by a gully on the N.E. face, arranging things so that Bonney was the last to arrive (not difficult). The summit was a steep pointed snow pyramid, and as he climbed the last ten feet we placed an opened sardine tin on the slope above. The tin slid off down the slope with gathering momentum, and passed him at speed. Then, with a blush of fulfilment, the kamikaze sardines, still in perfect order, disappeared over the edge. We had by then untied his rope, and cannot understand to this day why he did not jump after them.

We paid dearly for our miscalculation. Back in Base Camp he built an automatic coffee grinder with two tins, an ice-peg and a twenty pound boulder, which got out of control and plunged into the egg powder. Then he made a bath, and Floyd was nearly carried off by a condor while bathing naked. Then he built a raft with our air-tight packing drums, sailed it to the far end of a lake and ran it aground. Finally, he set fire to his sleeping-bag in the middle of the night and Chase, five inches longer than his tent, straightened out in alarm.

Tomlinson spoke for all of us:

"Let's face it, as a human being you are a complete write-off. There is no point in taking you home. We have decided that you should be exposed on the mountain." We very nearly lost him in the camp below Chichiccapac when he became trapped under two inflated air-beds in a two-man tent. We managed to coax him to the upper slopes however, and we abandoned him while he was admiring the view. Let's not waste words on euphemisms.

Anyway, he caught us up at Miami as we were settling down for the night on the airport roof.

---

* There seems to be some misunderstanding here. Huayaccapac is actually the name of another mountain of the same name, which has two peaks each named after the one mentioned in the text. Huaynaccapac was an Inca prince.
— Ed. (Not me. Ed.)

I GET HIGH

MARK VALLANCE
(1978)

Starting up in business is like having 120 feet of rope out, no runners, and a 5b move in front of you. Sometimes it feels like that for weeks on end.

I prepared to jump. The weather was perfect; clear sky, hard frost, a scattering of snow. The camera team was in position and waiting, the radio mike turned on and recording. I climbed past the top Friend, feet above it, climbed a bit higher — "Hell, I'll give them a real show" — and I climbed a little higher still. Then I jumped. As the rope tightened my belayer was jerked upwards onto his Friend and the breath was knocked out of me. I was lowered to the ground — no need for 'a retake'.

The five minute episode on B.B.C.'s *Tomorrow's World* programme went out at the end of January 1978 and a six year secret was out.

I first met Ray Jardine in the summer of 1972 in Colorado on my way back from the Antarctic. We were both working for Outward Bound at the time and between courses we climbed together. Though I did not know it then, he was carrying the first prototype Friend around with him — four cams on a shaft with no stem and no trigger — it needed four hands to get it out!

We climbed quite a lot in Rocky Mountain National Park and Eldorado Canyon. In Eldorado I particularly remember having a hard time on Yellow Spur in a very battered and toeless pair of Robbins boots. The 5.10 face climbing beside Kor's old bolt ladder, 6,000 feet above the canyon floor, for someone who had just had a two-year lay-off from rock, was a joke. Climbing in the Robbins boots, I soon discovered, was just a Yanky ploy to give the 'know-all' British a hard time — trouble was I couldn't find any E.B.s.

I soon learned the technique of 'off-width' cracks, (Ray was really into 'off-width' at the time). Having learned the technique all I had to do now was build up my strength to be able to apply it. For this, frequent visits to the gymnasium and 'the wall' at the beautiful University of Colorado campus in Boulder were called for, followed by bouldering at Flagstaff Hill below the Flat Irons.

Another lesson I had to learn was 'ethics'. Being a know-all Brit, I thought I had ethics off to a fine art, (using aid was O.K. so long as nobody saw you). I was belayed to the bolts at the end of the first pitch of George Hurley's route on 'The Book'. We were doing an early free ascent and Ray climbed down, around and couldn't get back into the crack. "Why don't you just stand on my shoulder?" said I stoically, (Ray weighs 13 stone). "You're attached to the bolts. If I so much as touch you that'll make it A1."

My first experience of Friends was much later, in 1975. Ray was very secretive at this time, carrying a blue nylon bag around which clinked and rattled. It was another hot day and we were below Washington Column. I was sworn to secrecy before being shown the contents of the bag.

Ray's prototypes were an odd selection, some beautifully made, polished aluminium, carefully filed edges, sophisticated trigger attachments, 'J' slots for holding the triggers in the closed position ready to fit straight into cracks; others just slung together to test out a new idea, but retained in the armoury because they worked.

A climber, John Dill, who I shared a drink with one night, on hearing that I had been climbing with Ray said, "Have you climbed with any of his Friends?" "What do you mean?" I asked — it seemed like an odd question the way he said it. "Oh — I just thought you might have climbed with some of his Friends". Then it clicked — I was talking to one of the initiated. Even the name Friends arose out of the secrecy. Kris Walker wanted to ascertain whether Ray had the bag of Friends with him whilst they were with a number of other climbers. "Have you got the bag of Friends, Ray?" The name stuck.

That day's climbing on the Column we made the first ascent of Power Failure and I learned a good deal about the Friends. One of the belays was from two No. 4s in a vertical crack. As I hung there in my slings the Friends seemed to move — my God they did move! I kept absolutely still — sweating. Then I started to get cramp and had to shift my position. They moved again. I watched, fascinated. If I moved upwards they swivelled to point at me. However I moved they aligned themselves with the load. We had to go back next day to finish off the route and I got a really dirty 5.8 pitch and Ray got a beautiful little finger crack but we spotted a really big straight-in crack over to the right, which we climbed the next day and called Dwindling Energy. The big crack was a mind-blower with a 100 feet of — but for Friends — unprotectable jamming, followed by a layback to a stance under a roof which provided the crux at 5.11 to land us on Sudden Comfort ledge.

Next day it was my turn for a hard lead and I chose Gripper down on Arch Rock — great to be able to just climb and leave the protection to the Friends. Later on it was really frustrating climbing with other people and not having the Friends — seeing the opportunities and not even being able to talk about them. I'd hoped to do Nabisco Wall but by the time I'd got up the long layback of Waverly Wafer, having forgotten my chalk on what was an exceptionally hot day and nearly fallen off at every move — we roped off; but if we had had Friends...

We talked at length about getting the Friends on the market and Ray said he'd got various plans. I gave him some money to send me a set as soon as they were available and even suggested that it might be possible to make them more economically in England — the big problem was getting them on the market at a realistic price. When you think that a wired nut costs from one to two pounds and it is just a lump of aluminium with two holes, wire rope and a swage — Friends with their twenty-seven parts, as many holes to be drilled and scores of assembly operations were going to be very expensive. About a year later Ray sent me a letter to say that if I personally made the Friends he would give me a world-wide licence to produce. Six months later Ray was in England and we spent a hectic two months working on the details and doing a lot of climbing. Ray really liked gritstone and did a lot of routes.

I couldn't find anything hard enough for him. Jim Moran commented to me later that Jardine just eats cracks. This followed a day at Cratcliffe when we did all the routes and Jim had been most impressed by the protection point he'd seen in the layback of Five Finger Exercise "I've never seen anyone get a nut in there before," said Jim. "Was it any good?" "Oh yes — pretty good," said Ray non-committally.

At the Roaches we did Sloth as our first route. "Fantastic" said Ray and promptly climbed it again — I think he'd have carried on climbing it all day if I hadn't told him that there were some hard climbs nearby.

Eventually Ray did find a problem to work on — The Baldstones Roof — a climb which involved every trick in the book and which Ray finally graded 5.11c. After our second evening working on this problem we'd packed it in and gone over to do Ramshaw Crack, which Ray climbed in less than a minute muttering "5.10b!"

We spent one evening looking at colour slides and I was most impressed with a series of a huge roof in Yosemite — 'Separate Reality'. The slides were of exceptional quality and very impressive. I mentioned that he ought to send one to Ken Wilson for *Mountain* magazine. "Do you think they're good enough?" said Ray innocently. Less than two weeks later *Mountain 56* came out with possibly the most impressive free climbing picture ever taken on the front cover.

A year later when the business was well under way, I sat below this huge roof hoping that Ray would fall off because I really didn't want to second it. He got almost to the lip and reached for the stopper that he knew would fit in at the lip. It didn't fit. He tried again and fiddled about — it still wouldn't go in. He tried the move swinging his feet down and levering up to hook his foot round the lip and fell off. Thank God — now we could go back to camp. "The crack was wider," was Ray's excuse. I marvelled at such ingenuity. This was a new one on me. I've studied all the ways of climbing down gracefully and thought I'd heard every excuse. But there had been a fair-sized earth tremor a few days previously.

Much of the work that we did on Friends during the summer of 1978 was inconclusive. We couldn't find anyone to extrude the hard cam alloy or a supplier of suitable high tensile bolts. Everything seemed to be too expensive. When Ray left for the States I'm sure he must have been thinking that another attempt to get Friends off the ground had failed.

About two weeks after Ray left I started getting replies to the scores of letters we had been sending out, and suddenly everything started to fit into place. Now I had to go for it, the start of the long 5.10. I borrowed all the money I could and got the bank to give me a second mortgage on the house, I had some notepaper printed and started to place orders for components. I then took a deep breath and gave up my job — no runners on this climb — either success or a big fall.

1985

PETER HARDING
(1975)

Maybe I never should have answered the advertisement.

CLOGGY GREAT WALL AND OTHER MODERATES. BEGINNERS. ANY PARTY. SATISFACTION GUARANTEED. 5 (NEW) POUNDS*, 600 (OLD) POUNDS (OR 2 DEUTSCHMARKS).

J. ALLTON. REGISTERED CLIMBING GUIDE.

* INC. VAT. (SPECIAL RATE FOR O.A.P.s).

But that was how I came to meet Joe (Lead 'em) Allton, famous T.V. personality and rock climber.

Of course he had needed to drag me up, despite all the modern gear, but we had struck up a rapport and, eventually, I had been conned into an Alpine season.

I insisted on a rock venue after asking Joe about his reputation as the fastest ice man in Britain. I gathered that this must have been earned when working as a delivery driver for the Longon Refrigeration Company's fleet of supercharged mini-vans.

We put our permit applications to the Ministry for Sport early, specifying the Tre Cima di Laveredo, and were fortunate to be allocated July 13th to 14th inclusive.

Nothing harder than the Direttissima Allton had promised as we brought the helicopter down near the new 600 room Climbotel.

As we steered our power wheeled climbing caddies laden with gear, round to the foot of the North Face, I still had misgivings. Stopping at the Parkplatz, below the vertical sweep of the Dibona ridge, Lead 'em sat about unloading all the tackle, finally 'mechano-ing' the caddy frames together to make a size-able frame tent.

I set up the 'Atomicooka' portable bivouac oven, turned up the heat to Regulo 7 and put in two 'Freezifood' synthetic dinners. Meanwhile Lead 'em hammered in four 'Supachrom' pegs and attached the computerised 'Autosecond' automatic seconding machine. He clipped himself on to five of the titanium nitryl fibre climbing filaments issuing from the top of it, plugged the micro-transmitter/receiver module into the socket in his new irridescent blue helmet and set off at a rate of knots in a vertical direction. The powerful Magnetronic soles of his J.B.s made little noise other than the characteristic 'plink', 'plink', as he moved rapidly upwards. At 70 metres he whipped out his 'Hot-Shot' automatic bolt gun, fired in a couple of the latest poly-mite coated gobos attached a collapsible stance seat and sat swinging in space. The loudspeaker in the 'Auto second' crackled and Lead 'em's voice spoke out, "O.K. I'm ready: send up the grub."

The dinners were almost done. I gave them a few seconds more at

Regulo 9, then, taking one pack out of the oven, I attached it by the hauling ring of the packet to a 'Minikrab', clipped it to one of the ancilliary service ropes and pressed the No.1 'Haul' button on the 'Autosecond'. I watched it go skywards for a few metres, then set about my own meal. It's great what they can put into a one cubic centimetre 'Freezifood' pak these days. Two Tournedos steaks, three veg, a container of Gaelic coffee and one goodly portion of plum duff. Difficult to believe they are all man-made protein from DuPont. Suddenly a squelchy 'plonk' on my climbing helmet punctuated the gastronomic enjoyment. Lead 'em, deadly accurate as always, had trundled a brussel sprout on to me.

"Bloody got you," a voice crackled out of the 'Autosecond' speaker. "We're off when you're ready."

I packed the 'Atomicooka' into its hauling sack, connected it to a free filament and pressed the appropriate haul button. Within five minutes I had organised the hauling of all gear, apart from the frame tent which was one of the new disposable 36 hour self-destruct job, only taken in case bad weather made any climbing illegal. Finally I arranged the 'Autosecond' to haul itself, with me attached to its base by two krabs, up to join Lead 'em.

Masses of gear were now fixed to pegs and gobos some 70 metres above the scree. "Now mate," said Lead 'em. "We start the climb proper."

Allowing me time to connect up the 'Autosecond' to four bolts and myself to a water-soluble plastic channel peg, he led off on a diagonal overhanging traverse to the right. The 'Autosecond' ticked away smoothly whilst I sat comfortably on the stance seat reading *Mountain Life*. The odd hum, whistle and expletive cracked from the speaker as Lead 'em moved upwards. The run-out meter registered 96.5 metres above several overhangs and roofs. From the speaker: "This is your leader calling. Come up when you like, but don't forget to switch the 'Autosecond' to manual." "Yellow second to blue leader, Roger, Wilco. Ten four point five, over and out!" I replied.

After the gear hauling routine, I slipped the machine on to my back like a rucksack and set off.

With the aid of finger Fi-Fis, B.UR.P.S.*, T.W.E.R.P.S.+ and some old fashioned etrier work, I eventually reached Lead 'em on a small ledge above a fair sized overhang. I was, in two words, demoralised and knackered.

"Good pitch that," he said, even though there were only sixteen overhangs and four roofs.

"This, my friend Lead 'em bloody Allton, is not the bloody Direttissima Route at all," I said vehemently.

"No," he remarked. "Thought you might enjoy a new one. The only real problem is going to be in avoiding the Direttissima, Super Direttissima, Direttissima Variant and the old Comici staircase."

I observed that the wall above was quite blank, but way over to the right, I espied a rusty peg from which hung an old-fashioned nylon tape

* Bonington Ultimate Rock Pop Stickers
+ Tall Wall Engineering Real Purpose Staples

sling. On the left a thin crack was sealed solid with the now illegal jammed nuts, their wire strands sprouting like the legs of abandoned North Sea oil rigs in a Scottish loch.

"Super Direttissima Route," observed Lead 'em. "The only way to avoid it, is to pendulum over to that groove beyond."

Taking two 'Mac Grip' hand-operated rock suckers from his 'sack, he plip-plopped up the blank wall above for 30 metres. Then hanging from one sucker he put in a ring bolt from his selector type Mk 2 bolt and leeper gun. Clipping one rope through the ring, he shouted, "O.K. put the seconder onto abseil."

I pressed the appropriate button and watched the abseil integrater dial. Lead 'em was lowered down slowly. "Give me 20.4 metres and calculate the swing setting," he said. I took two readings from the photoelectric range-finder needle, took out my pocket computer and fingered a quick calculation. I set the 'Auto-second' green dial to 20.4 and the red pointer to 51.9 metres.

Lead 'em came to rest some 20 metres above my head, swinging gently.

"Now," he said "actuate the pendulum sequence."

I programmed the 'Autosecond' whilst Lead 'em plip-plopped with his suckers back up to the left.

"Right," he announced. "Ready for Action." I pressed the button marked Z and saw the illuminated tell-tale flash "All Systems Go!"

Lead 'em certainly did go. Releasing his suckers, he penduled down and across, deftly firing in a 30 second evaporation type mini-bolt at the end of his swing. With the fastest draw I have ever witnessed, he produced his rock screw applicator pistol from a shoulder holster and established a stance with three medium 'Hi-Tense' beryllium rock screws. (Euro Standard 11/78/3B.)

"Whizz oh!" he said. "It would have been bloody well impossible to get across without using that old peg or the holds on the Super Direct Route, especially since the Commission for European Climbing banned the use of nuts."

"If you don't mind," I shouted, "I'm going to keep my hand in at the old-fashioned stuff, by climbing across the Super Direct."

"You're going to miss a gripping pendulum," said Lead 'em.

Established on the next stance, or more correctly, hanging, from the base of the 'Autosecond', which was in turn, attached to the three rock screws, I surveyed the next pitch — a horrible, crumbling reach of rotten red coloured rock. "I'd sooner scramble up 200 feet of vertical custard in frogman flippers than even try to climb that lot," I groaned.

"Not to bloody worry!" smiled Lead 'em. Carefully, he extracted from the depths of his duvet, a small rocket. Setting it pointing upwards in two ring pegs, he clipped a chromolly self-tapping ring spike, complete with krab and rope end, into the warhead. Connecting up to a hand operated ignitor, he started to count down. "5, 4, 3 — Lift off!" Woosh! We choked in clouds of pungent smoke as the rocket departed skywards with filament screaming out of the 'Autosecond'. "New Mark 3 Bonatti Bazooka," said Lead 'em. "Range up to 200 metres. Homes into solid rock only, at whatever height you set on the dial. Better gear than the Whillans Whizzer!" He continued: "Once attached my bloody waist rope to one by mistake when trying 'em out on Cloggy. Whisked me up 70 metres until it banged in right between two novices soloing up Woubits Left-Hand. Bloody marvellous. The buggers were gripped rigid!"

The rope filament suddenly stopped. "Here we go then mate." Lead 'em leered, and clipping on a Magnadrive Jumar Escalator, the well-known solar powered automatic prusiker. He gyrated upwards. Eventually I followed in similar fashion.

Lead 'em had made a stance on two pegged-in alloy foot plates at the foot of a gigantic crack. "Good jamming above," he said. "We'll need a No.2. setting on the old 'Crackerjams.'" Forthwith he pocketed his bionic crack width gauge and took out his crack jamming tools. One in each hand, he set off.

The smooth-sided crack was a uniform 30 millimetres wide, having been produced by controlled neutron activation fracture to the latest recommendation of the Technical Sub-Committee of European Climbing (N.E. Italian Division). It was vertical for at least 64 metres. Inserting his left hand jamming iron, Lead 'em squeezed the pistol-type grip, locking it into the crack, and pulled up to insert the other. Hand over hand, with the rythmic clicking sound of the 'Crackerjam' actuating toggles, he swung up easily. At 66 metres he paused to arrange a runner, using his alloy, lever-type, semi-automatic bong fixer. Thus reassured he pressed on over a large roof. Suddenly the speaker on the 'Autosecond' crackled a startled 'Whoops!' Rope filament screamed out of the top of the machine and the whole device became alive with red and green flashing lights. 'Alert!' flashed the illuminated tell-tale. The print-out spewed perforated paper tape announcing 'Leader falling!' Fascinated (and scared stiff) I dragged my eyes from the 'Autosecond' and looked up. Lead 'em was plummeting towards me, legs and arms flailing, still gripping a jamming iron in one hand. With a screech and some blue smoke, the disc brake on the right hand side of the 'Autosecond' glowed red, and finally locked up as Lead 'em came to rest smoothly, 3 metres above my head. "Bloody marvellous!" he said, "I'm taking that bloody jamming iron straight back to old man Brown's Supermarket in Llan bloody beris just as soon as we return. That's the second time it's let me down."

"Yeah!" I moaned "if we do return — get me a new pair of those synthetic Tibetan Yak wool under-pants!"

Lead 'em quickly stuck his jamming iron back into the crack, deftly produced a spare and clambered back up the fissure.

After some twenty minutes I heard a distant voice from above, "What the hell has happened? I'm waiting for you to follow."

I looked at the 'Autosecond'. The rope register run-out dial reading was 257 metres and still going strong. The illuminated tell-tale flickered on and off 'Fail', 'Fail'. The printout paper read '3XHE-OPQA:? "Oh no!" I ejaculated, "The damn device is doing its own thing!" I rattled it, flicked all the switches,

John Hunt and Jancis Allison at the C. C. Dinner in 1991. Photo: Derek Walker.

Dave Viggers making the first ascent of Brief Encounter (E2 5b), Rusty Walls, Pembroke during the weekend of one of the Range West briefings in 1996. Photo: Ian Smith.

'Boisterous' Bob Allen on Jolly Sensible Arête (E1), Sitting Bull Buttress, Pembroke.
Photo: Ian Smith.

Above: George Band (left) and Hamish Nicol using the window of the Ling Hut as a shaving mirror in June 1988. Photo: Dave Atchison.
Below: Left to right, Cliff Fishwick, Trevor Peck and Barrie Biven. Photo: Biven Collection.

shook it, kicked it, but no joy. I shouted up, "Pull, I'm climbing," and with all the gear plus the sick machine on my back, I took my old Mk 5 crack plugs and moved up laboriously, with a lot of rope (and nervous) tension.

"Bloody well fused." I spluttered, joining Lead 'em at the foot of a fearsome looking dièdre. "Strewth," he gasped, "What a time for the bloody second to go kaput!"

For two hours or more we pored over the instruction manual on the Gee Whizz Electric Company's 'Autosecond' Mark 2. Lead 'em scratched wired circuit diagrams on the rock with a carbon fibre micropeg.

"It must be the trionic transistor in the secondary feed back circuit that has fused the main core laybrinth and shorted out the primary energising matrix," said Lead 'em. "You could be right," I agreed, having recently done a six week crash crouse on cybernetic climbing aids at the Old Age Pensioners' Polytechnic.

"I only sent it over to Yosemite Electronic Climbing Gear Inc. last month for a complete overhaul," spat Lead 'em. "We'll have to bivvy."

Using our peg and bolt guns, we rigged the hammocks, one above the other on the left wall of the dièdre. I got to work with the 'Atomicooka' and expanded an emergency 'Cragfast' foodpak — fillets of sole bonne femme with mussel and oyster sauce plus lemon tea and two portions of crêpe suzette. As Lead 'em pronounced when we were ready for kip in our 'Sputnick' lunar-heated bivvy suits. "Bloody Marvellous!"

Memory fades on the detail of the following morning. I recall that we slept in until 10.45 a.m., before shaving with the Brut facial hair eradicators built into the shafts of our peg hammers. I remember best the bit that made my day. We were near the top and the overhanging rock had relented to very broken ground. "I can't go on," moaned Lead 'em. "It's these damn jugs and the angle of the rock," he went on, "I always go dizzy when it goes off the vertical this way and I don't trust these bloody great natural holds. We'll have to abseil off."

"Not bloody likely!" I yelled, and led through for the final pitch of 20 metres. Thus the description in the new 1990 series *Citizens' Climbing Guide Books* Volume 14 reads: 'Indirect Route. First Ascent. J. L. E. Allton* and P. R. J. Harding+ leading through. July, 1984. Grade 9 Sup. Plus A6/36.8. 486 pegs. 42 bolts. 10 golos'.

* Guide (First Class). Bachelor of Mountaineering (Wales).
+ Pensioners, Climbing Permit No. EB/146/3C (Restricted).

THE EAST PEAK OF LLIWEDD
THE AVALANCHE ROUTE

J. M. ARCHER THOMSON
(Vol. XI No. 43 March 1909)

Lliwedd has always been a mountain of mystery, partly owing to the bewildering perplexity of the face, and partly owing to the fact that its imposing crags, though seldom treacherous, are frequently deceptive. Thus a discussion of its possibilities, begun in 1883, is revived every year without the least diminution of interest. After several ascents of the East Peak by strong parties in the Easter holidays two years ago, the idea prevailed that fresh variations might yet be made, but no completely new route was likely to be found. The Great Chimney, the Black Arête, the West Wall testify to the accuracy of the former surmise, for though fully half-height climbs with marked features of their own, they are variations in the sense that a section of a known route had to be followed first to find them. The latter conjecture was less well grounded. The Avalanche Route begins from the scree and continues without trespass to the summit. Its addition further illustrates the historical fact that Lliwedd, like Freedom, has "part by part to man reveal'd the fullness of her face." The rashness of prediction is a temptation to predict. It is probable that a few secrets yet remain to be wrested from the mountain, but great perseverance will be essential to the task.

In September, 1907, E. S. Reynolds and I, with the advantage of the training given by a new route up the Slanting Buttress and the varied problems of a long climb across the Central Zone of Lliwedd, turned our attention to the central slabs of the East Peak.

Between Route 1 and what is now called the Central Chimney Route, a deep chimney about 80 feet in height was found, cutting the wall above the scree. An opening is given by this chimney which affords by its position a proper and, by its steepness, an appropriate introduction to the climb which lies above. At one point an obstruction forces the climber out on to the left wall, but he can first hitch his rope over a useful spike. A few yards west of its exit the mountain throws down the gauntlet in the form of a massive rib. When Reynolds, who had joined me, had obtained anchorage to his liking, I scrambled over the prominent corner, and was disappointed to find the view curtained off by a subsidiary rib. There were, however, just sufficient holds to permit what seemed to be a traverse to Nowhere. Once round the second corner, Utopia appeared in the shape of an elementary ledge on a wide expanse of exposed slabs. On reaching this I was glad to find a belaying-pin for the rope, of which some sixty feet had now run out. My companion was delayed, I believe, by some re-arrangement of the rucksack, but the indistinct sounds that reached me gave me the impression that more rope was needed. I therefore descended to a spot where I could hold the rope on a knob with one hand and at the same time sit on a sloping wrinkle. The interval was not dull. To light a pipe with the free hand proved a lengthy task of absorbing interest. This done, the air around suddenly vibrated; I was pleasantly fanned by a flutter, accompanied by a tremulous booming closely resembling the low notes of an organ. Nothing was visible and the noise slowly subsided and ceased.

J' écoute,

Tout fuit,

Tout passe,

L' espace,

Efface,

Le bruit.

The cause was plain when a crash was heard and a great boulder and numerous satellites were seen chasing each other down the scree directly below. My shouts elicited no response, neither were they audible to my companion round the rib, but they startled an innocent wanderer a mile away on Crib Goch, who repeated them in order and with needless verbal accuracy to the company assembled in the evening. It was then learnt that a party of three young climbers were at the time finishing their ascent on the Terminal Arête.

On the arrival of Reynolds, beginning a few yards west of the knob, I climbed up the slabs in the direction of a little ledge, discernible above. The distance proved longer than it appeared, and at length I began to speculate whether the dwindling line of holds in front or the limits of the rope behind would be the first to bring me to a standstill. Neither did so. The ledge was reached without drawing upon the reserves of strength or the last few feet of a 90-foot rope.

The accommodation on the ledge was scanty; neither a sitting nor a standing posture gave the requisite security, but a trial of the former revealed the existence of a singularly sharp spike of rock hidden in a tuft of heather. With feet below and arms upon the ledge 1 could now play the rope round the pointed spillikin. The second man came up unfalteringly. The next move was made along a vein of quartz which soon lost itself in a buttress set with overhanging projections, and presenting a seemingly impassable barrier. A direct assault upon the rocks on the east side was the only alternative to retreat. They receded but little from the vertical, and the difficulty was accentuated at a point where it became necessary to make a stride of abnormal length, and while at full stretch in an exposed position with one handhold for a mainstay, swing the weight across on to the right foot. About fifty feet from the last anchorage I reached the semblance of a niche (2380 feet), and seated here on a solitary grass tuft, with the rope drawn tight over a solid bollard of rock, could await my companion with the utmost composure of mind. In response to inquiries as to what was to be done next, I could only guess the position of my companion and extol the true-fixed quality of the high hold for the right hand. Soon after I caught sight of a hat a few feet below me. The nook is one of those from which each newcomer must necessarily evict the man already established, so, having no alternative, I exchanged the seat in the eyrie for a stance on the belaying-bitt. From this aerial spot the view was unique. I seemed to be standing on a vertebra of the backbone of the mountain. An impossible crag rose directly above, and smooth slabs shelving away on either side presented an outline of delicately undulating curves. This romantic environment produces on the mind an impression of isolation at a great height.

I stepped from my perch to the rocks on the right, and rounding a corner, encountered a vertically fluted wall. The position thereon was extraordinarily exposed, for there stretched below 300 feet of open face which betrayed no trace of ledge or furrow. By stepping warily in and out of the shallow grooves I found it possible to work upwards on small holds in a slightly oblique line, and within fifty feet of the bollard I chanced upon a knob of rock which enabled me once more to hitch the rope.

The issue hardly remained any longer in doubt. The climb began to change in character, and we were soon approaching at a quickened pace the level of the Cairn Traverse, almost embarrassed by the choice of good things provided here by Nature for the support of man.

It is a feature of this route as of Route 1 that two climbers see little of each other in the course of ascent.

The Traverse leads to an easy slope of rock, now called the Terrace, which occupies approximately the centre of the face. Several interesting routes are within reach, and unless these are already known, it would not be amiss to choose one of them.

From the Terrace there rises a formidable wall, marked with red or coppery tints. It occurred as an afterthought that, if a breach could be made, an appropriate continuation would be given to the climb. My first attempt failed, for at the height of ninety feet a tempting and necessary hold could not be tested without risk of disturbing the balance. After careful descent to the Terrace, a rudimentary ledge was discerned near the Shallow Gully — the west boundary of the wall. The formation here rudely resembled the surface of a clustered pillar; it seemed that the furrows would afford footholds, while the balance could be maintained by gripping the ribs. This proved correct, but the higher I rose, the lower I found the relief sink; the holds diminished in consequence, and, when sixty feet of rope had run out, had dwindled down to the minimum limit.

On the right, the recess of the Gully gave a corner to the wall; round its angle one step could be seen, and the existence of others conjectured. By inserting the toe of the left foot into a little nick, and thrusting the right foot across to the distant notch, I could just bridge the blank interval. It was not necessary to remain long standing on tip-toe, spreadeagled on the face. From two slender finns of rock, pressed between the fingers and thumbs, sufficient purchase was obtained for the gradual transference of the weight to the stance. The left hand could now just reach a knob, but a tentative effort showed the impossibility of setting foot on the next notch. It became a necessity of the situation to pay homage to the mountain, and "crook the pregnant hinges of the knee" — a method belauded in books on climbing, but generally hazardous on difficult slabs. Here, however, it happened that the freedom of the next movement was not seriously compromised, for the expected holds presented themselves, and brought me up the remaining twelve feet to the ledge.

The rucksack made variations, but Reynolds followed my route unerringly up to the level of the nick. He could advance no further. After hitching the rope I descended a little and suggested a leap. To this bold course he readily assented. At a given signal each of us made a vigorous effort, and he alighted very cleverly on the notch. It was now explained that the hold representing the minimum limit, though useful to me, who had previously put on shoes, could not be utilised by a boot. My companion was plainly the better judge in the circumstances, and to his opinion I am most anxious to give special prominence.

The ascent of the Red Wall is more exposed and longer than that of the Devil's Kitchen. It is, however, safer, inasmuch as the rock is of excellent quality. No frantic struggle is entailed, but the muscular tension can nowhere be relaxed. In a word the whole operation is one of much delicacy.

The upper half of the wall, far less steep and smooth, afforded the pleasure of an interlude, and gave access to a long shelf now called the Gallery (2,720 feet). Two obvious lines of ascent therefrom were already appropriated to other routes, and as the excellent grey chimney at the east end was already known to me, our choice fell on its virgin sister. In this yellow, angular recess the climbing proved ideal, writhing and bridging alternated, and Reynolds could wedge in securely at the foot of a prostrate sentinel, while the vertical finish was tackled. At its exit the aneroid registered 2800 feet. Here we built a cairn. Our revels now were ended. We proceeded leisurely up easy rocks and in ten minutes reached the familiar summit, conscious of a deepened respect and affection for the "vast mural steeps of Lliwedd."

A general appreciation of a new climb is often difficult to form. The Great Gully of Craig Yr Ysfa was described in this *Journal* as "the most entertaining gully climb in Snowdonia." Subsequent confirmation of this view by others, with extension of area to include Cumberland, encourages me to say this much without hesitation, that the Avalanche Route is the most exposed climb in England and Wales. An attempt in windy weather would be indefensible, and the ascent should be reserved for a day when the conditions are wholly favourable.

LLIWEDD

L. P. SHADBOLT
(1956)

"The climber goes to scale the cliffs of Lliwedd
Where many feet before his oft have trod,
But which of all the many routes he diwedd
Is only known to Thomson — and to God."

FOLLOW YOUR 'GHOST'

A. W. ANDREWS
(1954)

A new ascent is of course always exhilarating, but with the present guide-books very little is left on British crags. In the Alps most guideless climbers have to be explorers. And it is that side of climbing that still appeals to many. To them I suggest choosing an easy way up Lliwedd and wandering where your "ghost" leads. At least you may have the excitement of losing your way in the labyrinth, and find that, as the best story-tellers say, the way into fairyland is not by the barred gate, which you are trying to force, but the open door.

> Something must still be added to give zest
> To tales of stones, where each is like the rest;
> As men of old when blinded in the maze
> Of Lliwedd's tangled and perplexing ways,
> Had to use more embroidery, for none
> Could tell, when they got home, what they had done,
> And, as true lovers should, kept a sure hold
> On careless tongues and kissed but never told.
>
> But now, the probing of a grasping hand
> Has torn the birch tree from its anchor's stand,
> The "Thank God Hold," for those of hope bereft,
> Swept every rib and pinnacle and left
> No stone unturned, so that the Wayfarer
> Might walk thereon, and tread the shining stair
> That leads to Paradise, the stepping stone
> To Heaven, if Heaven could still be won.

BUCHAILLE ETIVE MOR AND THE CROWBERRY RIDGE

(extract)

E. A. BAKER
(Vol. III No. 9 September 1900)

Our climb starts from the lowest part of the middle of the buttress, at a place marked by a stone man, and ascends at first by an indefinite sort of crack, where the rocks are much broken. For about 80 feet, though the face is exceedingly steep, it offers no great difficulty. At a height of 30 feet a little ledge provides safe anchorage. Above it a yet steeper section of cliff leads to a platform, measuring about 12 by 2½ feet, which we marked by a stone man. Here begins the severest portion of the climb, some 70 feet of open face, very nearly vertical, and for the most part almost destitute of good holds, those that exist being shallow, and sloping the wrong way, so that to cleave to the rock at all calls for a sustained effort in balancing. It is a place that makes demands equally on a leader's caution and audacity. Should any party prefer not to tackle this arduous pitch, they may descend into the gully from the corner of the platform on the right, and traverse back again along some objectionable ledges to the higher platform on the ridge, so re-gaining the direct route.

There was a general unroping here, for the usual 40 feet of rope be-tween each man was quite inadequate for this formidable stretch. George Abraham led up it in admirable fashion. Anxiously we watched him quit the platform to the left, stepping out on to a tiny ledge with his left toe, and, moving cautiously leftward and gradually up, disappear from our sight. The rope went out inch by inch, and we waited patiently for a shout to tell us that the distant platform was won. At length the eighty-footer was nearly all paid out, and the welcome shout fell from above with a summons to Puttrell to come on. Now, with a brief pause for photography, there was another period of waiting, but not the anxiety of having a man climbing on a hope-less length of rope above us. Next the rope-end was flung down for the cam-era and some of the impedimenta to be swung up, and then it fell for me. Lower down the rocks were splintered and loose to a large extent; they were perfectly sound just here, but the solidity entailed extreme paucity of holds. After the short traverse to the left, just at the beginning of the 70 feet, a shallow depression, breast-high, sloping outward and not allowing any grip, has to be utilized as a hold by pressing the hand squarely downward, and is the only fulcrum to be had for lifting the body over four and a half feet of vertical rock; and situations not a whit less sensational occur again higher up. In fact, there is hardly a place where there is at the same time handhold or foothold enough to admit of a comfortable pause for breath. The rocks are slabby, moreover, and were still wet and greasy, in places, with rillets left by the rain. Standing on an open face, on the edges of cracks or excrescences, to be measured by fractions of an inch, one sees as a vague background far below, as one looks for foothold, a wide stretch of precipitous hillside, jutting crags, and snowy gullies. But the thrilling sight only nerves one to quiet and sustained effort, though a bulky rucksack pulling backwards almost outweighs the psychological encouragement of the rope. Our admiration for the leader's conquest of this intimidating pitch waxed enthusiastic. Ashley Abraham came up last, and pronounced the climb, so far as we had done it, to be at least equivalent in difficulty to the direct route up the Eagle's Nest Arête on Great Gable.

A GREAT EFFORT

J. M. EDWARDS
(1941)

In the last three years three people have asked me how I climb. Hence this personal article. They said also that it was the state of mind and not the mechanics that they thought important, and that if each man would write of himself under this head then others coming after might know better what to imitate and what to avoid. A primary condition for this, of course, would be to lay aside any modesty that one had at any other times assumed.

It will be best to describe directly a given instance.

I will not weary you with the preliminaries. There were none. Everything had been in order, the customary had occurred. I had come here for the week-end to climb, had got up, dressed, eaten a good breakfast with a good appetite and having nobody to climb with had gone out for the day alone. I had considered carefully which cliff to visit and chosen a near one not to make too strenuous a day. This involved walking along a stretch of road, then a slope up towards the cliff.

The slope I took by stages. Three hundred yards then a rest, three hundred yards then a rest. During the last war it was explained to me that the British soldier marched by stages and it has been my chief method since. It is easier. Some people prefer to go up hills at a steady ten miles an hour, as if they were an army tank cruising or Scott hauling sledges in the Antarctic. I do not. During each rest I gazed at the cliff exploring from a distance how a route might go. Then when quite near the cliff I stopped again and looked up at it more slowly, heavy with the fresh air, and it looked at me, and it slid about in my eyes as a cliff sometimes does, and was difficult to focus. I shall go there and there, I thought and then perhaps coming to the steeper portion, I shall go there, or perhaps it will be too hard for me to go there, then I shall not go there but will go there instead by what appears so far as can be seen from here to be a dirty and a bare sided finger crack, but which may not be so, or otherwise examining the rock closely when we are there, rubbing the nose against it, there may be some third or fourth way, not guessed at from a distance. But first I thought, husbanding my energies I will rest here for a little time where stability can still be assured without effort or trouble by sitting down. So in the middle of the mountains upon a pile of rocks I sat down. A certain tendency to inertia in the mind can have great force.

Do not mistake me, the choice of cliff and of pastime had been free, it was unhampered by any conditions either of expediency or friendship, there was no particular unhappiness on me at this time beyond the normal. Yet I sat down. And as I lifted my head, stones, blocks of rock, sky, cliff faces lay round the field of vision arranged in various ways.

Then later I got up and walked to the foot of the cliff meditating carefully where to start. Then tied the rope on, flung the loose end down the slope and arranged it so that its coils should open without snags. This took some time, due to a complex cluster of small rocks in the way which needed re-arranging before I could be sure that the rope would come clean across them. Then I moved on to the rock itself.

Now perhaps you looking on might remark of these actions that none of them had been done in any rapid or decisive mould. You would be right. Perhaps that is why there was no great resultant from them. After twenty minutes I had advanced about fifteen feet and was trembling slightly, not too sure of my position. The rock now before my face was ordinary rock, surfaced at an angle of sixty to seventy degrees, fairly smooth. Heaven was above, the earth a few yards beneath, and I remember nothing of either. As for myself the fore part of my right foot was planted well on a square ledge, the heel overhung into the air and demanded a constant muscular effort at the calf; my left foot was three feet higher and one and a half feet to the side put against a small sloped piece of grooving. In appearance therefore, had anybody been passing, I was about to step up. In practice I had been trying to do this for ten minutes but had not yet succeeded. It seemed simple, the need was clear, holds were there, but they were small and I am not a man in any way to make a move until satisfied that it is safe, so that to remain in this statuesque and silly position was my only choice for the time being. Every minute or two when my right leg began to tremble I pulled the left leg down from its unserviceable height, bent myself this way and that a little to relieve the strain, then put the leg back again, using the action also as a gesture of purpose.

But any man must be to some degree hard pressed before he gives up on a point where his heart is set: so I began to struggle. Oh, good heavens, good heavens I thought, what on earth am I to do, this is not very good, you are being a coward, an arrant coward and this cannot, must not continue, I have time and again pointed out that you are being very silly but you do nothing, you do nothing except stand there with that fixed and ridiculous stare a few feet from the foot of this wretched precipice. But I still accomplished nothing. Then I began to struggle again. I thought, what is wrong, there is something missing, there is no spirit, I am heavy and unable to move; perhaps if I launch out and become sufficiently frightened; in fact I am sure that once over the border there would be no holding me. So I made several attempts to launch out, but nothing happened. Then I thought perhaps if I eat my sandwiches that will improve me, but no no for shame, it is not yet half-past eleven how can I eat them now, yet there can be no harm in it, give yourself a change, I said eat them all and that will be a load off your mind, then you will not have the temptation to eat again until you get home. So standing still on my footholds and feeling firmer than I had done for some time, I got the tin of sardines out of my pocket, twisted the lid off in the usual way but carefully because of the position, and ate the fish one by one with my mouth. This took some time. Then drained the tin, put it back in my pocket and turned to the rocks once more. Now how will it go I thought, every excuse is exhausted. And I tried again. No, it is no good, I said, it is no good: here I am fifteen feet from the ground on easy rocks as I said before, it is after lunch but in my own bones there is no more energy than there ever was and my whole soul is as flat as a carpet, what am I to do: perhaps if I were to recall former victories or to picture glory, but how can you do that when you are alone, perhaps if I shouted and sang, but you know you were never able to shout or sing: now if there were an onlooker, that would make an effort worthwhile: perhaps is there anyone in sight: no, not a soul, not one in the whole valley: there is no representative of the human race, none to praise, nobody to look surprised at cowardice or to laugh at folly, to provide me with gibe or comparison or stage: there is a sheep, but the sheep do not know about these things, a little bird but she is away out of sight already. So I stood on waiting, unable to move. It is difficult to describe what it feels like to be so, to describe that extreme desolation that may be left behind in the human brain when it is without anything working in it to spur it on. I stood on that hold for a long time. Then quickly, with the sweat standing out on my skin and my heart beating, I moved up on to the next holds and then the next and then I did not see what to do and the movement stopped again.

The view had changed. There was heather now in front of my eyes, and some of the thin dust that goes with it. I took a handful of the heather in my right hand. It seemed firm but when bent back it snapped and broke off. A bad material. I made a final effort. Look at yourself I said, and do you know what this is, that it is schizophrenia, the split mind: I know but I do not care I said: it is stupid: what could you do if you did get ten feet higher up, the rocks have not started yet to become difficult, take yourself off from this cliff: oh, this climbing, that involves an effort, on every move the holds to be spotted and often there are none, then every limb placed, the body set into the one suitable position found but with trouble, then with the whole organism great force must be exerted, before anything happens, and this to be done while the brain is occupied sick and stiff with its fears: and now you have been doing this for well over an hour and a half and the strain must be telling: get down therefore.

My mind made up, it only remained to go, not always an easy thing to do. But as it has often been remarked God may be merciful, and is so sometimes when you least expect it and on this occasion it happened that feeling in behind the heather I almost immediately found a good enough spike of rock for my rope and was able to get back down again in no danger. Then I walked a little way up the hillside slowly, rested and walked home.

But the resilience of man is great, and his ingenuity. So I was not done yet and on the way back setting to work I soon picked up my pride in this way, by thinking, today the victory has been to the devil, but tomorrow is not to him yet, also by thinking, it has been said that the secret of life is in detachment from it, good.

STREET ILLEGAL

JIM PERRIN
(1978)

You would say I was not well. My life was in pieces and I was too shocked to recognize the case. But this is a broader perspective, and bye the bye. I had been on Romney Marsh for a few days, trying (and failing), to get into the bed of a girl with large, sensual hands and a calm manner. We had smoked a lot of dope, touched once or twice without vibrancy, walked in greening fields, and little else.

> Posthabui tamen illorum mea seria ludo.
> ('For trifling sports I quitted grave affairs'. Virgil, Eclog. VII 17)

It was a willed thing. Very early on a March morning I left, drove fast along the South Coast, stopped briefly in Salisbury for tea near the Cathedral, and dreadful cheesecake, then drove on to Cheddar.

I parked at the upper end of the layby beneath Coronation Street. This I thought a wise precaution. In from the base of my ribs there was a certain thrilling tightness. As if the day for it had come. You have a thing suggested to you, perhaps even years before, and you know with a sense of terror that one day you have to put yourself on those rails. In my case it had been seven, maybe eight, years before, when I had first done the route with Frank Cannings. On top, he had said that it would be the great route to solo, and at the time he could have done it. I had just laughed, but really shuddered, really been brought up sharp inwardly by the thought.

This day there was the momentum: I was down there inside somewhere quietly weeping and all the while there was something inexorable going on. Firstly I put on my E.B.s, and fiddled with the laces several times to get the right balance between rigidity and comfort. Then I took two double tape slings and one shorter one, put them round my neck, checked my chalk bag, put it over my shoulder, made sure the tapes were not tangled.

All this had been rather deliberately and slowly done, as if to wear down a bit of the momentum. I now sat in the car, took out the blanking plate where the radio would have been, reached in and brought out a tobacco tin. I cut myself two lines of coke on the lid. Not too generous on this, I thought, take it easy. Also I unwrapped a piece of silver foil from a cigarette packet, which should have had some speed inside, but it had got damp and soaked into the paper, so I ate the paper.

I now sat back, shut my eyes, and breathed in and out deeply to get relaxed. Now as I said, there was this part of me subdued and very frightened, and there was a sort of manic overdub on the basic rhythm of everything. I was really zapping along now and actually couldn't have given a fuck about anything; I was laughing. So I set off and steam rollered it, pretty quietly up through the ivied bits, but then very powerful and determined, out over the two bulges. On the bolt ledge I steadied my breathing, no more, just deeply in and out as I stood facing inwards, then up the crack and out, round the Shield. It was easier than I'd ever remembered it. Across the Shield I was so relieved I thought 'Good, take a blow,' clipped in two slings, knotted, adjusted them, and sat there. It was not a wise thing to do. Up to this point I'd been motoring, really moving fast and well. And now I broke the rhythm of the thing, sat down, and the subdued me broke back with a terrorized sense of the place I was in. I wept. I mean this literally. Once in the slings, with the car park three hundred feet below, I was so scared that I wept.

Leniter ex merito quicquid patiare ferendum est.
('Let pain deserv'd without complaint be borne'. Ovid, Her. V 7)

It was something of a grey March afternoon with a suggestion of dampness about it and a little seepage from the crack in the bulge above. I was sitting there blubbering like a two year old, wanting my coke, my dog, horizontal earth under my feet, in just about reverse order.

The need was, to get a perspective on something. The hysterics didn't last long, but once they had gone I couldn't get back to being fast and loose. I was holding myself very tight, very hard, using a lot of control. I tried to focus out but there was nothing vital to focus on. The greyness — rock, sky, road, was everwhere. Even the grass had a wintergrey sheen. Not so much as a woodlouse faltering out of its crevice. This frightened me a bit because if I just relaxed, I could relate to it, resign myself to it, and not give a fuck. I was letting myself down gently into being the objective correlative of a dead and inert world. I rose on an inner scream, and it modulated into a vicious controlling anger. Out of my slings and working myself on to the rock again, it was all wrong. I was absolutely tight. My moves were bad, jerky, hurried, and imprecise. It was like watching a bad climber who might just make it.

I saw Chris King once on Right Unconquerable and it was the same sort of thing. His runners were coming out, he was right out at the edge of control, you were aching for him to make it, but the thing was so fine, so nearly not. Curiously, pathologically interesting, yet distasteful, as I would imagine a dung-beetle to be.

The groove and sidestep bulge were prolonged as something out of a nightmare. At the bulge my fingers felt to be slipping in the crack. I took the crack above very slowly, lumberingly, feeling almost safe. The last wall was damp and protracted. I was beginning to expect to make it, and holding back. At the top I crawled and bit grass, laughing.

Ridetque sui ludibria trunci.
('And soaring mocks the broken frame below'. Lucan, IX 14)

After a little while I got up and made my way down to the road. I now felt desolated by it all. There was nothing cathartic in it. I felt worse than before. It seems odd to me that you, as readers, will evaluate it, say this or that about it, as though it mattered, which it did not. Just something, some sequence of psychic events, combining with opportunity, produced it. Nothing changes by it. I doubt if I could ever do it again. Except that some day the rhythm builds up, the whole crazy edifice shifts, you cut loose, don't give a fuck, and you're away.

Dulce est disipere in loco.
('Wisdom at proper times is well forgot'. Horace, Od. IV, xii 28)

"NOW I KNOW WHY"

BOB ENWRIGHT
(1991)

The summer of 1978 gave plenty of opportunities for honing up our fitness ready to meet the challenge of Yosemite in August/September. The last week-end we could get a decent walk and a rock route to test our abilities saw Trevor, Rick and myself leaving the car-park of the Brotherswater Hotel, striding out for Dove Crag and our intended route, Extol.

About halfway to the crag where the path crosses a small stream, I sat down and looked at the scenery. At least that's what I told myself I was doing. In reality I needed a serious rest. The other two were up ahead with thoughts of not being the last to get to the climbing. Trevor was always a competitor.

On that small, warm rock, I wondered if I had done enough to get fit for the untold rigours that lay ahead in the Californian sun. Before I got too depressed at the thought of being a burden on the team, I continued on, to the shadowy rocks at the foot of a wet-looking first pitch.

"Yours is the sharp end," said Trevor, as I surveyed the unpleasant preliminaries. He'd decided the big second pitch was his, as Rick was leaving the heroic stuff to us. In the event, I ended up leading the whole route which made me feel good and banished the morning's depressions. That was, until the walk down, when I stumbled a lot and the 'unfit' feeling returned. Driving back along the motorway, my thoughts were... "I wonder why?"

Yosemite was everything we'd been told, and more. Tuolumne Meadows gave us some memorable days, but the two I recall most were our last in the park before becoming tourists in 'Frisco' and 'L.A.' The Chouinard/Herbert Route on the Sentinel was magnificent. Rick having to lead everything above the 'Afro-Cuban Flakes' with a very shaky head-torch, then having to talk me up carrying the sack, in the pitch black dark. Finding our way from the summit, at midnight, down a very narrow gully to a welcome stream was the best route-finding I've been involved in. All credit to Rick for this. At the stream, after much drinking of its sweet water, we decided not to risk the last 1,500 feet in the dark, and slept until a combination of the cold air, morning light and small lizards licking the salt from our cheeks, woke us and we continued the descent. Again, Rick was quite a distance in front as I was stumbling and feeling unfit. After two weeks of intense rock, walking and descending (roping down the east face of El Cap was demanding), I thought, "Why?"

Feeling unfit at various times when walking to and from crags became 'the norm' and I stopped thinking about it. Until 1981. This was the year the company I worked for moved factory, with the usual stresses this can cause.

I began to feel very tired. So much so that I fell asleep at the wheel of my car when the traffic lights were on red! Apart from causing much merriment with my workmates and at the pub, it suggested to me that 'expert' help might be useful.

The consultant's words were, "I wish I was as fit as you," and despite several hours of tests and examinations, which of course inflated his fee, I was pronounced physically sound, but "may be suffering from a slight case of overwork and don't overdo it in the mountains, lad."

Skiing in Andorra with Rick's newly-formed winter holiday company was an invigorating experience. Fitness of the legs is paramount in this sport, but by early afternoon I couldn't push the ski edges into the snow when turning. The "Why?" question began reappearing, but not seriously enough to stop me doing some of my best climbing over the next few years. Good seasons in the Alps and memorable summers in the Verdon Gorge, the Vercors and on other French rock. Discovering how to stop quickly on skis encouraged boldness and high speeds, making winter in the Alps very exciting, but the dreaded afternoon tiredness returned quite often.

1987. A new love, a wedding, a honeymoon in Chamonix, Vercors and Verdon. No climbing, of course, just amongst the mountains with my new wife. The two loves of my life. Together. Perfect. But, whilst walking through the long tunnel in the Verdon Gorge, I was again stumbling over small stones in the dark.

The biggest stress factor of all began later in the year when I left the security of a multi-national company to start my own. Seven days a week with only a few days off for climbing whenever they could be justified. Winter skiing still provided the ups, but the downs were there if I let them encroach. Some super days on Gogarth repeating routes I'd done 10 years previously, fired up the fingers and even encouraged the odd E4. This made the confidence roll in and, when time permitted, several good, if stumbly, weekends were stolen. One such opportunity came when Rick Johnson phoned and asked if I fancied a week-end in the Pyrenees.

I was working in London on the Friday morning, drove out to Gatwick and flew to Toulouse where I was collected by one of Rick's ski coaches delivering a party of nuns back to the airport from Lourdes. The coach trip to Lourdes is a story all on its own, but meeting Rick with the resort car was very welcome. We drove to Bareges and the end of the roads as we know them, to collect a turbo four-wheel drive machine left by the custodian to convey us to the hut. My turn behind the wheel. It was dark, very steep and precipitous, on rock strewn tracks, in a strange vehicle. Exciting is not the word. However, the refuge was reached incident free. The refuge was a magnificent building in the heart of the Pyrenean National Park amid splendid mountain scenery. We had three days of superb rocksport. Walking down at the end of each day with the sun setting, throwing shadows and reflections into the many small lakes beside the path, I felt that too much work and not enough play had taken its toll on my body. Rick was regularly half a mile in front, constantly having to wait for me. Dusting myself off innumerable times

Above: Nat Allen (left) and Ivan Waller and **Below**: Left to right, Trevor Jones, Ivan Waller and Hugh Banner at the C. C. Dinner in 1991. Photos: Derek Walker.

Above: One of *the* great British climbing partnerships, Peter Harding and Tony Moulam, photographed at the C. C. Dinner at the Maynard Arms, Grindleford in 1995.
Below: A triumvirate of Grand Old Men of British climbing, Jack Longland, Ivan Waller and A. B. Hargreaves at the C. C. Dinner of 1991. Photos: Derek Walker.

Jim Curran à Hoy. Photo: Gavin Crowther.

The influential, quiet insurance clerk, Colin Kirkus, a touchstone figure in the annals of C. C. history. Photo: Mrs Eileen Kirkus (now Greenwood).

after falling in the thin powder snow that lay over the rocky terrain, I made a vow to get my legs very fit.

Early summer 1990, a trip to Wasdale with my old friend Alan Thompson, resulted in us doing half a dozen excellent middle grade routes on Kern Knotts. Then came the walk back to the valley with the recurring question... "I wonder why?" A heavy fall on the path beside the little church necessitated a drive to the hospital emergency department where a number of small stones were removed from under the skin on the palm of my hand.

Later the same year I thought I would let the private medical insurance scheme I was in pay for another go at finding out the reason for my tiredness and inability to walk in a straight line. After three days in hospital undergoing check after check, in and on an array of very sophisticated equipment, the consultant (not the same one as nine years previously) visited me.

He spoke softly. "I've got good news and bad news. The good news is, you are very fit and will probably live your alloted three score years and ten."

I looked at him and said, "That's nice to know. I'm ready for the bad news." Equally softly, but with firmness came the reply, "You've got Multiple Sclerosis."

I thought for a few seconds then, quite calmly, said, "Thank you for the diagnosis.

Now I know why..."

A WET WEEKEND IN WALES

NORMAN ELLIOTT
(1989/90)

[At Capel we asked the A.A. man how long the weather had been like this; he replied that he had only been there three months.] J. S. T. Gibson **(1938)**.

Friday night. The gale submerged the A5 near Capel and we felt the familiar pangs of disappointment at arriving in the Pass in the rain. The weather forecast had predicted correctly and judging from the lack of vehicles in the pub carpark most climbers and walkers had decided to give this January weekend a miss.

Quite sure that tomorrow was a write off we fortified ourselves at the bar before making a drive and a dash (all of 20 yards) through the deluge to the light and warmth of Ynys Ettws. Inside the hut, a welcome, a fire, a bottle of Scotch and conversation with the few other brave souls quickly subdued the sound of the maelstrom outside. We were not then all that surprised when my watch showed 11am the next morning. A quick look outside confirmed that it really had set in, although a lightening towards the coast gave grounds for hope, if not optimism. A quick breakfast accompanied by the trills from Ronnie's Irish pipes and we determined to at least go and see what Anglesey was like.

"Coming for a look at Gogarth?" said Terry to a startled Daphne, who had arrived earlier that morning, having set off from London at 3 a. m. so as to miss the traffic. "What are you going to do?" she enquired. "Well we thought we'd have a go at Britomartis if it's dry. It's a route we've been meaning to do for some time — it's supposed to be very good."

A short time later and the three of us were driving across the Menai. Daphne's engaging conversation broken only by the cascading voices from the tape singing Rutter's of Requiem Mass — a truly beautiful composition that we had played endlessly since discovering it some months earlier and yes, the weather was getting better. A strong drying wind cut across the island charging the white horses towards Castell Helen as we drove into South Stack car-park.

Our walk across the headland to Wen Zawn soon had the blood warming against the searching winter wind. Arriving at the crag there was just one other party in evidence: the leader was just finishing the top pitch of Wen and his second was deeply ensconced in the crack like some dark chough sheltering from the frigid updraft.

I glanced at my watch as I zipped it into the rucksack pocket. Just enough time, I thought, as I clipped into the rope and followed the other two down. The abseil follows the line of The Trap, and it was good to see Daphne smiling up from the belay ledge a safe distance above the churning sea.

Britomartis starts just around the corner and the first moves are considered the hardest as one makes an exposed traverse across a steep undercut to reach the soaring vertical crack which splits this steep wall and forms the first pitch. I made the swing down followed by moves which were dripping dark wet and immediately out of sight of the second. The rock felt chilled as I crabbed across to the cleft and prepared to move upwards.

It was then the wave hit me.

Water battered me from every direction with a force which slammed the chest into the rock and left me chocking on the oily Irish sea. The initial shock was immense as I clutched, shuddering, to the steep holds. Water poured from sodden clothing, the soaking weight of which now threatened to pull me off. Protection, to say the least, was now vital, and I managed to sink a large nut into the back of the fissure, clipping in as my hands froze and floundered on the streaming run-off. Thoughts of Arnis Strapcans being taken by the sea just round the next corner shot through my mind as I moved up to place another runner which I hoped would take me out of reach of another pounding. Sliding up I slithered in another Rock and sat back in the harness to contemplate what to do next. Everything was soaked, hair, boots, rope, slings and every stitch of clothing. I considered throwing my 'sweat' shirt into the sea as its weight alone acted like a drag anchor against the possibility of upward movement. It was cold, very cold. 'Silly sod', I thought, 'that will teach you to climb without socks in January'. If only my hands could be dried. I reached automatically into the chalk bag only to encounter a handful of grey wet slime which I threw at the incoming waves like a soggy ill-formed snowball.

It was at this point Daphne put her head round the corner some 30ft away and eyed my dripping state critically. "Is he all right?" Terry enquired from behind her. "It's better not to know," was her curt reply. She shouted round to me, "Would it help if you had a dry chalk bag?" and quickly I was pulling it across and using its contents to blot up hands and rock boots. Another five minutes of drip-drying and I was ready for the rest of the route.

To say the climb is only VS+ it is remarkably steep so I took a lot of care to arrange good protection whenever I could. About 80ft up the crack is what Steve Ashton in his topo guide describes as a 'smelly hole'. I had just passed this feature enjoying for the first time the exposed position from the large flakes that the route is noted for, when without warning the wall fell away. I'd tested the holds, and they must have seen regular traffic, but they chose this moment to break away, taking a square metre of the face and me with them. The fall thankfully was only about 10ft into space, and I was left hanging from my last runner which had remained attached to sound strata only an inch below the cleavage line of the rotten flake above.

Daphne looked around the corner for the second time, now some distance away, enquiring after my health. I nodded and she disappeared from sight, conversation with Terry proving more interesting than my welfare. By now I was angry and stormed up past a little overlap to the belay ledge.

Now this narrow stance is far from commodious and I eyed with suspi-cion the three manky belay pegs. Ever since I snapped off a piton by hand like a piece of muesli bar at Bosigran I have had a dread of sea-cliff pegs, and for the life of me I didn't fancy a belay here at this late time in the afternoon. It was whilst I was deciding what to do that a helicopter from Valley beat its way by. The winchman sat eyeing me with clinical regard just 100 metres away, his professional detachment only emphasising my lonliness. 'Just hope you don't ever have to come any closer', I thought and pressed straight on up the second pitch.

The initial moves were quite hard into a triangular niche, followed by an exposed traverse along a ledge system leading to the final groove. The climbing up the ledgey angle was relatively easy. It needed to be as the protection was poor and the ropes were dragging like hell. The total length of these two pitches according to the Paul Williams's guidebook is 190ft, quite an achievement on a 165ft of rope, I reasoned as I exhaustedly pulled the straining rope on to the platform. Sure enough, Terry had been traversing into the groove whilst I climbed the final few feet. A tug o'war followed gener-ating a little body warmth as Terry rapidly heaved his way up the climb, pulling over the top as the sun which had just pretended to appear for the first time that day immediately set in an orange ball to be replaced by a rising moon and the intermittent search beam of the lighthouse.

"Daphne's going to be late for her C.C. Committee meeting," chuckled Terry as I yelled at the darkening sea for Daphne to start climbing. We need not have worried, as she shot up the route, determined not to be left to the night. She arrived out of the gloom to a heroine's welcome, but immediately confessed that she had left a middle-sized Friend stuck in the crack. "Never mind," I said, "That's what gear is for — better it than you." Knowing full well that it belonged to Terry, a gesture of magnaminity seemed in order as I sensed his loss and long face in the dark.

Back to the car by the full moon to dry clothes and warmth, the now cerebal sea rapidly retreating as we hurtled back to Llanberis. A quick good-bye to Daphne (who was only an hour late for her meeting) and last orders at Pete's Eats had lentil and bean curry banishing the last vestige of chill.

It had been in its way a great day so far and it was still only 9 p. m. We had arranged to meet some friends who were camping below Snowdon at Glaslyn, so dragging ourselves away from the Padarn we shouldered our packs and walked slowly up the Miners' Track throwing our moon-shadows on to the path.

It's good to have warm friends and friends who are warm, on occasions like this, although they did let us walk nearly round the lake before answer-ing our yells. The usual banter, a mug of wine and a warm sleeping bag never felt better.

I slept fitfully, dreaming of huge waves and helicopter rescues as Terry snored his way into his usual foetal position at the bottom of the tent.

Sunday morning and another sea, this time of mist, lay below us, Snowdon splendid in its white topping above. So up the Gribben with the best Brocken Spectre I have ever seen projected onto a rising tide of cloud over the Trinity Gullies. The ground was coated with deep hoar-frost driven into diamond currents over the summit rocks. Never have I enjoyed the top of Snowdon more. Sea level seemed a long way away.

On arriving back home on Sunday evening we sorted out the still wet climbing gear. Imagine the delight on Terry's face when he discovered it was my Friend that had been left on Britomartis. As he reminded me, "After all that's what Friends are for!"

A SEA CHANGE

DAVID HOPE
(1994)

It had been a good week with the confidence rising continually as we pushed our grades beyond former limits. The final day was to be fitting then, and, awakening to the same blue skies of previous days we lingered over breakfast and a second mug of tea. Even on such a day the Great Zawn is a forbidding place but we blended in with ease that summer, fingertips and fists hardened to its coarse crystals and searing cracks. We scampered rapidly over the approach, anticipating, driven almost, to the abseil point.

We pulled the ropes through. There were no hints, no shivers of apprehension, nothing to indicate the day ahead, but as we stood on the edge of the crevasse I was vaguely aware that the sea had a rougher edge to it, a few white horses, a choppier, irregular rhythm not quite in tune with this sunwashed morning. Not threatening but disturbed. Ignoring it, we stood on the other side of the crevasse joking about how desperate we'd first thought that jump to be, years ago, now just routine. Soon, the gear racked, he went to work from the boulders on oddly wet rock to reach the foot of the groove.

It was, as the guide stated, greasy but also running with water, against all expectations. A slip brought a quick runner and a few feet further, another, as the slime oozed an uncomfortable atmosphere into the air. For some unaccountable reason I checked the belays, though there was no need. A fleck of spray caught my ear and salt water slipped into my left eye, stinging. The day was hot, the sky cloudless, but I felt chilled. The rope slid out a few more feet and grunts and swearing gave evidence of an unexpected thrutch on this supposedly straightforward pitch. Although not concentrating fully on the rope I mechanically inched it out. The shine was off what was going to be the start of a great day. A scatter of spray dotted the back of my T-shirt and its companion swell took my left foot. I swore and shook the saturated leg, taking a step back and glancing seaward. The vagueness of my earlier apprehension distilled into something firmer, for the sea was not playing the game today as the weather was. Besides, we'd got the tide right as well, so why am I getting wet? The air had changed too, the quality of the sound deeper, booming, oceanic. And then came the first wave. I recoiled in shock, soaked to the skin, staggering back a little and inadvertently tugging the rope. A strangled cry of surprise came from above demanding attention and no pulling. I apologised and stepped back onto a higher boulder, freeing more rope with a wary eye seawards. I added my own comments of haste, amazed at the sea change, changing to ones of shock and cursing as another, bigger wave slapped me to the bed of the zawn in an angry swirl.

"Make it snappy, I'm getting soaked down here."

A grunt and a few more feet, and then the belay ledge, but not before two more angry swipes had left me shivering, scraped and a little worried. Both of these had hit the groove and had to climb the blooming thing. I ought not to have looked out to sea but I was under compulsion, sensing fully what was going to be there. A black, brooding sea was rolling great crashing fists of Atlantic into the mouth of the zawn, hiding the lower sky and darkening the already gloomy floor. A lull in the waves allowed me to get in the groove and up it a few feet. The runner wouldn't come out and I caught the full force of the wave and a mouthful of salt, swallowed in the gulp of a breath. Coughing and retching I shouted for a tight rope which was duly delivered with much mirth from above. The next one drove the breath from my body and I noticed with grim satisfaction that the spray had caught him as well. 'Serves him right for laughing,' I chokingly thought, and then I realised that that wave should not be reaching him. 40 feet up and that wave reached him? With disbelief I watched myself as if from afar as the water casually brushed my hands and feet from the rock in the next rush. I dangled, twisting in the rope and now, very much frightened. Fighting for breath, every time I opened my mouth I drew in water and spat and choked and gasped frantically.

"For Chrissake sake, the effing rope!" I screamed, not realising that he too was dripping. The ledge arrived courtesy of the swell, lifting and throwing me, a crumpled scrap, at his feet. I grabbed automatically at the belay rope and hauled myself to my feet, as he tied me in.

"What the hell is going on?" he shouted trying to make himself heard above the roar.

"I don't know and I don't care," I yelled into his ear, "but we're not going to climb out of this at 6a so we'd better figure out how to get off."

It was difficult to communicate because the sea was thumping and clawing at us almost continuously. I looked up through salt-smeared eyes to see them breaking 20 feet above us. Realisation came quickly. We had to get across the traverse to the crevasse and then reverse the jump to the abseil platform. It was difficult to think straight, or to organise, rock expelling breath by its sheer force, numbing us with its cold. Breathing was an epic in itself, as each blow submerged us for what seemed like hours while lungs shrieked for air. With eyes closed under each onslaught it was difficult to gauge the time for the next air so a throat full of water would leave us rasping in air, unable to time the next hit or gasp, catching us in mid breath and exhausting us further. We were just hanging from the belay as it seemed pointless to try and stand on the ledge, but we somehow couldn't work out the next stage, given the fury of our surroundings. It was then that I thought we might not make it out.

Time was suspended as we grimly fought to stay upright in each rush of the ocean. Somehow we established the idea that we would have to traverse across the teeth of this foaming monster and found ourselves counting the seconds between each breaker. The first attempt was a skidding lurch across the wall lunging for any hold to purchase enough time before impact. The wave took him with one hand clawing vainly at a crack and bodily flung him upright some five feet until the rope stopped his rise. The force on my belay plucked me off my feet and as I lurched sideways the plate locked and he dropped, catching a glancing blow with his thigh before going under the next. I hauled him in and held him tight with one arm against the ledge as the next wave washed over us and seemed to keep us submerged for a lifetime. As it withdrew we sank great coughs of air into our lungs, each seeing real fear mirrored in our eyes. He got angry.

"Come on you swine!" he screeched. "Can't you do better than that? Come on! What about a real wetting?"

I grabbed him by the hair and shook him out of his hysteria, the pain getting through. Calmer now, though with flecks of spittle flying, he turned to face the gap again.

We tried to establish the best landing point on the platform only to realise that it too was raging white with massive sheets pumping back and forth across it rumbling up the abseil. But we'd pulled the ropes through and without the security...? One thing at a time now, we've got to get there first.

And so our efforts assumed an almost dreamlike quality with him setting off aiming for the last far point as the sound receded into the background and all that became important was our two sparks flickering, fighting against the damp. Almost outside ourselves we watched our torn hands clutch and clutch again while the sea played with us, dancing us around on the foam, batting us back and forth between breaker and granite, submerging us until we thought we'd burst, flinging us brutally against the hardened walls of this liquid prison. Our hopes began to fade as salt tears mingled with salt waves, a final enslavement seemed to beckon. How long, how long? The aches in my body told me that we were still alive. Time did not matter. Small details stood out. I watched his camera snap from his harness and into the embrace of the sea. I counted our ropes' abrasions waiting for them to become the inevitable, almost natural end. I sucked my torn knuckles wondering at the life in their salt taste and once, only once found my thumb in my mouth as my eyes, storm wide with wonder, watched him make another effort. This time he almost made the ledge by the crevasse only to slip and fall away. A despairing lunge caught an edge with his left hand and a great sobbing moan escaped his lips before the next wave caught him and flung him on and beyond the crevasse to flounder on the platform. I shouted for all I was worth.

"Get up! Get uuuuup! You've made it. Get to the wall before the next one."

He hadn't heard, I'm sure, but instinct saw him clawing his way across on hands and knees, only to be bowled over and thudded sickenly into the back wall. Please no, I whimpered to myself, please don't take him back. Pleeeease no. I cried on in silent misery but the waves relented and he appeared staggering on one knee, his arm over a good lip in a hollow on the platform.

I don't recall how he made the few yards to the foot of the exit route but somehow he was tied in on nuts and laboriously pulling in the ropes against the snatching of the waves. I didn't want them to come tight. This place was my security. So what if each wave tore my feet away? To commit myself to a swim in these towers of fright seemed an absolute lunacy. I talked myself into it. Check your harness. Check. Are the knots OK? Yes, OK. Which nut will come easiest? That has to be the last. OK that one. Take that one out now. Come on, come out. I collapsed at the futility, weeping in raging, barking laughs, spitting out each wave as it engulfed me. You stupid fool, I thought, just untie and go, leave the nuts, treat yourself to some new ones. In the event the sea took my hand and as I unclipped the final one I was flung up into the air and descended head first.

He told me later that I was screaming in abject fear, but I have no recollection. I was just thinking that I hate swimming. I can swim, but I dislike it as an activity and this was a stupid way to die. I came to, bobbing, gasping and thrashing the disorientated surface, seeing only white and blue around me. Where was the crag? And then a mule kicked me in the back as I was slammed against the wall below the crevasse. I hung briefly on the now tight rope as he held me, and managed to turn and face the ledge, having enough presence of mind to watch the next wave drive in and jump on it, flailing wildly with my arms. I dropped onto the platform and with a combination of scratching and dragging, made his belay.

We were still being hit but now the full force of the attack was being curbed by the wall of the platform. At least we could breathe in relative comfort without fighting to stay on our feet and slowly I nutted my way up the exit route, slumping often into the slings to rest. At the top it was some while before I could trust myself to stand and fix the belay, finally coming to with his calls to my ears. God, I ached. Spent, but secure, we slumped on the upper rock platform and slowly stirred.

Pushing the tears from my eyes I glanced across at him as he dragged himself into a sitting position and sagged back against a boulder. He tried to grin. I noticed that he'd chipped a tooth and his gums were flecked with red above a swollen and discoloured lip. A sliver of blood and mucus was smeared across a cheek from his nose and a dull wet glow of red in his matted hair was beginning to seep out over his left temple. One sleeve of his T-shirt hung by a couple of threads above a rent seam, almost down to his waist, and angry weals displayed the effects of abrasive granite across his ribs. He swallowed awkwardly, trying to speak but only succeeded in croaking until he'd properly cleared his throat.

"My God," he whispered, "You look a right mess."

RESCUE

A. J. J. MOULAM
(1985/86)

Mist caressed the mountains as we sat in the smoke room of the little hotel, which huddled close to a tiny lake, in a fold in the hills. Everyone had come in early as the day had been so wet and dismal, but now we relaxed in front of an almost uncomfortably hot roaring fire which made a welcome contrast to the cold hard weather outside. Talk was animated, as the climbers savoured their drinks and, as I waited for the dinner gong, odd scraps of conversation came to me over the general hum. "You remember that hard move on Bowman's Buttress? You know, where you step..." "Then I pulled up, more or less a one-arm pull..." "I shouted 'Keep it tight'..."

I settled back in my chair, content and warm, and thought of my day; of how hard I had found the climb, of the discomfort as the first trickle of rain found its way down my neck, of the exhilaration in accomplishing a difficult move despite nearly frozen hands. Then I realised in retrospect, contrasting my current feeling of well-being with the agony of the climb, how worthwhile it had been. It was always like this.

I glanced out through the tiny window in the thick Welsh wall to the bare hillside. The cloud bank rolled majestically up and along the grey wet slope. A broken down wall ran straight up, with decision, to the track, and... yes, there was someone moving on the mountain. I got up and shifted my position so that I could watch the stranger's approach. He seemed to be coming very quickly, and it was getting dark. He ran lightly down a patch of scree, scarcely displacing a stone, and then on down through the heather and bracken, so well in balance that he appeared to glide down through the wreaths of mist on the still fellside. He disappeared behind some boulders, and then struck straight and direct, for the road. I lost interest and went back to the bar to refill my tankard.

I had just regained my seat when the door slammed open and the runner burst in. He was dressed all in grey. His grey anorak had its hood pulled tightly round his face. All I was aware of was a pair of hurt pale grey eyes looking out from an ashen pallor. His trousers were grey and mudstained, and his boots and socks looked the same colour in the poor light. The only relief to the overall greyness was the red glow of the fire and the newcomer's black hair that protruded, dripping wet, from his hood.

Even after these few seconds he stood gasping in a steadily growing pool of water. A hush fell on the bar, the fire crackling unnaturally loudly and counterpointing the drip, drip, drip of water from the apparition's clothes.

"There's been an accident", he said in a choked, distressed voice. The bar became a babel. "Where?" "How serious?" "How?" And then a rush for the drying room to curse and pull on our soaked clothing. It was particularly bad for me as I had cunningly found a place for my garments above the stove, and everything was clammy and steaming, like a turkish bath.

The supervisor of the mountain rescue post questioned the distraught messenger and then rang the police, the ambulance and a doctor. Quickly the unknown man helped to put the first-aid rucksacks in the Land Rover, and struggled to fasten the stretcher to its roof. At last we were all ready and piled into the various cars with our ropes. The convoy drove up the pass to the car park and, the stranger was already there, with the stretcher ready on the ground. He commandeered the front and set off at a great pace as the rest of us took places at the other end and sides. Through the stile, with some awkwardness and then on up into the mist we toiled. From my position at the back I could only just see the leader; he hardly seemed to be there. But he was certainly a fine walker. It was an effort to match his pace as we stumbled through the boulders and the bewildering fog.

Would he never tire? On he forged, never looking back, and I could have done with a rest. My wet trousers chafed my legs and the new rain had just penetrated my dry underclothes. My feet were soaked and cold rivulets had started to run down my chest. Why on earth did I climb? Surely the others must be tired? But that relentless grey back still strode on at its punishing pace.

The track levelled out and became less well marked across a steep scree slope. We had left the tourist route and were now moving along where only climbers go. Above us steep and broken cliffs rose, as we perceived in occasional clearer spells, and a cold wind started playing round us. My bare hands were suddenly chilled, but I had no opportunity to put on gloves. I glanced back and saw the other members of the rescue team straining to keep up with us; despite them having no loads we had left them well behind.

It became darker and the path descended a little. We threaded our way between mini lakes, and then up again through ankle-torturing boulders and fallen rocks. An eerie chill came over us, despite the exertion, as the scree became steeper and more unpleasant. Then, before I saw it, I felt the presence of a body. There it lay, on a bed of stones, in the queer sad crumpled way of the obviously dead. We put the stretcher down by the corpse and I turned to commiserate with the grey stranger. But he had gone. And only then did I recognise the amazing resemblance between the dead man and the unknown who had brought the news.

'Postscript'

"When Antæus was wrestling with Hercules and was thrown again and again, he rose with renewed strength each time he touched the ground. So did we. We got renewed vitality from personal contact with our mother earth, in her best and noblest forms."
President C. E. Mathews's 'Toast to the Club' (Vol. 1 No. 4 June 1899)

NO MERE CLIMBERS' CLUB

LEHMANN J. OPPENHEIMER
(Vol. III No. 11 March 1901)

To the Editor of the *CLIMBERS' CLUB JOURNAL*

MANCHESTER, March 16th, 1901

DEAR SIR,
The majority of our members have probably read the notes by Mr. Douglas Freshfield in the February number of the *Alpine Journal* in which (under cover of discussing the future of the Alpine Club) the aims of our own Club are seriously misrepresented and the members held up to ridicule. For the profit and amusement of those who have not read the paper I should like to quote a passage: "Any step on our part that will emphasise the fact that this is no mere Climbers' Club, but a Mountaineers' Club, will be a good step. Let us leave youths who depict themselves engaged in 'Stable Traverses' (where, let us hope, a soft and convenient receptacle awaits members of unstable equilibrium) to be reformed by their President, Mr. C. E. Mathews. If anyone is capable of the task, he is. But let us preserve our primitive tradition and maintain this as a Club of mountain enthusiasts, etc."

I am not aware that when our Club was formed the name was chosen to distinguish it from a mountaineering Club — on the contrary, its principal object was stated in the initial circular to be the encouragement of mountaineering, particularly in England, Wales and Ireland. Mr. Freshfield, however, makes the distinction, and points to the Climbers' Club as exhibiting tendencies which its illustrious parent should avoid. These supposed tendencies appear to be twofold — a spirit of rashness and self-confidence, and an absence of enthusiasm for the mountains considered as other than physical playgrounds.

Now, sir, I should like to know which of these is exhibited in the Wastdale "Stable Traverse": surely not the first — there is difficulty certainly, but no danger in it, and the mountaineer who occupies otherwise idle moments in such practice will be the less liable to come to grief when on the crags.

How does the case stand with regard to the second tendency? Is a capacity to perform the traverse to be considered incompatible with an enthusiasm for the mountains? Are the tastes for sweets and savouries mutually exclusive? I do not even see why a development of one faculty should necessarily be accompanied by a weakening of others. Does a strong mathematical faculty preclude a man from appreciating poetry and music, or does the appreciation of these fall as the faculty rises? It is satisfactory to remember that one of the greatest of mountaineers, Mr. Mummery, while confessing that he would "still climb, even though there were no scenery to look at, even if the only climbing attainable were the dark and gruesome pot-holes of the Yorkshire dales," in the same breath declared that he would continue to revel in the enjoyment of mountain grandeur though debarred from all thought of climbing. Of the fact that he did actually combine both enjoyments he has left no lack of proofs in his deeds and writings. I believe, sir, that the majority of our members have still an eye for nature, although they belong to a "mere Climbers' Club." I am aware that there are amongst us some who consider the delightful tramp to the foot of the rocks "a beastly grind," and are careless, once the climb is accomplished, of the view a hundred feet higher, from the mountain top. They are rather to be pitied for what they miss than held up to scorn. In every Club there are black sheep — even in the Alpine Club. If I am not mistaken it includes amongst its members the writer of the review in our *Journal* to which Mr. Freshfield took such strong exception (justifiably, I think, if the reviewer was serious, which seems more than doubtful).

However, these notes by Mr. Freshfield, though unfair and unkind towards us, may lead to our gain if they stimulate any lagging mountain enthusiasm amongst us. We may congratulate ourselves, at the same time, that "a high climbing qualification" has not yet become here, as in the Alps, "to a great extent a money qualification."

APPENDIX

JOURNAL EDITORS

E. R. TURNER	1898 - 1904
A. W. ANDREWS	1904 - 1911
SIR ARNOLD LUNN	1911 - 1914
N. T. HUXLEY	1914 - 1915
C. MYLES MATHEWS	1915 - 1920
GEORGE LEIGH MALLORY	1920 - 1923
RAYMOND GREENE	1923 - 1926
H. R. C. CARR	1926 - 1928
MALCOLM PEARSON	1928 - 1929
J. D. HILLS	1929 - 1937
ELLIOTT VINEY	1937 - 1940
F. A. PULLINGER	1940 - 1946
A. D. M. COX	1946 - 1949
F. H. KEENLYSIDE	1949 - 1954
A. K. RAWLINSON	1954 - 1959
J. NEILL	1959 - 1965
N. A. J. ROGERS	1965 - 1969
F. A. WEDGWOOD	1969 - 1971
T. I. M. LEWIS	1971 - 1974
J. H. LONGLAND	1974 - 1976
K. J. WILSON	1976 - 1977
W. O. CONNOR/G. MILBURN	1977 - 1978
G. MILBURN	1978 - 1987
I. J. SMITH	1987 - 1991
D. J. CUTHBERTSON	1991 - 1997
T. K. NOBLE	1997 -